SUMMITRY IN THE AMERICAS
A Progress Report

RICHARD E. FEINBERG

SUMMITRY IN THE AMERICAS
A Progress Report

Institute for International Economics
Washington, DC
April 1997

Richard E. Feinberg, *Visiting Fellow* in 1996, is Dean at the Graduate School of International Relations and Pacific Studies, University of California, San Diego. He was Special Assistant to the President and Senior Director, Inter-American Affairs, National Security Council, where he was a principal architect of the Summit of the Americas. He also served at the Departments of State and Treasury as well as with the House Banking Committee. His publications include *The Intemperate Zone: The Third World Challenge to US Foreign Policy* and *Subsidizing Success: The Export-Import Bank in the US Economy*.

INSTITUTE FOR INTERNATIONAL ECONOMICS
11 Dupont Circle, NW
Washington, DC 20036-1207
(202) 328-9000 FAX: (202) 328-5432
http://www.iie.com

C. Fred Bergsten, *Director*
Christine F. Lowry, *Director of Publications*

Typesetting and Printing by Automated Graphic Systems
Cover Design by Michelle M. Fleitz

Printed in the United States of America
99 98 97 5 4 3 2 1

Library of Congress Cataloging-in-Publication Data

Feinberg, Richard E.
Summitry in the Americas: A Progress Report / Richard E. Feinberg.
p. cm.
Includes bibliographical references and index.
1. America—Economic integration. 2. Summit of the Americas (1994 : Miami, Florida). 3. United States—Foreign economic relations—Latin America. 4. Latin America—Foreign economic relations—United States. 5. United States—Foreign relations—Latin America. 6. Latin America—Foreign relations—United States. 7. Free trade—America. I. Title.
HC94.F44 1997 96-40437
337.1'7—dc21 CIP

ISBN 0-88132-242-3 (paper)
ISBN 0-88132-246-6 (cloth)

The views expressed in this publication are those of the authors. This publication is part of the overall program of the Institute, as endorsed by its Board of Directors, but does not necessarily reflect the views of individual members of the Board or the Advisory Committee.

To my children, Sonya and Aaron,
who have the biggest stake
in the success of summitry in the Americas.

Contents

Preface xi

Acknowledgments xv

Overview 1

Plan of the Book 4

1 Why Did It Take 200 Years? The Intellectual Journey to the Summit of the Americas 7

with Javier Corrales

The Western Hemisphere Idea 13

Early 19th Century: Hemispherism Aborted 14

Pan-Americanism in the Late 19th Century 18

Imperialism and Anti-imperialism: The Early 20th Century 20

A (Brief) Hemispheric Revival: The Years Before and After World War II 23

The Cold War Years 26

Building Bridges: Summits and Charters 31

The Revival of Hemispherism 34

The Remaining Obstacles 37

The Role of Leaders 38

2 Near-Term Antecedents 39

The Democratic Wave 40

The Clinton Administration and Promotion of Democracy 42

Regional Integration Gains Legitimacy 44
Latin American Readiness 49
Early Thinking in the Clinton Camp 52

3 Creating an Initiative 55
The Spark 56
Mexico City 59
Deadlines and End Runs 60

4 US Trade Policy 63
Presidential Preferences 65
Chilean Accession to NAFTA 68
Caribbean Basin Parity 69
Division and Delay 71
Final Approval 75
Setting an End Date 77

5 Decision Making and Decentralized Functionalism 79
The Deputies Committee 80
Policy Formulation and Coordination 82
Working Groups and the New Agenda 84
Working Groups: A Closer Look 88
Democracy 90
Economics 91
Environmental and Social Issues 93
Policy 93
Operations, Logistics, Media 94
The Vice President 95
The President 97

6 Hemispheric Diplomacy 99
Forging Bonds 102
Cascading Modular Multilateralism 103
Latin American Reactions to the Summit 105
The Vice President in South America 107
Mexico 110
The Vice President in Central America 112
The Caribbean 113
South America Again 114
Canada 115
Conclusions from Round One 115
Round Two 116

The Emerging Hemispheric System: First Assessment 127

7 Free Trade Area of the Americas **131**
Designing Procedures 133
Intensive Consultations 134

8 The Spirit of Airlie House **139**
Pre-Airlie Consultations 140
The Final Offensive of the Rio Group 141
The Triumph of Cascading Modular Multilateralism 144
Compromise and Consensus 146
The Success of Airlie House 148

9 Miami **151**
Setting the Scene 152
The Rhythm of the Summit 154
Leaders' Meeting 154
Consensus on FTAA 2005 155
Sustainable Development and Democracy 156
Dangers Averted 157
Signing of the Summit Texts 158
First Step toward Implementation 160

10 From *Dichos* to *Hechos* **161**
Two New Engines: The Summit Implementation Review Group and Responsible Coordinators 163
Putting the Plan in Action 164
The Free Trade Area of the Americas 175
The Interim Scorecard 181
Problems Requiring Mid-Course Correction 182
US Government Implementation 183

11 Making Hemispheric Summits Work **185**
US Interests and Strategy 187
Hemispheric Diplomacy 192
Gaining Brazilian and Mexican Cooperation 195
Summitry and Hemispherism 196

Appendices

Appendix A Summit of the Americas: Chronology of Events 202

Appendix B Memoranda for the Vice President and the President: Proposed Hemispheric Summit 206

Appendix C Fourteen Summit Agenda Initiatives Presented by the United States to Governments of the Hemisphere 208

Appendix D Summit of the Americas: Declaration of Principles 213

Appendix E Summit of the Americas: Plan of Action 218

Appendix F Summit of the Americas Partnership for Prosperity: Democracy and Free Trade in the Americas 244

Appendix G Leaders at the Summit of the Americas 245

Appendix H Responsible Coordinators for Summit Implementation 246

Appendix I Glossary 247

Index **249**

Tables

Table 1.1 Ideas in favor of and against hemispherism 10
Table 2.1 Expansion of intraregional trade, 1988-94 50
Table 10.1 Implementation of the Plan of Action 165

Figures

Figure 4.1 US decision making on trade policy 76
Figure 5.1 US government policy planning 86
Figure 6.1 The Miami process 104
Figure 10.1 The postsummit inter-American system 162
Figure 11.1 Proposed US government organization for the 1998 Santiago summit 190

Preface

The Institute has conducted extensive research over the years on economic development in Latin America, and on the growing momentum toward economic integration between North America and Latin America. In 1986, we published one of the first blueprints for restoring economic progress in the region: *Toward Renewed Economic Growth in Latin America,* by Bela Balassa, Gerardo Bueno, Pedro-Pablo Kuczynski, and Mario Henrique Simonsen. In 1990, John Williamson's *Latin American Adjustment: How Much Has Happened?* laid out and assessed the impact of "the Washington consensus" on Latin American economic recovery.

On the trade side, the Institute has of course prepared some of most influential analyses of NAFTA and the prospects for extending free trade arrangements throughout the hemisphere. On the former, Gary Clyde Hufbauer and Jeffrey J. Schott first wrote *North American Free Trade: Issues and Recommendations* (1992) as a guide to the negotiations and then analyzed the result in *NAFTA: An Assessment* (1993). With respect to a broader hemispheric pact, Hufbauer and Schott wrote *Western Hemisphere Economic Integration* (1994) as a blueprint for the subsequent Summit of the Americas in Miami in December 1994 that launched the effort to construct a Free Trade Area of the Americas. They are currently updating that analysis in light of developments since the Miami summit.

This new book by Richard Feinberg tells the story of the Miami summit. At that meeting, heads of state of the 34 democracies of the region pledged to negotiate a Free Trade Area of the Americas by 2005. They also agreed on an extensive agenda of cooperative initiatives on issues including the defense of democracy, fighting corruption, and preserving the environment. The Miami summit could turn out to be the defining moment in the modern history of the Western Hemisphere.

This book also assesses the first two years of implementation of the Miami initiatives, with recommendations on improving the process of summitry in the Western Hemisphere. Its particular focus is the second summit of the Americas, scheduled for Santiago in March 1998. The analysis integrates the negotiating goals and strategies of the United States and the major Latin American countries, offering a rare synthesis of hemispheric decision making and diplomacy.

Richard Feinberg is uniquely positioned to write this book. As the senior staff member of the National Security Council responsible for Latin America, he took the lead in proposing the Miami summit and overcame a great deal of bureaucratic resistance in achieving Administration agreement to do so. As a distinguished social scientist, Feinberg's analysis of the decision making and diplomacy surrounding the summit and it followup offers important new insights into inter-American relations at a crucial time in their evolution.

The Institute for International Economics is a private nonprofit institution for the study and discussion of international economic policy. Its purpose is to analyze important issues in that area and to develop and communicate practical new approaches for dealing with them. The Institute is completely nonpartisan.

The Institute is funded largely by philanthropic foundations. Major institutional grants are now being received from The German Marshall Fund of the United States, which created the Institute with a generous commitment of funds in 1981, and from The Ford Foundation, The Andrew W. Mellon Foundation, and The Starr Foundation. A number of other foundations and private corporations also contribute to the highly diversified financial resources of the Institute. The AVINA Foundation provided support for this study. The Dayton Hudson Foundation provides general support for our trade-related studies. About 16 percent of the Institute's resources in our latest fiscal year were provided by contributors outside the United States, including about 7 percent from Japan.

The Board of Directors bears overall responsibility for the Institute and gives general guidance and approval to its research program—including identification of topics that are likely to become important to international economic policymakers over the medium run (generally, one to three years), and which thus should be addressed by the Institute. The Director, working closely with the staff and outside Advisory Committee, is responsible for the development of particular projects and makes the final decision to publish an individual study.

The Institute hopes that its studies and other activities will contribute to building a stronger foundation for international economic policy around the world. We invite readers of these publications to let us know how they think we can best accomplish this objective.

C. Fred Bergsten
Director
April 1997

INSTITUTE FOR INTERNATIONAL ECONOMICS
11 Dupont Circle, NW, Washington, DC 20036-1207
(202) 328-9000 Fax: (202) 328-5432

Acknowledgments

This book is at once historical interpretation, policy analysis, and prescriptive advice. It is also a personal memoir. Any book written by a participant in the events he or she is describing will inevitably reflect the perspective of that participant-observer. I have sought to correct for this inherent bias by conducting extensive interviews with other participants in the summitry process from the United States and throughout Latin America and the Caribbean, including official and nongovernmental actors. I also sought balance and insight from relevant scholarly work.

During the "Miami process" leading to the 1994 Summit of the Americas, I made many good friends whose contributions are recognized in their proper place in the story. It was a special privilege to work closely with two distinguished foreign service officers, Anthony Gillespie and Alexander Watson, with the always gracious Thomas "Mack" McLarty, III, and with two of the stories' chief protagonists, Al Gore and Charlene Barshefsky. It was also an honor to sit across the table, at times negotiating texts and at times breaking bread, with such accomplished Latin American and Caribbean diplomats as Roberto Abdenur, Richard Bernal, Fernando Petrella, and Sonia Picado.

As a visiting fellow at the Institute for International Economics, I was privileged to benefit greatly from the collegiality and wisdom of its superb fellows, including Geoffrey Carliner, I.M. Destler, Ellen Frost, Morris Goldstein, Gary Hufbauer, and Jeffrey Schott. Many of the individuals I spoke with from around the hemisphere, in informal conversations and structured interviews, are cited in footnotes, while others requested anonymity. Individuals who provided valuable comments on drafts include

Bowman Cutter, Jorge Dominguez, Robert Pastor, Riordan Roett, Nancy Soderberg, Alexander Watson, and Robert Zoellick. Among my new colleagues at the University of California, San Diego, who brought their well-trained intellects to bear on my drafts, are Dain Borges, Paul Drake, Stephan Haggard, and Miles Kahler. Joseph Tulchin helped me with my historical research and Lael Brainard improved my understanding of the APEC process. Javier Corrales, my coauthor for chapter one, taught me a great deal about summitry's place in the broader context of the history of hemispheric relations, a topic on which much heat but little light has been shed. My description and assessment of summit implementation owes a tremendous debt to a network of researchers (appropriately recognized in chapter 10) assembled by the Institute for International Economics and the University of Miami's North-South Center. Any author of a book of this scope knows the importance of competent and industrious research assistants of the quality that I was blessed with at the Institute for International Economics and the University of California at San Diego: Katharine Brewer, Barbara Kotschwar, Susanna Sitja Rubio, Raymond Greene, Tamera Marko, Jordan Plawner, and Pedro Villegas. I also wish to thank William Leary of the National Security Council's Office of Records and Access Management for his professional assistance and rapid clearance of my manuscript. Of course, I alone am responsible for any remaining errors of fact or interpretation.

I owe a special debt of gratitude to C. Fred Bergsten for his constant encouragement, advice, and support—without which this book would not have been possible. Nor could I have met my many deadlines without the loving companionship of my wife, Diane.

Overview

President Bill Clinton's decision in late 1993 to convene a summit of his counterparts from around the Western Hemisphere the following year marked a turning point in hemispheric relations—a moment in which underlying historical currents and individual initiative converged. Vice President Al Gore, supported by national security adviser Anthony Lake but working outside normal bureaucratic channels, had approached the president directly with the idea of hosting the summit. In a speech in Mexico City on 1 December 1993, Gore invited Latin American leaders to attend and made the case for deepening the ties that bind Western Hemisphere countries.

The result was the Miami summit of December 1994, in which participating heads of state pledged joint commitment to democracy and good governance, economic integration and free trade, the eradication of poverty and discrimination, and sustainable development. The summit launched the Free Trade Area of the Americas and called for completion of negotiations by 2005. It also elevated new issues—including anticorruption, money laundering, civil society, and women's rights—onto the hemispheric agenda and dramatically expanded the scope for collective action in the region.

The first objective of this book is to explain the timing and historical importance of the Miami summit. How did the conditions of the early 1990s differ from those extant during earlier initiatives in inter-American relations? Why did the United States propose such an initiative at this juncture? What was the reaction in Latin America and the Caribbean?

The 1994 summit was the first in a generation. Two previous summits, held in 1956 and 1967, failed to fundamentally alter the course of hemispheric relations; since then, the region has changed greatly. During earlier summits, roughly half of the leaders were military-backed strongmen. Key issues were the size and shape of US aid programs. North-South division prevailed—industrial countries provided economic assistance and eventually trade preferences, but primarily out of security concerns rather than a vision of mutual economic gain. In contrast, by 1993 the hemisphere had become overwhelmingly democratic, and the North American Free Trade Agreement (NAFTA) was opening a door to economic integration that transcended old divides.

Clearly, the time was ripe for a broader initiative. As Gore put it in his Mexico City address, "We will seek to make explicit the convergence of values that is now rapidly taking place in a hemispheric community of democracies, a community increasingly integrated by commercial exchange and shared political values." Throughout Latin America and the Caribbean, there had been a turn toward democratic governance and more open markets. In sharp contrast to the authoritarian wave of the 1970s, by the early 1990s there were Central and South American democracies in power that guaranteed periodic elections and considerable freedom. Only the Caribbean states of Cuba and, for a time, Haiti resisted these democratic trends. In the economic realm, governments were shedding statist, protectionist policies in favor of market-oriented economic reforms, opening their economies to international trade and reinvigorating subregional integration arrangements that were generally consistent with global market integration.

In contrast to earlier fears that the international economy was dangerously unstable and harshly unfair, by the early 1990s Latin American policymakers and intellectuals increasingly perceived their integration into the international economy to be not only inevitable but on balance beneficial. Latin America's elected leaders—interested in fortifying their democracies and opening their economies—welcomed the support of the world's largest market economy and most powerful democracy. Whereas in the past many Latin American politicians sought to discredit their enemies by identifying them with the United States, by the 1990s Latin American leaders strengthened their domestic positions through association with US presidents.

Shifts in US policy were part of this hemispheric convergence. With the end of the Cold War, the US government abandoned opportunistic arguments of past administrations that had served as apologia for authoritarian stability and threw its support behind human rights and democracy. In the economic realm, the United States in the 1980s reversed field and turned toward bilateral and regional free trade arrangements, making NAFTA possible and US policymakers more receptive to Latin American entreaties for a special hemispheric trading arrangement. Strategically, some US policymakers, including Presidents Bush and Clinton, increasingly perceived this more democratic and friendly Latin America as an opportunity—a next-door neighbor that could provide political allies and profitable markets.

A second objective of this book is to describe the policy processes—within the US government and among the countries of the hemisphere—that created the Plan of Action endorsed in Miami. Drawing on his experience on the Clinton administration's National Security Council staff, the author offers an up-to-date understanding of how the US executive branch makes policy toward Latin America. The book's discussions of functional issues, such as international trade, narcotics, and environment, shed light on policymaking processes of broader application. The importance of the functional agencies, the problems of bureaucratic coordination, and the dichotomy of authority and expertise are examined in the context of the post-Cold War period.

The book's descriptions of hemispheric diplomacy are intended to illuminate the contemporary attitudes of the major countries and regions in the Western Hemisphere. These attitudes are dramatically different from what they were at the time of previous summits in 1956 and 1967, and even from those that were most prevalent in the 1980s. Therefore, innovative ways to build winning coalitions, involve diverse constituencies, and overcome remaining conflicts of ideology and interests will be required if the opportunities for hemispheric reconciliation are to be realized.

A third objective of this book is to assess the outcomes of the Miami summit and offer recommendations for improving and institutionalizing summitry in the Americas. The Miami summit produced a declaration of principles and a plan of action that contained 23 initiatives replete with over 150 action items. Yet countervailing forces (antihemispheric bias, nationalism, protectionism, bureaucratic obstruction)—in the United States and key Latin American countries—and the lack of a decision-driving crisis continually threaten successful implementation of the Miami initiatives. The ultimate judgment on the Miami summit will depend on the degree to which its spirit of cooperation endures, its texts are implemented, and the process of summitry continues.

This book will argue that summits are crucial to the pursuit of vital US and Latin American interests and that institutionalizing the summit process begun in Miami is the only foreseeable way to maintain momentum in Latin American relations. From the author's perspective as a promoter and planner of the original summit, this book also offers recommendations on how the process can be improved and how it can be made part of the ongoing policy agenda in the United States, much as the summits of the Asia Pacific Economic Cooperation (APEC) forum have become for that region.

In his State of the Union address in January 1997 and through his announcement of trips to Mexico City and Latin America in 1997, President Clinton again has signaled his intention to keep hemispheric relations on the radar screen of US foreign and economic policymaking. The next scheduled summit—to be held in Santiago, Chile, in March 1998—will test the hemisphere's commitment to diplomatic goodwill and the concrete goals and objectives first established in Miami.

Plan of the Book

Chapters 1 and 2 set the historical context. In these chapters, US-Latin American relations are reinterpreted as a struggle between those who favor hemispherism—that is, closer ties among nations, with the goals of bolstering republican institutions and promoting mutual prosperity—and those who fear, distrust, or disdain their neighbors. Hemispheric history is not simply a tale of the United States pitted against or in favor of Latin America but reflects a more complex picture of the United States and the countries of Latin America harboring both hemispherism's opponents and proponents. Only rarely have the prohemispheric forces been ascendant throughout the region, and it was during those periods that hemispheric cooperation made the most progress.

Chapter 3 draws on the author's personal participation in the summit initiative and describes the circumvention of the executive branch bureaucracy that resulted in the presidential decision to convene a Latin American summit. Lacking in strong bureaucratic constituencies, free of major conflict, and facing the ever-present antihemispheric forces, Latin America was not a strong candidate for presidential attention. Indeed, a senior-level group had brushed aside the idea just before Vice President Gore leaped to embrace it.

Chapters 4 and 7 analyze the process that culminated in the US decision to negotiate hemispheric free trade by 2005. The delays and obstacles thrown up during the bureaucratic process strongly suggest that, without the summit, the United States would not have bound itself to negotiate a Free Trade Area of the Americas by a set deadline and regionwide free trade would probably have remained a vague aspiration, not a solid hemispheric consensus.

Chapters 5 through 9 describe the Miami summit diplomatic process, which produced the most far-reaching documents in the history of hemispheric diplomacy. An unusual mixture of strategies—bilateralism, geography-based plurilateralism, and issue-specific coalition building—produced initiatives that had the support of a winning coalition of states and many nongovernmental actors. This highly experimental Miami process was not without its flaws, but it did capture the energies of the region's international agencies, functional ministries, and organized civil society.

Chapters 8 and 9 detail the final vice-ministerial meeting at Airlie House in Warrenton, Virginia, as well as the private discussions among the leaders in Miami.

The two final chapters describe post-Miami implementation and offer recommendations for making summitry work better. The Miami summit revealed a rich new texture in inter-American relations, which now included international agencies (the Organization of American States, but also several economic and social agencies), the cabinets and ministries of governments, and public-private sector partnerships. Drawing on the work of an independent team of researchers, the author concluded that, of twelve of the more salient initiatives, very good or good progress was being made on four initiatives (civil society, anticorruption, energy, and pollution prevention), and modest progress was being made on seven others (democracy, human rights, narcotics and money laundering, education, women's rights, capital markets, and trade). Little movement was registered in biodiversity. Chapters 10 and 11 identify significant impediments to full implementation: the excessive number of action items; inadequate financial resources; lack of measurable goals, priorities, and timetables; slippage within the international agencies; weak monitoring mechanisms; and the absence of a central coordinating mechanism capable of overseeing implementation.

The challenge for the future is to build on successes while correcting for the flaws that remain in hemispheric summitry. The 1998 Santiago summit presents another major opportunity to advance the consensus agenda legitimized in Miami. The concluding chapter proposes initiatives to keep US policy focused on this goal and lays out ideas on how the leaders can make progress at the next Summit of the Americas.

1

Why Did It Take 200 Years? The Intellectual Journey to the Summit of the Americas

with Javier Corrales

In 1990, Mexico made a daring proposal to the United States: the establishment of a free trade zone between both nations. This was not the first time that a Latin American nation had approached the United States with the intention of securing a special bilateral relationship or economic alliance. Ever since their independence from Europe, many Latin American nations had hoped at some point to construct a special relationship with their powerful northern neighbor. For nearly two centuries, the United States typically shied away from such ties.

This time, however, the United States reacted differently. First, President George Bush embraced Mexico's proposal to negotiate a free trade agreement and in his Enterprise for the Americas Initiative (EAI) envisioned expanding free trade throughout the hemisphere. President Bill Clinton completed the North American Free Trade Agreement (NAFTA) negotiations and in a bruising domestic political battle persuaded the US Congress to ratify the agreement. Clinton went further: he authorized Vice President Al Gore to invite the democratically elected presidents and heads of governments of the Americas to a summit meeting to discuss ways of deepening hemispheric cooperation through economic integra-

Javier Corrales is Visiting Assistant Professor of Political Science at Amherst College, Amherst, Massachusetts. His area of research is comparative and international politics of Latin America. He has been a consultant for the World Bank, the Inter-American Dialogue, and the Harvard Institute for International Development. He is presently writing a book on the role of Executive-Ruling Party relations in the politics of economic reform in Argentina and Venezuela in the 1990s.

tion and a shared commitment to democratic institutions. Gore extended the invitation during a 1 December 1993 speech in Mexico City. All invitees promptly accepted, many hoping that the summit would open the doors to closer relations and perhaps even an economic alliance with the United States.

That the members of the Western Hemisphere accepted the invitation to an inter-American summit was not new. Prior convocations of Pan-American meetings were typically welcomed—with varying degrees of enthusiasm—by the nations of the hemisphere. What was new this time was the Latin Americans' counterproposal: free trade should be the centerpiece of the summit agenda, if not the precondition for a successful summit. Never before had most Latin American nations been so keen on establishing a hemispherewide free trade regime that would include the United States and Canada. Initially reluctant (chapter 4), the United States eventually embraced the offer.

These two turning points in intrahemispheric affairs—the decision by Presidents Bush and Clinton to engage Latin America and Latin America's insistence that free trade be part of such cooperative efforts—are the basis of the declaration of principles and the associated plan of action proclaimed at the Summit of the Americas in Miami 9-11 December 1994. What explains these momentous decisions? What prompted the United States to look to Latin America as an area worthy of close political and economic ties? Why did 34 nations of the hemisphere agree to sign the most far-reaching document on intrahemispheric integration in 1994 but not before? In short, what explains the rise in the 1990s of what we choose to call "hemispherism"—that is, the active attempt by the nations of the hemisphere to redirect their foreign policies in favor of closer political and economic ties with one another with the joint goal of bolstering republican institutions and promoting economic exchange?[1]

---

1. Hemispherism, as we define it, is a type of regionalism. Andrew Gamble and Anthony Payne define regionalism as state efforts to "deepen the integration of particular regional economic spaces," *Regionalism and World Order* (London: The MacMillan Press, 1996), 258. Gamble and Payne and others rightly point out that regionalism in the Western Hemisphere in the 1990s is better described as "open regionalism" because it did not emerge as an alternative to globalization (as regionalism traditionally tends to be). See, for example, Louise Fawcett and Andrew Hurrell, eds., *Regionalism in World Politics: Regional Organizations and International Order* (New York: Oxford University Press, 1995), and Economic Commission for Latin American and the Caribbean (ECLAC), *Open Regionalism in Latin America and the Caribbean* (Santiago: United Nations, 1995). Although this regionalism is based on regional preferences, and membership is closed to extraregional countries, it is trade-creating and potentially consistent with General Agreement on Tariffs and Trade (GATT)-World Trade Organization (WTO) principles. In addition, the summit texts call for hemispheric cooperation as a step toward globalization. They go beyond traditional conceptions of open regionalism because they are not exclusively concerned with economic issues; they also tackle political and social concerns. That is one reason we prefer to use a different label for this concept.

An answer to these questions lies in the evolution of intellectual traditions in inter-American relations (table 1.1).[2] Historically, the notion that it is in the best interest of the nations of the Western Hemisphere to seek close ties with one another had been a powerful intellectual tradition throughout the Americas. But it typically failed to dominate in the United States and in Latin America. Rival intellectual traditions always reined in hemispheric integration projects. In the late 1980s, however, the intellectual climate throughout the Western Hemisphere changed dramatically. For the first time, the balance shifted in favor of hemispherism. This shift occurred through a simultaneous process of idea strengthening and idea attrition: intellectual traditions in favor of hemispherism gained prestige, while traditions that conspired against hemispherism lost ground. The result was what Vice President Al Gore called "a new moment" for the leaders of the hemisphere to decide in favor of closer cooperation.[3]

The Miami texts proudly trumpet the four major intellectual traditions that experienced idea strengthening: the joint commitment to strengthening republican institutions, economic integration and free trade, the eradication of poverty and discrimination, and sustainable development. Never before had so many nations of the hemisphere come to accept these values and goals simultaneously.

However, jointly embracing a series of common goals and objectives was not sufficient for all 34 nations to sign the summit texts. It was also necessary for the ideas that discounted the benefits of hemispherism to lose appeal. In the United States, perhaps the most important was the notion that Latin America represented a problem rather than an opportunity. Until the 1990s, the United States had generally looked elsewhere—either to other regions of the world or simply inward to itself—in search of prosperity and security. Most US administrations concluded that Latin

---

2. An intellectual tradition can be defined as the combination of ideas, values, and images that prevail in a given society. Ideas, in turn, can be thought of as "social knowledge," or theories employed by intellectuals to explain social phenomena. Peter A. Hall, ed., *The Political Power of Economic Ideas: Keynesianism across Nations* (Princeton, NJ: Princeton University Press, 1989), 361. Values are the set of "ideological and ethical preferences" that shape the way individuals make normative judgments about the world. Mark P. Lagon, "Elite Values," in *US-Latin American Policy Making: A Reference Handbook,* ed. David W. Dent (Westport, CT: Greenwood Press, 1995), 67. Images are "patterns of perception" or "cognitive prisms" that allow individuals to filter, organize, and simplify the information received from the environment. Martha L. Cottam, *Images and Intervention: US Policies in Latin America* (Pittsburgh: University of Pittsburgh Press, 1994), 18. While scholars disagree on which of these elements—theories, values, and images—ought to be the focus of analysis, there is increasing tendency to agree that ideas play a causal role in foreign policy (see, for example, Judith Goldstein and Robert Keohane, eds., *Ideas and Foreign Policy: Beliefs, Institutions, and Political Change,* Ithaca, NY: Cornell University Press, 1993).

3. Al Gore, "Foreword," in *A New Moment in the Americas,* ed. Robert S. Leiken (New Brunswick, NJ: Transaction Publishers, 1994).

Table 1.1 Ideas in favor of and against hemispherism

Period	In favor of hemispherism (most prevalent in)	Against hemispherism (most prevalent in)
18th century	The Western Hemisphere idea (US and LA)	
early 19th century	No-transfer resolution and the Monroe Doctrine (US) The United States is regarded as a political model (LA)	Isolationism-neutralism (US and some LA nations) The no-benefits doctrine (US) Multiple partnership options (LA) • Bolivarianism: Spanish-American unity under the United Kingdom, without the United States and Brazil • Europeanism: bilateral alliances with Europe • Latin-Americanism: Spanish-American unity • Internalism-isolationism • Quarrel-thy-neighbor: mistrust neighbor states
late 19th century	The new Pan-Americanism is born (US) Strengthening of (economic) liberalism (LA)	Camouflaged imperialism (US) Conservative Yankeephobia: cultural rejection of the United States (LA)
early 20th century	Some strands of anti-imperialism are prohemispheric (LA)	The rise of modern Yankeephobia: anti-imperialist thinking (LA) The rise of the guarantor-client image of inter-American affairs (US)
post-World War II	Acceptance of nonintervention principle (US) Internationalism-globalism (US and LA) LA is seen as a reliable (military) ally (US) Prestige of the US's (anti-totalitarian) foreign policy (LA) Prestige of democracy (US and LA)	North-Atlanticism replaces hemispherism (US) The demise of economic liberalism (LA)

continued on next page

Table 1.1 (continued)

Period	In favor of hemispherism (most prevalent in)	Against hemispherism (most prevalent in)
mid-1950s to mid-1980s	Developmentalism theory in vogue (US)	LA as less strategically important than Eurasia (US)
	Pro-Latin American Cold War hawks (US)	Illiberal politics in LA revives the no-benefit doctrine (US)
	Pro-US conservative forces (LA)	LA as a problem and as a nonreliable partner (US)
	The rise of a democratic left (some LA countries)	The end of prodemocracy foreign policies (US and LA)
		North-South divide more important than East-West conflict (LA) • Self-reliance instead of self-help • Nationalism (embedded in state and party institutions) • Rebirth of Yankeephobia • Overexpanded view of sovereignty and nonintervention • Decline of democratic ideas • Aid addiction and trade as aid
late 1980s	Prestige of democracy again (US and LA)	Drugs, crime, and illegal immigrants (US and LA)
	Southern states experience the (trade) benefits of hemispherism (US)	Indecision about trade with low-wage nations (US)
	Proliferation of pro-Latin America think tanks (US)	Persistence of illiberal politics in LA encourages the no-benefit doctrine (US)
	New approaches to debt: the return of trust (US and LA)	Revival of conservative Yankeephobia (LA)
	Redefinition of the concept of sovereignty (LA)	Lingering rent-seeking tendencies (LA and US)
	From "trade as aid" to "trade instead of aid" (LA)	
	The Washington consensus and the Latin American amendment (US and LA)	
	Opposition forces trust the US (LA)	

LA = Latin America

America was simply a low-priority problem that had to be ignored, quickly resolved, or utilized for ulterior motives. Intrahemispheric relations should remain cordial but not too close because strong ties would bring little benefit. The United States preferred a Latin America bound to it but shied away from reciprocating with equally close ties. Promoting order and combating political vulnerabilities were valued above pursuing integration. The United States typically paid attention to the region during great crises (World War II, after the Cuban Revolution), reverting to declining interest the rest of the time.[4]

For the rest of the countries in the hemisphere, the traditional suspicion that close ties with the United States (and even among themselves) invariably favored the stronger party hindered hemispherism.[5] This fear of asymmetrical gains and losses also accounted for the often exaggerated exaltation of nonintervention by Latin American diplomats since the late 19th century. As will be argued, this fixation on nonintervention precluded Latin American participation in collective efforts necessary for hemispheric security, prosperity, and democracy. The United States typically interpreted this lack of cooperation as corroboration of the unreliability of Latin American nations as partners.

This chapter subscribes to the notion that intellectual traditions indeed shape policy. It does not purport to present an exhaustive history of hemispheric relations, nor does it deny the importance of other economic, structural, or institutional factors that have molded them.[6] It recognizes that US-Latin American relations have indeed been shaped by interests,

---

4. See, for example, Robert A. Pastor, *Whirlpool: US Foreign Policy toward Latin America and the Caribbean* (Princeton, NJ: Princeton University Press, 1992); Federico G. Gil, *Latin America-United States Relations* (New York: Harcourt Brace Jovanovich, Inc., 1971); Michael Kryzanek, *US-Latin American Relations,* 3d ed. (Westport, CT: Praeger Press, 1996); and Martha L. Cottam, *Images and Intervention.*

5. According to many neorealists, when a nation estimates that a counterpart might gain more from cooperation, it is less inclined to cooperate: the fear that relative gains made by the other could be used against one's disadvantage precludes cooperation (e.g., see Robert Powell, "Absolute and Relative Gains in International Relations Theory" in *Neorealism and Neoliberalism. The Contemporary Debate,* ed. David A. Baldwin (Columbia University Press, 1993). However, some neorealists offer a less reductionist view of "gain." For example, rather than define gains and losses strictly in terms of military capacity, Joseph M. Grieco argues that nations worry about any type of gain. See Joseph M. Grieco, "Understanding the Problem of International Cooperation: The Limits of Neoliberal Institutionalism and the Future of Realist Theory," in *Neorealism and Neoliberalism.* In Latin America, this more expansive definition of gains and losses is worth upholding because Latin American nations are often more concerned about cultural and symbolic gains and losses in inter-American affairs.

6. For recent essays representing different approaches to US-Latin American relations, including literature reviews, see David W. Dent, ed., *US-Latin American Policy Making.*

conflicts, opportunism, and crises, as most of the literature on the subject makes abundantly clear. Rather, this chapter aims to highlight the intellectual context of hemispherism. When the prevailing intellectual climate was against it, hemispherism simply could not flourish, even if it was supported by important presidents (for example, during the Alliance for Progress in the 1960s), or probable given structural and systemic factors (as in the early nineteenth century). But when the climate shifted in favor of hemispherism, leaders were sometimes able to create stronger cooperation than structuralist realists would have predicted.[7] This is precisely what took place in the Americas in the early 1990s. We now examine why it took more than 200 years for this to happen.

The Western Hemisphere Idea

Before the birth of most American nations, the idea that the societies of the Western Hemisphere shared special bonds with one another was already alive. The core proposition of this "Western Hemisphere idea" is that the peoples of this hemisphere stand in a "special relationship to one another" that sets them apart from the rest of the world.[8] According to this view, the societies of the hemisphere share more than a geographic location; they also share the desire to pursue a common world project: the construction of nontyrannical, republican institutions under which citizens could extend their liberties and prosper free from the vestiges of European feudalism. In short, the Americas were the privileged antitheses of Europe. Security is also part of the Western Hemisphere idea. The idea assumes that the societies of the Western Hemisphere face a similar security dilemma in international relations: the world as a whole is not especially hospitable to the construction of the political project intended by the founding leaders of the Americas. Consequently, the societies of the hemisphere are natural allies who not only share a deep esteem for one another but also need one another to thrive in the world.

The Western Hemisphere idea was both revolutionary and powerful in international relations when it was born in the 18th century. It was

---

7. Structuralists suggest that entrenched structures of power asymmetries in US-Latin American and inter-Latin American relations are an inherent source of political conflict. Cooperation under these conditions is unlikely, unless the hegemon is willing to assume the cost. However, in the Western Hemisphere there have been numerous variations in the levels of hemispheric cooperation despite the little variation in power structures since the late 19th century. And, as this chapter argues, these differences in levels of cooperation have not depended exclusively on the willingness of the hegemon to absorb the cost. For a recent structuralist account of hemispheric relations, see Peter H. Smith, *Talons of the Eagle: Dynamics of US-Latin American Relations* (New York: Oxford University Press, 1996).

8. Arthur P. Whitaker, *The Western Hemisphere Idea: Its Rise and Decline* (Ithaca, NY: Cornell University Press, 1954), 1.

revolutionary because until then thinkers from both sides of the Atlantic tended to avoid establishing differences between the New World and the Old. The Americas were considered simply an extension of Europe. But in the mid-18th century, some Europeans began to disparage the New World as a degenerate and monstrous land. This prompted many intellectuals from both North and South America to defend the New World, thus giving rise to the Western Hemisphere idea. The idea that the Americas shared a unique destiny became one of the most powerful intellectual inspirations of the independence struggle in the Americas.[9] But, however powerful, this idea would have its detractors in each generation.

Early 19th Century: Hemispherism Aborted

In the early 19th century, it seemed for a while that the Western Hemisphere idea would become the dominant doctrine in the foreign policies of the new American nations. For example in 1811, menaced by European powers eager to conquer new territories or reconquer lost ones, the US Congress passed the No-Transfer Resolution, which stipulated that the United States "cannot without serious inquietude see any part of the said territory pass into the hands of any foreign power." In 1823, President James Monroe carried the idea further in his famous Monroe Doctrine, which contained hemispheric statements such as:

- American continents . . . are henceforth not to be considered as subjects for future colonization by any European powers. . . .
- With the movements in this hemisphere we are of necessity more immediately connected. . . .
- The political system of the allied powers [in Europe] is essentially different . . . from that of America. . . .
- We should consider any attempt on their part to extend their system to any portion of this hemisphere as dangerous to our peace and safety.

This was the fullest articulation of the Western Hemisphere idea by a US administration.[10] The free lands of the Americas, by virtue of geographic location, were deemed off-limits to Europeans, and the United States committed itself to nondespotical institutions in the Americas. Moreover,

---

9. For instance, Father Molina in his *Historia de Chile* (1776), Father Clavigero in his *Historia Antigua de México* (1780), Thomas Jefferson in his *Notes on the State of Virginia* (1785), and Alexander Hamilton in *The Federalist* (1788).

10. Pope G. Atkins, *Latin America in the International Political System*, 3d ed. (Boulder, CO: Westview Press, 1995).

the United States seemed to be aligning its own security, peace, and happiness with the destiny of the other American nations.

In Latin America, the idea of a shared destiny also had an auspicious beginning. For it to flourish, some degree of esteem must exist among all the nations of the hemisphere. During the first decades of the 19th century, esteem for the United States among Latin American nations was profound.[11] The founding leaders of Latin America compared themselves to their US counterparts. They, too, were motivated to seek independence by the notion that the societies of the Western Hemisphere had grown apart from Europe and by their strong esteem for republicanism. For example, the Mexican statesman Lucas Alamán stated that although nature had made the countries of America neighbors, "the similarity of their political institutions has bound them even more closely together, strengthening in them the dominion of just and liberal principles."[12] Many Latin American founding leaders and intellectuals considered the United States a model for designing their own constitutions.[13] They also shared the same security concerns that worried the United States: fear that European powers, which were interested in gaining or recovering lands in the Americas, would take back their hard-won independence. Some Latin American leaders even proposed formal hemispheric political and economic alliances against Europe.[14] Those who took note of the the Monroe Doctrine (for example, the government of Argentina) approved of it. The independence leader Simón Bolívar praised it. Brazil and Colombia even suggested instituting the Monroe Doctrine as a hemisphere doctrine. Brazil, Colombia, and Mexico also proposed to the United States establishing formal bilateral alliances.[15] The first hemispheric congress ever proposed, the Congress of Panama (1826), was a Latin American initiative.

Despite the strength of prohemispheric sentiments and interests in the 19th century, the nations of the hemisphere did not form close alliances.

---

11. José de Onís, *The United States as Seen by Spanish American Writers (1776-1890)* (New York: Hispanic Institute of the United States, 1952).

12. Quoted in Whitaker, *The Western Hemisphere Idea*, 2.

13. Even the not-so-pro-US Simón Bolívar looked to the United States as "a unique model of political virtues and moral enlightenment." Quoted in Carlos M. Rama, *La imagen de los Estados Unidos en la América Latina: De Simón Bolívar a Salvador Allende* (México: Secretaría de Educación Pública, 1975), 13. See also de Onís, *Spanish American Writers.*

14. The Chilean Francisco Bilbao went as far as to call for a common citizenship, a federal union, and the abolition of custom duties in the Americas. In 1810, the Lima-born, Chile-resident intellectual Don Juan Egaña conceived a "Plan for the General Defense of the Entire America," calling for hemispheric governments to contribute "arms, money, and men in case of the slightest attack from, or sedition originating in, Europe." In José Agustín Balseiro, *The Americas Look at Each Other*, translated by Muna Muñoz Lee (Coral Gables: University of Miami Press, 1969), 41-42.

15. Gil, *Latin America-United States Relations*, 62.

In the United States, there were two rival intellectual traditions: isolationism and what we call the "no-benefit" doctrine.

The ever-appealing notion of isolationism—the idea that it was in the best interest of the country to avoid "entangling alliances" with foreign nations—was a serious challenge to hemispherism in the United States. Originally cast as a doctrine to keep the United States free from the broils of Europe, isolationism was quickly extended to the entire globe by US politicians: the United States should remain neutral not just in European conflicts but in every international issue, including inter-American affairs.

An even stronger enemy of the Western Hemisphere idea was the belief that the United States stood to derive no benefit from close association with the other nations of the Americas. This "no-benefit" idea first appeared during the 1810s, when the United States debated its position toward the wars of independence in Latin America. In 1818, a leading advocate of hemispherism in the House of Representatives, Henry Clay, strongly condemned the administration for its hesitation to recognize and support the independence of the new American nations. Secretary of State John Quincy Adams responded by invoking not just the desirability of neutrality but also expressing in his diaries skepticism that the United States could benefit from such an alliance: "So far as [Latin Americans] were contending for independence, I wished well to their cause; but I had seen and yet see no prospect that they would establish free or liberal institutions of government. They are not likely to promote the spirit either of freedom or order by their example. They have not the first elements of good or free government. Arbitrary power, military and ecclesiastical, was stamped upon their education, upon their habits, and upon all their institutions . . . I had little expectation of any beneficial result to this country from any future connection with them, political or commercial. We should derive no improvement to our own institutions by any communion with theirs."[16]

The no-benefit doctrine resurfaced again a few years later in the debate over the Congress of Panama. In defiance of Bolívar, who wanted the congress to be a forum of Spanish-speaking countries, the presidents of Colombia, Central America, and Mexico invited the United States and Brazil to participate, thereby transforming the congress into a Pan-American affair. President John Quincy Adams wanted to send delegates, but he encountered fierce domestic opposition, especially in the US Congress. To get approval for the mission, Adams had to assure Congress that the United States would remain free of any commitments. In the end, Congress authorized the mission, but the delay prevented the US delegate from arriving in time. So the United States was absent from the first true

16. Thomas L. Karnes, ed., *Readings in the Latin American Policy of the United States* (Tucson: The University of Arizona Press, 1972), 17.

Pan-American gathering as a direct result of the isolation and no-benefit doctrines. These doctrines proved to be decisive influences on US foreign policy toward the region during most of the 19th century.

The Western Hemisphere idea also had opponents in Latin America, where governments and citizens were intensely divided over at least five foreign partnership options: Bolivarianism, Europeanism, Internalism, Latin-Americanism, and Quarrel-thy-neighbor.

Simón Bolívar was a strong advocate of unity among Latin American nations to preserve independence. But he was equally emphatic about excluding the United States and Brazil from this union. Brazil was to be excluded because of its Portuguese heritage and because it was a monarchy rather than a republic. The United States was to be excluded also because of its British heritage and because it was deemed too weak to provide reliable protection against Europeans. Instead, Bolívar hoped that England would become the military protector of a South American federation. Thus, Bolivarianism was a violation of the Western Hemisphere idea on two counts: the exclusion of non-Spanish-speaking nations, and the inclusion of a European tutor.[17]

Rather than seek closer ties among the nations of the hemisphere, some Latin Americans advocated developing strong bilateral ties with European powers. The first major foreign policy preoccupation of most was to be accepted in the international (European) community of nations. This fixation on securing Europe's blessing made leaders avoid decisions that might upset the Europeans.[18] Close alliances within the hemisphere, which might be construed by Europeans as too hostile or separatist, had to be bypassed. Some South American nations hoped to establish formal bilateral alliances with European powers, often in defense against neighbors or domestic enemies, or as partners in their efforts to fulfill their own "manifest destiny."[19] The Europeanists, however, were themselves highly divided over which European power to seek ties with: England, France, or even Spain.

As in the United States, isolationism appealed to many Latin American circles in the early 19th century. Latin American isolationists argued that national efforts should be directed first toward internal problems such as

17. There were various attempts to create Bolivarian congresses in the 19th century: the Lima Congress (1847-1848) attended by Bolivia, Chile, Ecuador, New Granada, and Peru; the Santiago Congress (1856) attended by Chile, Ecuador, and Peru; and the Second Lima Congress (1864-1865) attended by Bolivia, Chile, Colombia, Ecuador, Peru, and Venezuela.

18. Harold Eugene Davis, "Relations During the Time of Troubles, 1825-1860," in *Latin American Diplomatic History*, eds. Harold Eugene Davis, John J. Finan, and F. Taylor Peck (Baton Rouge: Louisiana State University Press, 1977).

19. To varying degrees, most Latin American nations considered themselves territorially deprived. But unlike the United States, there was no consensus in Latin America that the pursuit of manifest destiny should be conducted without the help of a European power.

state building and domestic pacification. For them, hemispherism represented a distraction from the vital interests of the nation.

One of the strongest intellectual rivals of hemispherism is Latin-Americanism—the idea that the Americas are fundamentally divided into separate ethnic-cultural groups: those of Latin descent (including Spanish, Portuguese, and French) and the Anglo-Saxon. Whereas hemispherism calls for integrating the Americas on the basis of common values and goals, Latin-Americanism would separate the Latins and the Anglos on the basis of ethnic background.[20]

Almost every Latin American nation was born with uncertain borders. Territorial disputes further multiplied with the dismemberment of most of the first republics after the 1820s: Mexico lost Texas and Central America, Central America in turn broke up into five republics, New Granada broke up into Colombia, Venezuela, and Ecuador, and La Plata broke up into Uruguay, Argentina, Paraguay, and Bolivia. The uncertainty of territorial settlements, and the violence produced by secessionist trends, instilled some mutual mistrust among Latin American nations that in turn hurt hemispherism.[21]

The Western Hemisphere idea faced formidable (and perhaps more numerous) rivals in Latin America. Collectively, these ideas effectively paralyzed every hemispheric impetus. There always emerged a nation or an intellectual leader ready to question the motives of any such initiative or protest the inclusion or exclusion of the United States, Brazil, a neighbor, or any European power for that matter.

Pan-Americanism in the Late 19th Century

After virtually ignoring most of the southern continent for more than 50 years, the United States began to take a serious interest in Pan-Americanism in the 1880s. In this "new Pan-Americanism," as Mecham calls it, the United States now took the initiative and broadened its scope (that is, keeping extrahemispheric actors out of the region), to include the creation of institutions to facilitate political cooperation, regional commerce, and peacemaking promotion within the hemisphere.[22] Secretary of State James G. Blaine, a leading Pan-Americanist, persuaded the administration to

---

20. Latin-Americanism differs from Bolivarianism in that it calls for unity among all nations of Latin America, including Brazil, and rejects the inclusion of Great Britain.

21. This reveals the complicated relation between Latin-Americanism and hemispherism. Although Latin-Americanism posed a challenge or an alternative to hemispherism, some degree of Latin-Americanism (that is, sisterhood among Latin nations) is also a precondition of hemispherism.

22. J. Lloyd Mecham, *The United States and Inter-American Security, 1889-1960* (Austin: University of Texas Press, 1962).

convoke the first official Pan-American Congress.[23] Latin Americans welcomed the proposal for institutions of cooperation, but were less enthusiastic about hemispheric trade, being hesitant to give up their secure trade with Europe for uncertain New World markets. Some were receptive to peace maintenance but efforts in this direction were thwarted by countries engaged in serious territorial disputes, such as Chile.

A significant booster of hemispherism was the strengthening of political liberalism in Latin America. Latin American liberals identified closely with the United States and hemispherism in general. A good example of this liberalism is Domingo Sarmiento, an Argentine version of Alexis de Tocqueville, who traveled to the United States looking for the sources of US democracy. Liberals did not propose that Latin America slavishly imitate the United States, but they all shared esteem for the values embedded in hemispherism. Sarmiento, who became president of Argentina, symbolized the political inroads made by liberals throughout the Americas. Liberals also made economic inroads, ushering in the period of greatest export promotion and integration in the world economy since independence. By the end of the 19th century, the value of free trade became nonpolemical throughout Latin America, even among conservatives.[24]

Despite these leaps, hemispherism was again frustrated by the force of alternative intellectual traditions. Many in the United States came to support Blaine's new Pan-Americanism for reasons that had little to do with the Western Hemisphere idea. It represented an opportunity to compete against Germany and England for influence in South America and get hemispheric consent for US incursions in the Caribbean. For imperialists, Pan-Americanism was useful for keeping extrahemispheric forces out of the continent and amplifying the capacity of the United States to maneuver in the region. Some supported it because they saw the possibility of replicating Prussia's Zollverein in the Americas—a customs union under a single hegemon.

Another break on hemispherism was the expansion of Yankeephobia in Latin America. Although pro-US sentiments were gaining strength in Latin America with the rise of liberalism in the second half of the 19th

---

23. This was not easy. Between 1883 and the First Pan-American Congress (1889), more than five bills authorizing such a congress were turned down. Wilfrid Hardy Callcott, *The Western Hemisphere: Its Influence on United States Policies to the End of World War II* (Austin: University of Texas Press, 1968).

24. See Victor Bulmer-Thomas, *The Economic History of Latin America since Independence* (New York: Cambridge University Press, 1994). Latin American elites came to agree that the best hope for advancement lay with free trade and integration in the world economy. However, this enthusiasm for free trade was not automatic nor all-encompassing, because, as mentioned, not all Latin Americans were prepared to open up to the United States, and the United States, in turn, was not that committed to free trade (although far more committed than many Europeans).

century, anti-US sentiments were also growing. Except in Mexico, which had suffered severe military losses to the United States, Latin American Yankeephobia during this period was less a reaction against US imperialism than it was a conservative, Latin-Catholic, cultural reaction against the growing prestige of Anglo-Saxon, Protestant, liberal values throughout the world. Uruguayan philosopher José Enrique Rodó epitomized this position, warning his fellow Latin Americans not to "let yourselves be seduced by the material power of the Caliban [the United States]." For Rodó, the United States was a half-educated, spiritually deficient, and culturally mediocre empire. Latins should instead reinforce their Latinism-Hellenism and attend to the things of the spirit—the arts, the sciences, morality, religion, and so on.[25]

Another source of Yankeephobia was the cautious neutrality of the United States. The United States refused to implement the Monroe Doctrine during most Euro-American conflicts, or to take sides with any American country involved in a territorial dispute.[26] For most Latin Americans, Yankeephobia was therefore based on the presupposition that the United States cared little about the region, or at least their own country, and was more pro-European than it cared to show. And countries such as Argentina and Mexico saw the United States as a competitor for hegemony and an obstacle to their own manifest destiny. Thus, while many Latin Americans were welcoming the new United States commitment to the hemisphere, many conservative Latin Americans were unimpressed and even alarmed.

Imperialism and Anti-imperialism: The Early 20th Century

Between the 1890s and the late 1920s, hemispherism suffered major setbacks. In the United States, the image of Latin America as an unsuitable partner gained strength. In Latin America, Yankeephobia grew in scope and intensity, and universalism rather than hemispherism emerged as a dominant force.

Three political factors—two international and one Latin American—contributed to the surge of Yankeephobia in Latin America. The first was the by-then-unquestionable fact that by the late 19th century the United

25. José Enrique Rodó, *Ariel*, transl. Margaret Sayers Peden (Austin, TX: University of Texas Press, 1988).

26. Argentina, for instance, resented the United States for refusing to take its side during its conflicts with Brazil and during the British occupation of the Falklands in the 1830s. In the 1860s, the United States failed to deter the Spanish military incursions against Valparaiso (Chile) and the Chincha Islands (Peru). Cuban insurgents were frustrated by US refusal to help in the 1868 and 1878 wars against Spain.

States had become the most powerful nation in the hemisphere, far outstripping Latin America. This power asymmetry spawned resistance to the Western Hemisphere idea in the early 20th century. In some US sectors, it fueled the image of Latin America as a feeble, dependent region and of the United States as its superior and messiah. In parts of Latin American society, the possibility that "the big fish would eat the little ones," as Haya de la Torre said, provoked jealousy and fear.[27]

The second factor was US hyperinterventionism in the Caribbean. After the Spanish-American War (1898), the United States repeatedly intervened politically and militarily throughout the Caribbean and Central America. Although not all Latin Americans objected to this period of gunboat diplomacy, the overwhelming response of Latin American intellectuals was to raise the banner of anti-imperialism.

The third factor was the spread of socialist ideas throughout Latin America, especially after the 1910s.[28] Socialist ideas began to change the ways many Latin Americans perceived intrahemispheric relations in the early 20th century—rather than harmony of interests, US-Latin American relations were seen through the prism of class antagonism and exploitation. Socialism in Latin America thus encouraged the image of the United States as the embodiment of everything inimical to the region's progress.

Thus, a new and more powerful type of Yankeephobia emerged in the early 20th century that was a composite of the old repudiation of US culture and newer concerns about balance of power. By the 1910s harsh criticism of the United States became de rigueur among Latin American intellectuals.

Not surprisingly, hemispherism stumbled. Yankeephobia naturally translated into mistrust of Pan-Americanism, now seen as a US ploy to obscure imperialist intentions. Even US efforts to keep other countries out of the region provoked significant condemnation. For instance, in the British-Venezuelan conflict of 1902, when the United States acted to expel the British, many Latin Americans saw it as self-interested opportunism rather than a prohemispheric act. This view of US actions—condemning both action and neglect—persisted into the 1980s.[29]

During this period Latin America favored relations with countries outside the hemisphere. Universalism became especially appealing among governments that sought to compete with the United States for influence in the hemisphere, in particular Argentina, which preferred to cultivate its ties with Europe. The eagerness of most Latin American nations to

27. From Víctor Raúl Haya de la Torre, "¿Adónde va Indoamérica?," *Obras Completas*, 2d ed., vol. 2, ed. Luis Alberto Sánchez (Lima: Editorial Juan Mejía Baca, 1984).

28. See, for example, Charles A. Hale, "Political and Social Ideas in Latin America, 1870-1930," *The Cambridge History of Latin America*, vol. 4, ed. Leslie Bethell (Cambridge University Press, 1986).

29. See, for example, Pastor, *Whirlpool*.

participate in the League of Nations after World War I reveals the sway of universalism during this period. The appeal of universalism in Latin America also persisted until the 1980s; it became the policy choice of Cuba (under Fidel Castro) and, to some extent, most South American nations after the 1950s.

The Survival of Hemispherism

Yet hemispherism remained alive: six international conferences of American states took place between 1889 and 1928. Whatever the motives for its intervention, at least the United States was finally paying attention to the region. And many Latin American anti-imperialists felt the only way to curb the United States was by constructing hemispheric institutions of cooperation. For example, the anti-imperialist Argentine Foreign Minister Julio Drago, whose famous Drago Doctrine (1902) calling for a multilateral ban on all forms of interventionism was rejected by the United States, never lost enthusiasm for Pan-Americanism, which he believed was the only way to rein in the United States.[30]

Thus, not all anti-imperialists advocated breaking with the United States. The Cuban José Martí believed that although it could be a serious menace, the United States could also play a positive role in the region. It is not coincidental that Martí chose the United States as the headquarters for his effort to secure his country's independence. He declared: "On the one hand, there is our America . . . on the other, the America which is not ours, whose enmity it is neither prudent nor practical to encourage, and whose friendship, maintaining a firm decorum and wise independence, it is useful and not impossible to win."[31] Although never a full advocate of hemispherism, Martí eventually relaxed his skepticism of Pan-Americanism.[32]

Nonetheless, Pan-Americanism by the end of the 1920s was in trouble. Hemispherism entered an intellectual impasse, as became clear at the 1926 Pan-American Congress convened to commemorate the centennial of the Congress of Panama. Although a proposal was drafted to fortify hemispheric organizations, the United States and most large Latin nations refused to endorse it (thus displaying the isolationist/no-benefits traditions). The Mexican delegation proposed that the Spanish monarch Alfonso XIII be elected president of the congress (thus displaying Pan-Hispanicism). The motion to include the sovereigns of Great Britain and

30. The United States responded to the Drago Doctrine by counteroffering the Roosevelt Corollary (1904-05), which banned interventions other than its own.

31. Quoted in de Onís, *Spanish American Writers (1776-1890)*, 198.

32. Martí even praised "the mutual understanding" achieved at the First Pan-American Congress. See Balseiro, *The Americas Look at Each Other*, 133.

the Netherlands passed amid great applause (Bolivarianism, Europeanism, Universalism). At the opening ceremony, the most applauded speech came from the Honduran delegate, who argued that the congress represented an opportunity to test the fraternal sentiments of the "colossus of the North" (New and Old Yankeephobia). The prevalence of antihemispheric traditions kept hemispherism at an impasse.

A (Brief) Hemispheric Revival: The Years Before and After World War II

Between the early 1930s and the early 1950s, the intellectual climate across the hemisphere suddenly turned prohemispheric. Despite the difficulties posed by the Depression and the rise of trade wars throughout the world, political and security relations in the hemisphere improved steadily. More than ever before, US and Latin American leaders saw one another as partners (Good Neighbor Policy, 1933), talked about continental solidarity based on democratic values against military assault (Declaration of Lima, 1938), formulated a common policy against European perils (during World War II), built a system of collective security (the Rio Treaty, 1947), and formed a formal institution to address hemispheric affairs (the Organization of American States, 1948).

The evolution of hemispherism is not entirely explained by trends in economic interdependence in the Americas either. No doubt the rise of hemispherism at the end of the 19th century coincided with significant hemispheric trade, confirming the hypothesis that economic contacts generate international political cooperation. However, the reversal of hemispherism during the first decades of the 20th century occurred without a concomitant reversal of these economic trends. Quite the contrary, trade between the United States and Latin America expanded vigorously between 1900 and 1929. Hemispheric trade collapsed after the 1929 Depression,[33] and yet hemispherism begins to rise thereafter. In short, hemispherism did not always move in tandem with economic interdependence.

The rise of hemispherism after 1930 is better explained by the strengthening of several prohemispheric intellectual traditions. First, the big military power embraced antimilitarism. Under President Herbert Hoover in the late 1920s, the United States began to reconsider its position on military interventions, which were no longer seen as worth the cost. In 1933, President Franklin Roosevelt took this view further when he announced, "The definite policy of the United States from now on is opposed to armed intervention." Under this new Good Neighbor policy, the United States proceeded to withdraw its armed forces from Nicaragua (1933) and

---

33. Between 1928 and 1938, the trade ratio (the sum of exports and imports divided by the gross domestic product) of almost all Latin American nations declined significantly, in some cases by more than 50 percent. Victor Bulmer-Thomas, *The Economic History of Latin America.*

Haiti (1934) and refrained from overt military intervention in the region until 1965 (Dominican Republic).

Many scholars do not regard this shift as much of a departure. Peter H. Smith recently stated, "The Good Neighbor Policy can be seen not as a departure from past practices but as the *culmination* of trends in US policy toward the region," in essence, "a declaration of triumph in the imperial conquest."[34] Nevertheless, this presumed nonchange in US policy generated one of the most dramatic turning points in hemispheric attitudes. For the first time in decades, US foreign policy regained esteem among hemispheric intellectuals and statesmen, boosting Latin America's willingness to cooperate. Whereas only eight Latin American nations (mostly small ones) had sided with the United States in declaring war against Germany during World War I, most strongly aligned themselves with the United States during World War II.

The rise of hemispherism in the 1930s occurred because of a shift in US policy that, in turn, reflected a heightened concerned for hemispherism. In the 1930s, the United States steadily increased its level of commitment to the region while reducing involvement in other regions. The Good Neighbor policy became perhaps the only clearly enunciated US foreign policy at the time, and many foreign officials ranked hemispheric relations as the top US foreign policy concern.[35]

The second factor in the rise of hemispherism was the undermining of isolationism, brought about by World War II and the onset of the Cold War. Although the United States preferred to work through worldwide, as opposed to regional, international institutions, the aggressive internationalism of the early Cold War years ensured that it would neglect no region, including the Western Hemisphere.

Another development was the rise in the image of Latin America as a reliable ally. Until World War II, Latin America's noncommittal stand on issues of collective security made the United States question its loyalty and reliability, but during World War II Latin America proved its worth as a partner. The active collaboration of most Latin American nations with the war effort persuaded US leaders that Latin America could be trusted as an ally. This was a brief interruption of the "no-benefit" doctrine.

A final factor was the rise of antitotalitarian thinking. Just as the active cooperation of Latin American nations during the war impressed the United States, the US role during the war also impressed important Latin

34. Peter H. Smith, *Talons of the Eagle*, 65-66.

35. Smith, *Talons of the Eagle*, 66. There was, however, a major downside for hemispherism. This antimilitarism came with a certain US passivity toward authoritarian trends in the region. As Pastor says, Roosevelt "swung the pendulum from the extreme of interventionism to absolute silence on internal political issues," opening the space for the rise of dictators in Nicaragua, Cuba, and the Dominican Republic. Pastor, *Whirlpool*, 188.

American opinion leaders, even historical Yankeephobes. The socialist left, for instance, was impressed by the US-Soviet alliance against fascism; conservatives were awed by US decisiveness and military feats during the war. In addition, between 1944 and 1945, there were a record number of democratic transitions in Latin America, again producing a hemispheric convergence around democratic values.

Nevertheless, there were two counterweights to hemispherism during this period: the rise of North-Atlanticism in the United States and the decline of economic liberalism in Latin America. The war effort and the onset of the Cold War in Europe drew the United States and Western Europe together. By the late 1940s, this North-Atlanticism displaced hemispherism as the top US priority. By embracing North-Atlanticism, the United States dropped the notion that it shared more ties with the Americas than with any other region.

In Latin America, one of the most powerful prohemispheric intellectual traditions—the esteem for economic liberalism—disappeared after 1929. The collapse of international commodity and capital markets brought about by the Depression took a particularly heavy toll on Latin American economies. Many Latin Americans concluded that participation in the international economy was a major source of instability and even impoverishment. Moreover, a new economic paradigm emerged—the idea of declining terms of trade, which posited that the international prices of primary commodities (in which Latin American economies had a comparative advantage) were deteriorating with respect to the international price of manufactured goods (which these economies were importing).[36] Latin American leaders began to replace economic liberalism with the so-called import-substitution industrialization model, which was characterized by trade restrictions, exchange rate and capital controls, and countercyclical aggregate demand stimulus. And because Latin American nations recovered well compared with the North, the new model gained credibility. In addition, this new model found an institutional home in the United Nations Economic Commission for Latin America and the Caribbean (ECLAC), which further entrenched this tradition in the region.[37]

While economic liberalism was being buried in Latin America, it was regaining prestige in the United States.[38] A hesitant believer in free trade,

---

36. Although the "declining terms of trade" idea was not officially modeled until the 1950s by Raúl Prebisch, there is evidence that policymakers during the 1930s were already seeing the world political economy through similar lenses.

37. For Latin America's comparative economic performance in the 1930s, see Vittorio Corbo, *Development Strategies and Policies in Latin America: A Historical Perspective* (San Francisco: International Center for Economic Growth-ICS Press, 1992).

38. Judith Goldstein, *Ideas, Interests, and American Trade Policy* (Ithaca, NY: Cornell University Press, 1993).

the United States became the staunchest economic liberal after World War II. The idea that trade was advantageous for all—perhaps one of the least controversial points in Western Hemisphere thinking since the 1850s—became one of the most contentious issues after the 1940s. This explains why inter-American relations immediately following World War II contained an unusual degree of political and military cooperation, but very little progress on issues of economic integration.

The Cold War Years

The Cold War years proved to be difficult for hemispherism. Although only one nation (Cuba) decided to break completely with the United States, beginning in the late 1950s most Latin American nations significantly relaxed their loyalty to the United States and developed at least one major conflict. Likewise, the United States became increasingly disinclined to resort to hemispheric institutions for resolving international disputes. A series of antihemispheric intellectual traditions contributed to this view. First, many US Cold War hawks saw Latin America as an area of tertiary importance, at most. It had to be kept off-limits from the Soviets, but the region was seen as devoid of sufficient power or strategic interest to play a major role in the East-West struggle.[39] And the intensification of illiberal politics in Latin America after the 1950s (instability, authoritarianism, terrorism, unrest, etc.) erased whatever positive image of it the United States developed in the 1940s.[40] Illiberal politics in Latin America revived John Quincy Adams's view of the region as lacking "the first elements of good or free government."

While the United States began to see the world in terms of the East-West conflict, Latin American nations began to see it in terms of the North-South divide. Accordingly, the interests of the wealthy nations of the North (for example, the need for markets, natural resources, outlets for surplus capital) were seen as deleterious to the interests of the poorer nations of the South. Rather than promoting the well-being of the South, contacts with the North produced "structural dependency," in which the economy of one country depends on economic developments in another country.

---

39. The neglect of Latin America by some Cold War Hawks had two foundations. One was balance of power assessments: the feeling that US hegemony in the region was secure, or at least more so than elsewhere, and the assumption that the Soviet Union was respectful of the US sphere of influence in the Americas. The other was a derivation of the no-benefit doctrine: US injury from losing Latin America was not as serious as losing other strategically more important regions.

40. See, for example, Robert Packenham, *Liberal America and the Third World* (Princeton, NJ: Princeton University Press, 1973).

Consequently, Yankeephobia reached a new height in the 1960s. Whereas Haya de la Torre in the 1920s spoke of the "big fish" eating the "small fish," Juan José Arévalo in 1961 spoke of "the shark victimizing the sardine." This heightened mistrust of the bigger party proved catastrophic for hemispherism. As Arévalo argued, "International treaties are a farce when they are pacted between a shark and a sardine." Pan-Americanism was nothing more than an "instrument at the service of the shark."[41] This thinking, in turn, gave rise to a multitude of antihemispheric viewpoints.

One such viewpoint was the idea that to secure self-sustained development countries needed to pursue what Johan Galtung called "self-reliance": diminishing as much as possible the ties with the West in order to regain control over one's own resources.[42] Moreover, many Latin Americans gradually lost their enthusiasm for what they perceived as the US fixation with anticommunism. Although in the early years of the Cold War many Latin American nations eagerly agreed to US global containment strategies, by the 1960s they had second thoughts. Fighting the Soviet Union was increasingly seen as irrelevant to the problems of developing countries, a diversion of attention and resources.[43] Unlike the 1930-54 period, the crux of US foreign policy had no prestige in Latin America.

In addition, Yankeephobic nationalism became more powerful because it acquired stronger institutional homes. In the early 20th century, Yankeephobic nationalism was prevalent mostly among intellectuals. After the 1940s, however, the Latin American state "replaced the intellectual as the chief propagandist for nationalism."[44] Foreign ministries became filled with nationalists, heavily influenced by North-South modes of thinking, and even right-wing military rulers adopted nationalistic, anti-US foreign policies at various times after the 1960s. In addition, all Latin American political parties adopted the nationalist banner. As a result, anti-US senti-

---

41. Juan José Arévalo, *The Shark and the Sardines.* Translated by June Cobb and Raúl Osegueda (New York: Lyle Stewart, 1961), 13.

42. Johan Galtung, "The Politics of Self-Reliance," in *From Dependency to Development: Strategies to Overcome Underdevelopment and Inequality*, ed. Heraldo Muñozoz (Boulder, CO: Westview Press, 1981).

43. Robert E. Biles, "Perspectives That Make a Difference," in *Inter-American Relations: The Latin American Perspective*, ed. Robert E. Biles (Boulder, CO: Lynne Rienner Publishers, 1988); Robert Wesson and Heraldo Muñozoz, *Latin American Views of US Policy* (New York: Praeger, 1988).

44. John J. Johnson, "Political Change in Latin America: The Emergence of the Middle Sectors," in *Promise of Development. Theories of Change in Latin America*, eds. Peter F. Klarén, and Thomas J. Bossert (Boulder, CO: Westview Press, 1986), 94.

ment in Latin America acquired an unprecedented degree of institutionalization.[45]

The Latin American left's respect for US foreign policy also disappeared after the 1950s. They came to regard contact between a Latin American nation and the United States as a way to consolidate rather than change the status quo. Although some strands of the Latin American left advocated drastic rupture with the United States, they all shared a deep skepticism of the potential benefits of hemispheric cooperation.

In the early 20th century, Latin Americans tended to view sovereignty as the preservation of independence, in turn defined as the prevention of military assaults. In the 1960s, they expanded their view of sovereignty to mean the capacity to exhibit an independent foreign policy, especially in contradiction to US preferences. Thus, it became common for many Latin American nations to vote against the United States in international forums, increase contacts with Communist nations, and publicly challenge the United States over a wide array of issues. Sovereignty also came to be defined in terms of virtual freedom—if not virtual unaccountability—in economic matters. If the principles of property rights and reciprocity in international economic transactions were to be violated (as many Latin American nations did after the 1950s), then there were fewer incentives for other hemispheric nations to deepen economic ties among themselves.

The expanded definition of sovereignty served Latin American authoritarians rather well because it protected them against international accountability. Increasingly, Latin American dictators proclaimed that international condemnations of their regimes were blatant violations of the principle of nonintervention.

Equally important, the need to defend democratic values also lost appeal in the hemisphere. For the United States, the need to prevent a second Cuba superseded the need to defend democracy. As Kennedy declared in his analysis of the 1961 crisis in the Dominican Republic: "There are three possibilities in descending order of preference: a decent democratic regime, a continuation of the Trujillo regime, or a Castro regime. We ought to aim at the first, but we really can't renounce the second until we are sure that we can avoid the third."[46]

Latin American nations also sought ties with nondemocratic nations outside the hemisphere. In 1959, future Brazilian president Jânio Quadros visited the Soviet Union and promised to reestablish relations with gov-

---

45. For explanations on how institutions magnify the "stickiness" and impact of ideas, see, for example, Jorge I. Domínguez, ed., *Technopols: Freeing Politics and Markets in Latin America in the 1990s* (University Park, PA: Penn State Press, 1996); Goldstein and Keohane, eds., *Ideas and Foreign Policy*; and Hall, *The Political Power of Economic Ideas*.

46. Quoted in Packenham, *Liberal America and the Third World*, 165.

ernments irrespective of their political structures.[47] Indeed, Brazil's trade with the Soviet Union increased from 5 million to 65 million rubles between 1959 and 1963. Even the military leaders who took over in 1964 refused to cut the trade links with the Soviet bloc.

In the 1960s, Latin America also developed an acute case of aid addiction that also hurt hemispherism. Despite increased US foreign aid to Latin America after 1961, most Latin American nations remained unsatisfied, in part because an important derivative of the North-South perspective was the notion that poor countries were entitled to assistance in compensation for past wrongs and entrenched inequalities. Latin Americans also adopted trade policies that had less to do with promoting market forces than with securing trade subsidies from rich countries.[48] At the same time, the United States considered its economy relatively open to international trade and hesitated to grant special treatment to Latin American exports or to remove barriers to sensitive products from developing countries.

Despite these antihemispheric trends, hemispherism did not die during the Cold War years. Several prohemispheric international traditions—some of them new, some of them quite old—continued to circulate. In Latin America, for instance, conservative forces toned down their old Yankeephobia (that is, derision of US culture) because they, too, shared the US interest in containing communism. Moreover, although Latin America's aid addiction gave rise to some hemispheric conflicts, Latin Americans knew a reasonably pro-US posture was necessary to secure foreign aid. Finally, not all Latin American leftists were Yankeephobes. One of the most powerful political developments during this period was the strengthening of some anticommunist, anti-Castro, prohemispheric social-democratic parties in places such as Venezuela, Colombia, Costa Rica, and Puerto Rico. As Arthur M. Schlesinger Jr. argues, these political parties were eager to fight "both the oligarchs and communists" and still be friends of the United States.[49]

Various intellectual trends in the United States also ensured the survival of hemispherism during the Cold War. One was developmentalism—the idea that the promotion of economic development translates into more moderate, stable, and consensual political outcomes. For developmentalists, the best weapon against communism was to invest in development projects. In addition, a minority of Cold War hawks took it upon them-

47. Cole Blasier, *The Hovering Giant: US Responses to Revolutionary Change in Latin America*, rev. ed. (Pittsburgh: University of Pittsburgh Press, 1985), 33-36.

48. ECLAC, *Open Regionalism*.

49. Arthur M. Schlesinger Jr., "The Alliance for Progress: A Retrospective," in *Latin America: The Search for a New International Role*, eds. Ronald G. Hellman and H. Jon Rosenbaum (New York: John Wiley and Sons, 1975).

selves to chastise their colleagues for taking Latin America for granted and underestimating the strategic value of the region.[50]

However, most of the Cold War prohemispheric traditions were predicated, paradoxically, on notions that directly contradicted some basic tenets of the Western Hemisphere idea. In Latin America, for instance, the forces in favor of hemispherism valued it not for itself but simply as a means to other, more opportunistic objectives. Conservative Latin Americans toned down their Yankeephobia because they needed US blessing for their authoritarian designs. Many leftists moderated theirs not out of respect for the United States but to gain more room for maneuvering within their own countries and to keep the channels of foreign aid open. In the United States, both developmentalists and prohemispheric Cold Warriors justified increasing ties with Latin America by stressing John Quincy Adams's notion that Latin America was a potential headache. Engagement was necessary not because Latin American nations were reliable partners, but because they were unreliable: that is, likely to plummet into civil unrest and even communism if the United States turned its back.

US attention to the region was based largely on negative images and preemptive intentions. A stunning example was a long memorandum in 1950 by then-counselor of the State Department George F. Kennan to the Secretary of State. The memorandum begins, "Below are some views about Latin America as a problem in United States foreign policy. . . ." It argues that the region, from its geography to its social customs, is a source of aggravation and conflict with the United States: "It seems to me unlikely that there could be any other region of the earth in which nature and human behavior could have combined to produce a more unhappy and hopeless background for the conduct of human life than in Latin America." The social fabric of Latin America is so fragile that the region is extremely vulnerable to communist penetration, in fact, "the positions gained by the communists in Latin America are already sufficiently formidable to interfere extensively with the development of our normal peacetime relations on these continents." Kennan also argued that if war were to break out between the United States and the Soviet Union, Latin American nations might not become solid US allies (as they did during World War

50. In 1963 Nixon, for instance, emphasized the need to pay attention to Latin America and other developing regions: "Communism is on the move. . . . Where in the world today do we expect trouble? In the communist satellites of Eastern Europe? No, in the free nations of Latin America, Africa, and Asia." Quoted in *Globalism and its Critics: The American Foreign Policy of the 1960s*, ed. William Taubman (Lexington, MA: DC Heath and Company, 1973), 7. In the 1980s, Jeane J. Kirkpatrick, US Ambassador to the United Nations under President Reagan, also criticized the Pentagon for being oblivious to the rise of Soviet influence in Latin America during the 1970s. See "US Security and Latin America," *Commentary* 71 (January 1981).

II), but could succumb to civil war and even communist takeover.[51] In short, Latin America was not a trustworthy partner of the United States.

Kennan's memorandum represented the adaptation of John Quincy Adams's no-benefit doctrine to the Cold War. Quoting Adams, Kennan argues that Latin societies are not culturally inclined toward democracy, and thus US officials ought "to desist from all sorts of moralizing or public judgement" about domestic politics in the region.[52] The idea that inter-American ties should be built on the basis of democratic values disappeared. Both developmentalists and Cold War hawks came to accept a permissive attitude toward noncommunist authoritarianism in the region. For developmentalists, authoritarianism was a passing phase; for Cold Warriors, it was preferable to the alternatives. This disregard for democracy became an official tenet of US foreign policy with the 1964 Mann Doctrine (named for State Department official Thomas Mann), whereby the United States declared that it would tolerate any regime as long as it met two (easy) criteria: opposed communism and welcomed US corporations.

Building Bridges: Summits and Charters

Although the 1960-90 period was troublesome for hemispherism, there were efforts to build bridges.

Two summits of presidents of the Americas (Panama 1956 and Punta del Este 1967) occurred during the Cold War, reflecting the lasting power of the Western Hemisphere idea. But their shortcomings also reflected the prevalence of antihemispheric intellectual traditions.

The 1956 Panama meeting took place during a transition from high hemispherism to the huge divide of the Cold War years. The meeting was cordial, but its results were forgettable. President Dwight Eisenhower was interested in a "ceremonial and commemorative" meeting, where he could meet with Latin American presidents without having to visit each country. For Latin America's dictators, it was a not-to-be-missed photo opportunity with the US president. The United States was concerned about rising instability in the region and the overthrow of the Peronist government in Argentina. But most important, it wanted to preserve hemispheric allegiance to US foreign policy. However, none of this happened; hemispheric relations continued to deteriorate after the summit.

51. US State Department, *Foreign Relations of the United States: 1950*, vol. 2, The United Nations and the Western Hemisphere (Washington: Department of State), 598-624.

52. Instead, Kennan asks the United States to evaluate Latin American nations in terms of their external relationship, that is, their level of friendship toward the United States and behavior in the international arena.

In 1961, the nations of the hemisphere engaged in perhaps the most significant Cold War attempt to bridge the hemispheric gap. They signed the Punta del Este Charter, the multilateral launch of the Alliance for Progress. Like the texts that would be signed at the Miami summit, this charter called for greater international cooperation, deep domestic structural reforms, sustained economic development, more equitable economic distribution, and better public services. Both documents also incorporated the most pressing demands of Latin Americans at the time. Both agreements also excluded Cuba. If anything, US commitment was higher, at least in terms of foreign assistance: the US committed $20 billion to the region. Therefore, it constituted a meeting of the minds between US developmentalists and ECLAC-influenced Latin America.

But the alliance ultimately failed to bridge the growing divide in the hemisphere. As one of its main architects stated, the spirit of the alliance lasted at the very best less than 1,000 days.[53] The alliance could not avoid being a reflection of the prevailing anti-integration intellectual climate. It fell short of calling for dismantling import-substitution and antiexport policies in Latin America, and it was silent on what to do in the event of democratic reversals. More than an effort at integration, the Latin Americans saw the alliance as an effort to assuage their level of external dependence, and the United States saw it as an effort to promote containment ("the ultimate answer to Castro and Communism," in the words of Kennedy). For Latin Americans, the alliance was an opportunity to implement doctrines of state intervention and planning, proposed by the Economic Commission for Latin America; for the United States, it was an effort to purchase loyalty and good governance through aid. As argued, both goals were imbued with antihemispheric thinking. Moreover, the alliance was predicated on a high level of personalism rather than state-to-state respect: the Latin Americans were enchanted by the charismatic, youthful, Catholic US president, and Kennedy, in turn, was extrapolating too much optimism from his good personal relations with a few Latin American leaders (Rómulo Betancourt and José Figueres). As a result, the alliance proved ineffectual as a regime of hemispheric integration based on the promotion of democracy and free trade—in fact, it was never intended to be such a regime. The intellectual climate of the period conspired against it, and the alliance was, if anything, a true reflection of this climate.

The goals of the 1967 summit were decidedly more ambitious than Eisenhower's had been a decade earlier. This time, the initiative was Latin American (Argentine President Arturo Illía and Chilean President Eduardo Frei proposed the summit). Unlike Eisenhower, Lyndon Johnson pushed his diplomats to hammer out a substantive agenda. The participants hoped to resuscitate the moribund Alliance for Progress; the United States also wanted to regain Latin American loyalty to its containment objectives. The summit did produce some agreements on scientific, techno-

53. Arthur M. Schlesinger Jr., "The Alliance for Progress: A Retrospective."

logical, and educational issues and advanced the concept of the Generalized System of Preferences (whereby industrial countries grant temporary tariff advantages to developing countries) later adopted by the world trading system. The United States went so far as to support formation of a regional common market from which it was excluded. But the central objectives were not achieved. The Latin American Common Market did not prosper, the Alliance for Progress did not survive, and hemispheric loyalty toward the United States continued to decline in the 1970s.[54]

The two summits were supposed to usher in a new era of cooperation in the Americas, but each was more like a closing ceremony. The 1957 summit brought to a close the period of greatest political and military hemispheric cooperation ever (1933-54), and the 1967 summit ended efforts by pro-Latin American developmentalists and Cold Warriors to overcome the antihemispheric sentiments in the region. Despite strong presidential support and common interest, neither summit was able to counteract ensconced antihemispherism.[55]

By the mid-1980s, the inter-American system was moribund. Latin American nations did not regard their interests as harmonious with those of the United States.[56] The OAS was mired in dissent and inaction.[57] As James R. Kurth argued, the principle of nonintervention became the practice of unilateral intervention, and the principle of collective security became the practice of collective nonintervention.[58] Inter-American consultations over regional affairs were infrequent and unproductive. The Central American imbroglio and the Latin American debt crises reinforced the old US idea that Latin American nations were unreliable partners. US

---

54. Lincoln Gordon, "Punta del Este Revisited," *Foreign Affairs* 45, no. 4 (July 1967), 624-38; and Joseph S. Tulchin, "The Promise of Progress: US Relations with Latin America during the Administration of Lyndon B. Johnson," in *Lyndon Johnson Confronts the World: American Foreign Policy, 1963-1968*, eds. Warren I. Cohen and Nancy B. Tucker (New York: Cambridge University Press, 1994), 238-43.

55. The last Cold War US attempt to unite the hemisphere, the 1977 Carter-Torrijos Treaty transferring the Canal Zone to Panama, turned out to be a Pyrrhic victory for hemispherism. The US public was unprepared to think of Latin America as a worthy partner and therefore misread many of Carter's concessions, while Latin Americans could not relinquish their obsession with developing a foreign policy independent of the United States. See, for example, Pastor, *Whirlpool*; George D. Moffett III, *The Limits of Victory: Ratification of the Panama Canal Treaties* (Ithaca, NY: Cornell University Press, 1985); and Michael J. Hogan, *The Panama Canal in American Politics: Domestic Advocacy and the Evolution of Policy* (Carbondale: Illinois University Press, 1986).

56. Robert Wesson, "Summary and Conclusion" in eds. Robert Wesson and Heraldo Muñozoz, *Latin American Views of US Policy* (New York: Praeger, 1986).

57. See L. Ronald Scheman, *The Inter-American Dilemma: The Search for Inter-American Cooperation at the Centennial of the Inter-American System* (New York: Praeger Press, 1988).

58. James R. Kurth, "The Rise and Decline of the Inter-American System: A US View," in *Alternative to Intervention: A New US-Latin American Security Relationship*, eds. Richard J. Bloomfield and Gregory F. Treverton (Boulder, CO: Lynne Rienner, 1990).

involvement in the region in the 1980s pleased very few constituencies. Initial efforts to deal with the debt crisis were disparaged by neoliberals (for being too interventionist), by the left (for being too harsh), and by developmentalists (for being too shy). Efforts to deal with Central America produced even more malcontents: some Cold War hawks were dissatisfied with the results, administration officials were embarrassed over the Iran-Contra affair, and leftist detractors of US foreign policy reaffirmed their view that every time the United States intervenes in the region it ends up undermining progress. In short, in the mid-1980s, many leaders believed that no one seemed to gain from substantial hemispheric involvement.

The Revival of Hemispherism

But in the late 1980s the hemisphere's intellectual climate changed dramatically. Old enemies of the Western Hemisphere idea—Bolivarianism, isolationism, universalism, anti-interventionism, antitradeism, and even the no-benefit principle—began to lose appeal. The hemisphere began to converge over political and military affairs (as was the case in the 1940s), as well as in economic matters (for the first time since the late 19th century). Several factors contributed to this revival.

In the 1980s, the most dramatic political development in the hemisphere was the return of democracy in almost all of the countries of the hemisphere. Also impressive was the shift by the United States and Latin American nations toward more convergent views on debt abatement. In the early 1980s, many Latin Americans were enticed by ideas of reneging on international obligations or creating debt cartels (in essence, a type of Pan-Latinism), whereas and the United States was less conciliatory, refusing to consider debt forgiveness. But by the late 1980s, both Latin America and the United States adopted more constructive positions. Latin Americans agreed to domestic reforms, and the United States agreed to debt relief (under its Brady Plan).[59] For Latin America, this was the beginning of the end of the idea that Latin Americans owe nothing to, and share little with, the North. For the United States, this represented an erosion of the idea that Latin American nations are not to be trusted (especially with their finances). The debt crisis also revealed to the United States the importance of the Latin American economies to its own prosperity and the vulnerabilities of US bankers and exporters to fluctuations in the region's economic fortunes.

In the 1980s, Latin Americans began to think of nonintervention in less absolute terms. As new democracies, they discovered that absolute nonintervention could leave their governments devoid of international allies in the event of a coup attempt. Latin American nations came to

59. See, for example, William R. Cline, *International Debt Reexamined* (Washington: Institute for International Economics, 1995).

understand that collective involvement in the support of democratic efforts abroad is desirable in part because they, too, might need it. This shift in the definition of sovereignty became most evident in the 1991 Santiago Resolution of the OAS, which called for action in the event of "the sudden or irregular interruption of the democratically elected government in any of the Organization's member states. . . ."

In the mid-1970s, the US Congress and the Carter administration began to relax this risk aversion by seeking to promote human rights in the hemisphere. The Reagan-Bush years witnessed a growing bipartisan consensus behind promoting democracy.[60] Thus, by the early 1990s, one of the principal tenets of the Western Hemisphere idea made an unexpected comeback: unity on behalf of the collective defense of democratic values.

In the 1990s Latin Americans also redefined their view on trade, moving from trade as aid to trade instead of aid. Competitive hemispheric trade ceased to be seen as a form of entrapment and more as a route toward growth and, in some minds, even social equity.[61] Champions of economic nationalism and anti-imperialism in the 1970s and early 1980s such as Carlos S. Menem (Argentina), Carlos A. Pérez (Venezuela), Fernando Henrique Cardoso (Brazil), and Michael Manley (Jamaica) came to office after 1989 (Manley and Pérez for a second time) eager to open trade. To be sure, the smaller nations, especially in the Caribbean, asked (and received) some special treatment in intrahemispheric trade dealings, but the overall condemnation of trade with the bigger parties subsided significantly. At the same time, the United States relaxed its strict preference for global-multilateral trade agreements and came to view regional trade agreements as more effective mechanisms for liberalizing trade (chapter 2).

There was also a hemispheric change in economic thinking. By the early 1990s, most policy circles in Latin America, including top economists from ECLAC, advocated structural economic reforms favoring free markets, privatized public services, macroeconomic stability, and fiscal discipline along the lines suggested by several US economic advisers (dubbed the Washington Consensus).[62] Much has been written on whether this

60. For the evolution of prodemocracy efforts in the hemisphere see chapter 2, as well as Tom Farer, ed., *Beyond Sovereignty: Collectively Defending Democracy in the Americas* (Baltimore: The Johns Hopkins University Press, 1996) and Abraham F. Lowenthal, *Exporting Democracy: The United States and Latin America* (Baltimore: The Johns Hopkins University Press, 1991).

61. ECLAC, *Open Regionalism.*

62. See, for example, Sebastian Edwards, *Crisis and Reform in Latin America: From Despair to Hope* (New York: Oxford University Press, 1995); John Williamson, ed., *Latin American Adjustment: How Much Has Happened?* (Washington: Institute for International Economics, 1990); John Williamson, ed., *The Political Economy of Policy Reform* (Washington: Institute for International Economics, 1994); Bela Belassa, Gerardo M. Bueno, Pedro Pablo Kucsynski, *Toward Renewed Economic Growth in Latin America* (Washington: Institute for International Economics, 1986).

new model was imposed by the United States, has become accepted fully in Latin America, or is desirable for Latin American citizens. It is less often recognized, however, that Latin Americans have made their own amendment to the Washington Consensus: the state should be fortified in some areas such as tax collection and provision of social services for free markets and macroeconomic stability to endure politically.[63] Many market-oriented policy circles in the United States and elsewhere (including the International Monetary Fund [IMF] and the World Bank) have conceded that Latin Americans have a point.

A crucial obstacle to hemispherism in the 20th century, especially during the Cold War, was its rejection by most of the opposition forces in Latin America, who tended to see state-to-state contacts between the United States and Latin America as invariably favoring the status quo. In the late 1980s, opposition forces in Latin America began to discover that international involvement in domestic politics would result in greater pressure on governments to adhere to democratic procedures, protect human rights, and be more accountable. In effect, Martí-like thinking has returned: opposition forces recognize that US engagement in the region can be beneficial.

While society-based demand for hemispherism in the United States never became overwhelming, it did increase somewhat after the late 1980s. At one level, the United States became impressed with Latin America's new pro-US foreign policies such as Mexico's call for NAFTA, Latin American calls for US observers during electoral contests, the Andean countries' support for drug interdiction initiatives, and Argentina's sending of ships during the Gulf War. But at another level, demand for hemispherism also rose from within US society. With the end of the Cold War and the rise of multiculturalism in the United States, prohemispheric think tanks and advocacy groups proliferated.[64]

Political preferences in border states such as Texas, Florida, Louisiana, and California also changed. Traditionally, ties with Latin America appeared more threatening to the more conservative, agribusiness-oriented border states than to the more cosmopolitan, manufacturing-export-oriented northern states. In the 1990s, however, the aversion of border states to hemispherism subsided. They found their own export niches in

---

63. See, for example, Jorge I. Domínguez, ed., *Technopols: Freeing Politics and Markets in Latin America in the 1990s*.

64. Howard J. Wiarda, "Think Tanks," in *US-Latin American Policy Making*. For example, during the Cold War, most think tanks in favor of US involvement abroad were divided along two fault lines: procontainment vs. prohumanitarian and pro-strong ties with Latin America vs. pro-strong ties to other regions of the world. With the end of the Cold War and the rise of multiculturalism in the United States, the first fault line disappeared and the second one became less significant. The result was a greater convergence among US think tanks and advocacy groups in favor of involvement in Latin America.

Latin America by streamlining some agribusiness exports and diversifying their export base. California, Texas, and Florida, for example, were among the top four US states in terms of dollar gains in exports to Latin America between 1987 and 1993.[65] These new economic contacts also helped launch greater trade with Asia.[66]

In sum, a series of changes across the hemisphere boosted hemispherism. The United States and Latin America began to think along similar wavelengths in the early 1990s for the first time in decades. The consensus included not just security and political issues but also economics. The appeal of intellectual traditions adverse to hemispherism fell to an all-time low. Various sectors of Latin American society began to embrace collective involvement in international affairs, and in the United States, more people began to think of Latin America as a promising partner rather than as a region that had to be saved from underdevelopment, instability, and bad government. They also saw the need for collective international action on behalf of democratic preservation. This created the right opportunity for the 1994 Summit of the Americas.

The Remaining Obstacles

Nevertheless, some old antihemispheric traditions were still lingering, and new ones were surfacing. In the United States, there were three emerging antihemispheric trends in the 1990s. First, the ugly side of hemispherism was turning uglier—the unwanted flow of illegal immigrants, drugs, and crime from Latin America into the United States, especially the border states, was on the rise. And unlike trade benefits, these problems were more conspicuous to the average resident and easy scapegoats for larger problems.

Second, the US public remains undecided about the benefits of trade with developing countries. For some sectors of the left, freer trade with Latin America is a form of renewed imperialism, a threat to the environment, and an effort to exploit poor labor conditions abroad. For workers and business owners in industries that cannot compete with Latin America, free hemispheric trade is a menace to their livelihoods. As a

---

65. Texas topped the list (sales to Latin America and the Caribbean were up by $8.7 billion), followed by Michigan (up $4.9 billion), California (up $4.4 billion), and then Florida (up $4.3 billion). US Department of Commerce, Bureau of the Census, "US Exports to Latin America and the Caribbean, 1987-93. State Export Profile," Document ID no. 1487 (Washington, 1994).

66. Asian corporations have expanded their presence in border states in hopes of also profiting from new hemispheric businesses. For instance, by 1995 more than 17 firms from Korea, 45 from Japan, and 75 from Taiwan had opened up stores in Miami. Karen E. Thuermer, "Office Sting," *World Trade* (July 1996).

result, an antihemispheric, protectionist alliance of strange bedfellows—including liberals, labor, and businesses—has emerged. Although not politically dominant, this alliance has influenced the largest political parties.

Finally, the persistence of instability, corruption, insurrection, and financial woes across Latin America—especially in Mexico after 1994—has ensured the survival of the no-benefit doctrine. To the average citizen, John Quincy Adams's view that these nations "have not the first elements of good and free governments" seems applicable even today, despite the region's democratic and macroeconomic achievements.

Antihemispheric intellectual traditions have not died completely in Latin America, either. Mistrust of the United States still pervades many sectors of Latin American societies, including parts of the foreign policy establishments and bureaucracies. Many in labor and business remain equally unpersuaded of the benefits of trade with more powerful and competitive economies. Nineteenth-century Yankeephobic sentiments against US culture and values also persist.[67]

The Role of Leaders

Hemispheric achievements have always required the initiative of individuals.[68] Opportunities have existed for leaders to push the Western Hemisphere idea beyond what was structurally inevitable. In the late 19th century, for instance, the greater US presence in the Americas was probably an inevitable outcome of economic trends (the growth of trade). But the creation of international institutions for political cooperation (such as the Pan-American Union) during that period would not have happened without the vigorous initiatives of important leaders. Likewise, the creation of a system of collective defense (the Rio Treaty) and the establishment of a regional conflict-resolution organization (the OAS) at the end of World War II were the result of creative individuals who took advantage of favorable intellectual climates. The 1994 summit was also the result of a fortuitous combination of diplomatic initiative and the most favorable intellectual climate for hemispherism ever.

---

67. Conservative Yankeephobia extends beyond condemnation of US pop culture. It also rejects debates among educated circles of the United States about abortion, sexual harassment, gay rights, condom and needle distribution, care for the elderly outside the family, and assisted suicide, etc.

68. A study of the Group of Seven summits found that "the experience of Western summitry supports theories that stress the role of policy ideas. . . . To understand why nations cooperate at some times and not others, we must explore the ideas and the domestic incentives of leaders themselves." Robert D. Putnam and Nicholas Bayne, *Hanging Together: Cooperation and Conflict in Seven-Power Summits* (London: Sage Publications, 1987), 278-79.

2

Near-Term Antecedents

Chapter 1 traced through history the growing strength of prohemispheric attitudes in the United States and Latin America and the convergence of ideas that had created auspicious conditions for a hemispheric meeting. This chapter explores in greater depth the policy environment and actions taken by governments in the late 1980s and early 1990s that created favorable conditions for the Summit of the Americas.

In the United States, the Bush and Clinton administrations recognized that the shift toward democracy in Latin America opened new possibilities for dialogue on political values and warranted a definitive rejection of arguments that had served as apologia for authoritarian regimes. Increasingly, the United States was willing to take strong measures to protect hemispheric democracies and to act in concert with other countries and international institutions to deter anticonstitutional power grabs (Peru in 1992, Guatemala in 1993, and Haiti in 1994) and to preempt possible antidemocratic maneuvers (during elections in Venezuela in 1993 and in Mexico in 1994). US administrations also responded to the rise of pro-integrationist sentiments by announcing several free trade initiatives, including the North American Free Trade Agreement (NAFTA), the Enterprise for the Americas Initiative (EAI), and the proposed NAFTA parity for Central America and the Caribbean.

Latin American and Caribbean governments also responded to the new environment. Not only were elections becoming the normal way political power changed hands, but many governments were also increasingly willing to redefine traditional notions of sovereignty and to accept and even participate in collective actions on behalf of continental democracy. Governments were also implementing market-oriented economic reforms, opening their economies to international trade, and reinvigorating subregional integration, giving renewed life to the Central American Common Market (CACM), the Caribbean Common Market (Caricom), and the Andean Pact, while Brazil, Argentina, Uruguay, and Paraguay launched the Southern Cone Common Market (Mercosur). Increasingly, these trade pacts were perceived as building blocks toward a full-blown hemispheric free trade area.

The Democratic Wave

During the Cold War, the United States professed faith in democracy but was often willing to acquiesce in and sometimes even foster authoritarian regimes in pursuit of larger strategic objectives. Leftist political forces were typically perceived as actually or potentially allied with the Soviet Union and, after 1960, with Castro's Cuba and thus were viewed as strategic enemies of the United States. Fearing that communists were gaining influence in the Guatemalan government, the United States covertly plotted against the elected president, Jacobo Arbenz, contributing to his overthrow in 1954.[1] Similarly, Nixon and Kissinger worked actively to destabilize the elected government of Salvador Allende in Chile, fueling such severe political polarization that the usurper military regime remained in power for 17 years. In other cases, US policy was simply passive, dealing realistically with those strongmen and military-dominated regimes that occupied the halls of power. At the hemispheric summits held in Panama in 1956 and at Punta del Este, Uruguay, in 1967, where about half of the leaders had gained power through undemocratic means, US presidents dealt with the generals as a matter of routine.

Jeane Kirkpatrick elevated this opportunistic policy to the level of ideology in her famous 1979 *Commentary* article, which allegedly caught the attention of candidate Ronald Reagan and won her a senior post in his administration.[2] Kirkpatrick argued that authoritarian regimes were markedly distinct from—and morally superior to—communist regimes in that they were not totalitarian and were more liable to evolve toward democratic norms. Kirkpatrick justified US support for the military governments in Latin America and harshly criticized the Carter administration's human rights policies, holding Carter responsible for the Sandinista overthrow of General Anastasio Somoza Debayle in Nicaragua. In Kirkpatrick's eyes, Somoza was clearly morally and strategically superior to the pro-Cuban Sandinistas. Her authoritarian tilt influenced the early years of the Reagan period.

---

1. Stephen C. Schlesinger and Stephen Kinzer, *Bitter Fruit: The Untold Story of the American Coup in Guatemala* (New York: Doubleday, 1982).

2. Jeane Kirkpatrick, "Dictatorships and Double Standards," *Commentary* (1979): 34-45.

Ironically, the Kirkpatrick thesis celebrated US backing for military regimes just as they were about to vanish from the scene. The 1980s witnessed transitions to democracy throughout Central and South America. Military presidents were replaced by elected civilians in Ecuador (1979), Peru (1980), Honduras (1982), Bolivia (1982), Argentina (1983), El Salvador (1984), Brazil (1985), Uruguay (1985), Guatemala (1986), and Chile (1989). In tandem with these regional trends, the Reagan-Bush administrations ceased to exonerate authoritarian rule and backed democracy more fully in the Western Hemisphere.[3] When pressure grew in Chile in the mid-1980s for a return to democracy, the Reagan administration threw its support behind the prodemocracy forces. In Nicaragua and El Salvador, the Bush administration came to see democracy as a powerful instrument for the peaceful reconciliation of civil strife. In Panama, Bush intervened to oust dictator Manuel Noriega and to place Panamanian democracy on track. In each case, motives were mixed: in Chile, Reagan's neoconservative assistant secretary for inter-American affairs, Eliott Abrams, lent US support to prodemocracy forces in part to show consistency with human rights criticisms leveled against leftists elsewhere; in Central America, the Bush administration sought to extricate itself from the Central American quagmire and focus its energies on other parts of the world;[4] and in Panama, a new US president showed himself to be a decisive leader prepared to use force. But foreign policy is inevitably the outcome of a complex mix of motives, and by the end of the Bush administration the Washington bureaucracy had grown accustomed to supporting democratic forms of government and to working hard to keep the military in its barracks.

Prodemocracy policy became institutionalized through repetition and routine and through the development of operational programs.[5] The US Agency for International Development (USAID) provided electoral assistance, including special ballot paper and ink and aid to computerize voter registration rolls. The Departments of Justice and State collaborated in supporting judicial reform, including training judges and supporting local bar associations. The US executive branch was also influenced by the National Endowment for Democracy (NED), established by Congress in 1983 to promote democracy abroad. NED worked with four constituent

---

3. A good description of this evolution can be found in Howard J. Wiarda, "United States Policy toward Central America: A Retrospective of the Reagan Years," in *Latin America and Caribbean Contemporary Record*, eds. James M. Malloy and Eduardo A. Gamara (New York: Holmes and Meier, 1990).

4. For a frank discussion of Bush administration motives in Central American policy, see James A. Baker III, *The Politics of Diplomacy* (New York: G. P. Putnam and Sons, 1995), 47-60.

5. A review of political trends and US programs during the 1980s can be found in US Department of State, *Democracy in Latin America and the Caribbean: The Promise and the Challenge*, Special Report No. 158 (March 1987).

institutes formed by the AFL-CIO, the US Chamber of Commerce, and the Republican and Democratic parties, which, together with a widening array of nongovernmental organizations (NGOs) seeking to promote human rights in Latin America, wove a web of opinion that enveloped State Department officials.

With the end of the Cold War, the risk of supporting democracy had also declined sharply. Authoritarian regimes were no longer necessary to maintain order and keep communists at bay. The Marxist left was in disarray, and those hard leftist forces that remained had no Soviet Union to ally with. Gradually it became apparent that should leftist forces win elections, they probably would play by the new rules of the game. The dynamics of the global marketplace, domestic opinion grown tired of polarized politics, and emerging hemispheric consensus behind democratic norms combined to narrow politicians' margin of maneuver. The October 1992 election of Cheddi Jagan as president of Guyana was a telling example of this transformation in hemispheric politics. In the early 1960s Britain and the United States considered Jagan, a founder of the left-wing People's Progressive Party, a dangerous radical, and Britain worked for his defeat.[6] By the 1990s the United States barely noticed his election, and a much mellowed Jagan's main interest in the United States was to increase his nation's rice quota in the US market.

The Clinton Administration and Promotion of Democracy

The Clinton administration reasoned that democracy abroad was in the US interest because democracies were more likely to be reliable allies that adhered to international norms and were less likely to declare war on each other or to engage in dangerous arms races.[7] But in the making of Clinton administration policy toward the Western Hemisphere, the prodemocracy impulse was at least as much a reflection of idealism as it was of instrumentalist realism. Liberals in and around the Democratic Party concerned with human rights and democratic freedoms had focused special attention on Latin America, where democracy had a long tradition but where authoritarian regimes had systematically violated human rights in the 1970s. An early indication that the Clinton administration would hew to a tough prodemocracy line came early in the administration on

6. See Arthur M. Schlesinger Jr., *A Thousand Days; John F. Kennedy in the White House*, vol. 6. (Boston: Houghton Mifflin, 1965), 775.

7. For example, see White House, *A National Security Strategy of Engagement and Enlargement*, (Government Printing Office, February 1995), especially the "Preface" by William J. Clinton, pp. i-iii; also, Anthony Lake, "From Containment to Enlargement," address at Johns Hopkins University School of Advanced International Studies, Washington, 21 September 1993.

policy toward Peruvian President Alberto Fujimori. In 1992 Fujimori had shut down his congress and undertaken other unconstitutional acts to quell the opposition while his antiguerrilla campaign systematically violated human rights. The Bush administration had pledged US participation in a large international financial package for Peru, but the Clinton team decided to hold up final approval pending acceptance by Fujimori of several human rights conditions. Fujimori conceded, and a clear signal was sent that was noted around the hemisphere.

A second test came on 25 May 1993, when Guatemalan President Jorge Serrano attempted to shut down his congress and supreme court. Within hours, the White House released a firm statement calling for Guatemala to "immediately restore full constitutional democracy." The State Department soon announced not only a suspension of US bilateral aid but also threatened to suspend Guatemala's access to trade preferences, and the Treasury Department worked within the international financial institutions to halt approval of new loans.[8] At US urging, the Organization of American States (OAS) promptly dispatched a high-level mission to Guatemala City, where Secretary General Baena Soares helped persuade business and military leaders to back a peaceful return to constitutional rule. Soon Serrano was on a plane out of the country and the Guatemalan congress selected as president a former human rights ombudsman.

Amid coup rumblings in Venezuela on the eve of presidential elections scheduled for 5 December 1993, President Clinton wrote to President Ramón Velasquez warning that "any disruption in the democratic process would inevitably have an immediate and chilling impact on the full range of our bilateral relations," and a State Department envoy cautioned that economic sanctions would follow unconstitutional acts.[9] In the same vein, as Mexican presidential elections approached in August 1994 the Clinton administration pressed the Mexican government to permit international observers and made clear its preference for an honest ballot.

The September 1994 intervention in Haiti to restore Jean Bertrand Aristide demonstrated the Clinton administration's willingness to apply force to gain its democratic objectives (and, to be sure, to stem a migrant crisis). For the first time in the long history of US military action in the Caribbean Basin, the United States had obtained an "all necessary measures" resolution from the United Nations, in part to keep Latin American and Caribbean countries behind US policy. Coming just three months before the scheduled Summit of the Americas, the military action left unquestioned the intention and capacity of the United States to support democracy in the hemisphere.

---

8. On the US role, see John Goshko, "Christopher Says Pressure on Guatemala Bore Results," *The Washington Post*, 3 June 1993, A17.

9. James Brooke, "Venezuela Votes Today, Cautioned by Clinton," *New York Times*, 5 December 1993, 23.

Regional Integration Gains Legitimacy

There is a robust literature assessing the economic efficiency of free trade areas (FTAs);[10] but there is yet no authoritative study explaining why US policy in the 1980s turned toward bilateral and regional free trade arrangements, beginning with Israel and Canada and spreading in the 1990s to Mexico and then to the Asia Pacific and Latin America.[11] Decisions appear generally to have been made case by case, with the new pattern emerging only gradually.[12] Several trends in the international economy contributed to this paradigm shift: the shortcomings of the General Agreement on Tariffs and Trade (GATT), opportunities for strategic advantages, progress toward economic reforms, and new market openings.

Shortcomings of the GATT

Launched in 1986 after much wrangling, the Uruguay Round negotiations dragged on for nearly seven years in the face of repeated delays before concluding in December 1993. Even then, the GATT did not progress as far as the United States would have liked on such critical issues as dispute settlement, competition policies, services, and investment regimes and agricultural trade. These lengthy delays and substantive lacunae opened running room for impatient policymakers and aggressive foreign countries to propose new mechanisms for trade liberalization and rule setting.[13] Some of these regionalists sought to defuse the angst of the globalists who were concerned with preserving the most-favored nation (MFN) principle and avoiding discriminatory trading blocs by arguing that the threat of regional deals could be used to spur countries to complete the Uruguay Round. Specifically, the United States could showcase NAFTA

---

10. For good analyses of the economic case for FTAs in general and several regional examples including Israel, Canada, and Mexico, see Jeffrey J. Schott, ed., *Free Trade Areas and US Trade Policy* (Washington: Institute for International Economics, 1989). For a more recent assessment that includes discussions of the Asia Pacific Economic Council (APEC) and Western Hemispheric integration, see Robert Z. Lawrence, *Regionalism, Multilateralism, and Deeper Integration* (Washington: Brookings Institution, 1996). Neither book, however, focuses on US policymaking.

11. For an overview of the relationship between global liberalization and regional initiatives, see C. Fred Bergsten, *Competitive Liberalization and Global Free Trade: A Vision for the Early 21st Century*, Working Papers on Asia Pacific Economic Cooperation No. 96-15 (Washington: Institute for International Economics, 1996), 5-6.

12. Some US officials did develop a broader strategic vision to justify regional and bilateral free trade agreements. See James A. Baker III, "Geopolitical Implications of the US-Canada Trade Pact," *International Economy* 1, no. 2, January-February, 1988, 34-41.

13. For example, the US-Canada free trade agreement was attributed thus: "Frustrated with progress on the multilateral front, the United States in effect backed into the bilateral with Canada." Michael Aho, "Forward," in *Bilateralism, Multilateralism and Canada in United States Trade Policy*, William Diebold Jr., ed. (New York: Council on Foreign Relations, 1988), viii.

and the Asia Pacific Economic Cooperation (APEC) forum as viable alternative roads to liberalization. Regional arrangements could also be presented as catalysts to induce the Europeans to improve their offers in the final moments of the Uruguay Round negotiations.

Strategic Advantages

The United States signed three bilateral free trade agreements with countries with which it shares a special strategic or geographic relationship. The first, with Israel, derived not from US interests in the relatively small Israeli economy but from an intention to tighten diplomatic ties with a strategic ally in the Middle East.[14] Between the United States and Mexico and Canada, very long common borders create special bonds (cultural ties, border management, intrafirm trade, and investment) as well as unique problems (e.g., in environment, immigration and labor flows, and transportation).[15] The US desire to participate actively in APEC also obeyed important geopolitical considerations. The United States saw it as a mechanism for engagement in the Asia Pacific region after the Cold War. Nor did the United States want to allow Japan to dominate the region.[16] Although APEC's formal agenda was primarily economic, the United States has sought to use it to strengthen its political influence in the Asia Pacific.

Strong political motives also lay behind the Bush administration's interest in free trade with Mexico. Bush's secretary of state, James A. Baker III, wrote in his memoirs that NAFTA "would be the cornerstone of a new relationship with Mexico and enhance close ties on the whole set of issues that don't respect borders: narcotics, the environment, and immigration. And it would help advance other US objectives in Mexico, including the democratization of the political system."[17] The same political rationale would hold for advancing free trade with the rest of Latin America.

---

14. Howard Rosen, "The United States-Israel Free Trade Area Agreement: How Well Is It Working and What Have We Learned?," in Jeffrey J. Schott, *Free Trade Areas and U.S. Trade Policy* (Washington: Institute for International Economics, 1989), 97-119.

15. For a discussion of the weight of geographical proximity on trading patterns, including on US trade with Canada and Mexico, see Jeffrey Frankel, *Regional Trading Blocs* (Washington: Institute for International Economics, forthcoming).

16. Then-Secretary of State James A. Baker III explained his interest in APEC thus: "Above all, I was determined that any move toward economic integration in East Asia include the United States. At State, I would try to check any move by the East Asians to exclude us—gently if I could, not so gently if I must. But I wanted also to use broadened economic cooperation in more positive ways. Closer links to the economies of East Asia would help open up dynamic markets to American exports and investment. In addition, they would complement our existing political and strategic ties to a region that we had considered vital since the time of Teddy Roosevelt." James A. Baker III, *The Politics of Diplomacy*, 609.

17. James A. Baker III, *The Politics of Diplomacy*, 607.

Economic Reforms

The Bush administration saw free trade agreements with developing countries as mechanisms for promoting market-oriented economic reforms. Trade agreements would strengthen the political position of those reform-minded technopols who had been dismantling statist regimes and opening their economies to international trade and investment.[18] Free trade agreements would lock in reforms by tying them to international agreements that would be costly to violate. Bush administration Latin American economic policies were driven in large measure by the US Treasury Department, the agency within the executive branch that has the most systemic view of the international economy and which had used the debt crisis of the 1980s to promote economic liberalization throughout the developing world. In that protracted process of debt restructuring, Treasury leadership had become acquainted with leading Latin American technopols in the ministries of finance and economics and in the central banks. That leadership saw free trade as a means of strengthening their hands within their own governments and societies.

Market Openings

By the early 1990s, the Asia Pacific and Latin American regions had become the world's most dynamic growth areas and accounted for large and rising shares of US exports and investment. By 1992 US Under Secretary of the Treasury for International Affairs David Mulford, a principal architect of Bush's EAI and its vision of a hemispheric free trade zone, remarked that "Latin America is our fastest growing regional market—12 percent annual growth in the past five years. One dollar out of every seven dollars of exports from the United States goes to Latin America. And we are competitive there. The United States has a 57 percent share of industrial country exports of goods to Latin America, versus 11 percent for Japan."[19] US exports to Latin America surged from $30 billion in 1985 to $80 billion in 1993, increasing the region's share of total US exports from 12.5 percent in 1988 to over 15 percent by 1994.[20] US direct investment in the region also jumped during those years, rising at an average annual rate of 13 percent, from $63 billion in 1989 to $115 billion in 1994.[21]

---

18. For a discussion of technopols, see John Williamson, "In Search of a Manual for Technopols," in *The Political Economy of Policy Reform*, John Williamson ed. (Washington: Institute for International Economics, 1994), 9-13, and Jorge Domínguez, *Technopols: Freeing Politics and Markets in Latin America in the 1990s* (University Park, PA: Penn State Press, 1996).

19. David Mulford, address at The Heritage Foundation, Washington, 4 March 1992.

20. International Monetary Fund, *Direction of Trade Statistics*, various.

21. US Department of Commerce, *Survey of Current Business*, various.

Some US-based firms saw a strong link between freer trade and strategic investment opportunities. Firms could connect high-tech production in the United States with the more labor-intensive work in Latin America to produce a globally competitive product. NAFTA was one step toward uniting North and South at the level of the firm.[22]

Each of these four factors was significant, but even when taken cumulatively they did not make bilateral and regional free trade areas inevitable.[23] Political choices still needed to be made. There were strong advocates within the bureaucracy for adhering to the more traditional GATT-World Trade Organization approach. Moreover, powerful political forces in the United States staunchly opposed further trade liberalization altogether. Two US presidents had to make controversial decisions before US trade policy could head off in a regionalist direction.

The Enterprise for the Americas Initiative

The immediate origins of the EAI were President Bush's February 1990 counternarcotics minisummit in Cartagena, Colombia, and a presidential trip to Latin America later that year.[24] As with the Summit of the Americas, a presidential event helped focus the attention of senior policymakers, force decisions, and launch important new initiatives. At the Cartagena meeting, the heads of the Andean nations urged Bush to consider a post-Cold War economic policy toward the region. Bush gave the lead in designing this new policy to the US Treasury Department, where Under Secretary David Mulford held his deliberations closely and consulted minimally with other agencies.[25] The planned presidential trip of Septem-

---

22. Hufbauer and Schott argued that the most important objective of NAFTA was the synergy among the three economies that could generate important income and employment gains and enhance the international competitiveness of firms throughout the region. Gary C. Hufbauer and Jeffrey J. Schott, *North American Free Trade: Issues and Recommendations* (Washington: Institute for International Economics, 1992), 4.

23. Making a similar point, Kahler noted that "recent American investment in regional initiatives in both Latin America and the Pacific reflects more than an inevitable consequence of the growing economic importance of these regions. A new element in US foreign economic policies, these initiatives are uncharted and hard-to-predict features of future American policies (toward Europe)." See Miles Kahler, *Regional Futures and Transatlantic Economic Relations* (New York: Council on Foreign Relations Press, 1995), 12.

24. The most complete political analysis to date of the EAI is Joseph S. Tulchin, "The Enterprise for the Americas Initiative: Empty Gesture, Shrewd Strategic Gambit, or Remarkable Shift in Hemispheric Relations?" in *The Enterprise for the Americas Initiative: Issues and Prospects for a Free Trade Agreement in the Western Hemisphere*, ed. Roy E. Green (Westport, CT: Praeger Publishers, 1993), 143-58.

25. In his memoirs, then-Secretary of State Baker conceded that the EAI was "developed by Treasury with input from State." *The Politics of Diplomacy*, 606. At the time, bureaucrats at State, USTR, and Commerce all complained about being cut from the decision-making process and of being informed of Bush's announcement only hours before the event. Deputy

ber 1990 was the catalyst for President Bush's 27 June announcement of the EAI.[26]

The EAI comprised a multilateral fund within the Inter-American Development Bank (IDB) to spur private investment, some bilateral debt relief tied to continued economic reform, and "free trade agreements with the ultimate goal of a hemispherewide free trade system." All three components supported market-oriented, private-sector development. When he sent his EAI Act of 1990 to the US Congress, Bush emphasized its systemic objective: "For the benefit of all people of this hemisphere, the United States needs to reach out to support the efforts of these countries as each undertakes its own approach to economic reform."

The EAI trade component was closely associated with NAFTA. President Bush and Mexican President Carlos Salinas de Gortari had announced their intent to negotiate a free trade agreement only two weeks before the EAI rollout. In response to a personal request from President Patricio Aylwin, the Bush administration also announced that Chile was next in line for a free trade agreement. The US Trade Representative (USTR) established working groups with other countries to analyze their trade and investment regimes and to help them prepare for eventual trade negotiations. But with NAFTA negotiations in the limelight and further decisions on how and when other countries might negotiate similar agreements lacking, by the end of 1992 the working groups were virtually moribund. At the close of the Bush administration, NAFTA had been signed and would be ratified during the next administration. However, Chilean accession remained an unfulfilled promise and the proposed FTA from "Alaska to Argentina" were still just a dream.

The trade pillar of the EAI—its most ambitious and meaningful component—stalled for several reasons. Created by a few officials located primarily in Treasury, decision making did not allow for the consultations that create bureaucratic buy-in. There were many GATT-oriented officials within USTR who balked at an expansion of regional trading arrangements beyond the obviously special cases of Israel, Canada, and Mexico. (Indeed, many at the USTR had initially objected to NAFTA.) NAFTA took precedence, and if it represented a foundation for future free trade areas, it was also a roadblock to their immediate consideration. And as the 1992 presidential elections approached, the Bush administration began to shy away from negotiating additional trade agreements, which might not only complicate congressional ratification of NAFTA and the Uruguay Round but could also be unpopular with the protectionist wing of the

---

USTR Jules Katz was shown the final text just prior to the event and was told that his principal, USTR Carla Hills, could voice USTR's objections by calling the president. Katz had a reputation for opposing regional preferential schemes.

26. Bush made the announcement himself in the East Room of the White House. The trip subsequently was postponed until December 1990.

Republican Party, as well as with some blue-collar voters. During a mid-1992 visit to the United States by President Aylwin, Bush sided with USTR Carla Hills and decided against entering then into negotiations on a free trade agreement, to the embarrassment of his Chilean guest. As the US presidential elections approached in 1995-96, this same syndrome of trade fatigue and political calculation would slow implementation of the free trade plank of the Summit of the Americas.

Clinton Administration Follows Suit

The Clinton administration followed in the footsteps of its predecessor's trade policies in the Western Hemisphere. During the 1992 presidential campaign, candidate Clinton overrode the qualms of some of his political advisers and the opinions of organized labor and endorsed NAFTA, albeit with reservations that would require side agreements to protect the environment and workers' rights.[27] Clinton reaffirmed Bush's commitment to a free trade agreement with Chile. He did not embrace the EAI as such, but during the campaign and the NAFTA debates, he repeatedly spoke in favor of hemispheric free trade. Once in office, Clinton proposed a step toward NAFTA accession for the smaller countries in the Caribbean Basin: NAFTA parity legislation to give preferential access to their textile and apparel exports to protect the Caribbean and Central America from losing investment flows to Mexico.

Latin American Readiness

During the 1980s, many Latin American countries began to dismantle the import substitution model of industrial development they had adopted in the 1930s and 1940s. This model relied on state subsidies and trade protection to promote growth. As noted in chapter 1, disappointed with the results of import substitution and recognizing new global market forces, Latin Americans started to turn away from statism and toward more market-friendly strategies in the wake of the 1980s debt crisis. Many subsidies were slashed, state-owned firms were privatized, and government interventions were eliminated.[28] Fiscal deficits were reduced, and monetary policies became much more rigorous. Most important, tariff

27. For a description of this debate within the Clinton campaign, see Peter Behr, "Clinton's Conversion on NAFTA," *The Washington Post*, 19 September 1993, Business Section, 1.

28. The classic work on this reform process is John Williamson, ed., *Latin American Adjustment: How Much Has Happened?* (Washington: Institute for International Economics, 1990). See also Sebastian Edwards, *Latin America and the Caribbean a Decade After the Debt Crisis* (Washington: World Bank, 1993).

Table 2.1 Expansion of intraregional trade, 1988-94 (percent)

Trade pact	1988-92	1992-93	1993-94
NAFTA	8.2	16.5	17.3
Mercosur	24.8	39.5	12.7
Andean Group	22.2	30.9	7.2
CACM	15.0	10.1	11.9
Caricom	0.8	21.6	22.8

NAFTA = Canada, Mexico and the United States; Mercosur = Argentina, Brazil, Paraguay, and Uruguay; Andean Group = Bolivia, Colombia, Ecuador, Peru, and Venezuela; CACM = Costa Rica, El Salvador, Guatemala, Honduras, and Nicaragua; Caricom = Antigua and Barbuda, the Bahamas, Barbados, Belize, Dominica, Grenada, Guyana, Jamaica, Montserrat, St. Kitts-Nevis-Anguilla, St. Lucia, Trinidad and Tobago, St. Vincent, and the Grenadines.

Source: Direction of Trade Statistics, Bureau of Statistics, International Monetary Fund, for years cited.

rates and other forms of trade protection were cut, and foreign investment regimes were liberalized. Average tariff rates declined sharply between 1985 and 1992, falling by 92 percent in Colombia, 88 percent in Mexico, 74 percent in Brazil, and 46 percent in Argentina.[29] Economies became more open: trade as a percentage of GDP rose, regaining and eventually surpassing the levels attained before the debt crisis.

In the search for export markets, Latin American countries revived their long-standing interest in regional integration. In contrast to the last major integration effort of the 1950s and 1960s, these agreements were designed to be trade-creating, not trade-diverting. Rather than raise tariff rates against the rest of the world, Latin American countries accelerated their broad-based reduction of trade barriers in favor of neighboring states. As a result of these liberalizing measures and of recovery from the prolonged recessions of the 1980s, intraregional trade surged (table 2.1). Trade among Latin American countries rose from $32.6 billion in 1988 to $72 billion in 1994, and intraregional exchange accounted for a sharply growing share of total trade.

Just as the drive toward trade integration obeyed strategic and political motives in the United States, Latin Americans had reasons beyond the

29. Figures are for unweighted averages for tariffs plus paratariffs. Sebastian, Edwards, "Trade Policy, Exchange Rates, and Growth," in *Reform, Recovery and Growth*, Rudiger Dornbusch and Sebastian Edwards, eds. (Chicago: University of Chicago, 1995), 26.

immediate search for markets for their interest in free trade agreements with each other and with the United States. The economic liberalizers found support and comfort in trade agreements with like-minded leaders in neighboring states. These agreements created bonds among natural allies and gave them strong legal and political arguments against domestic critics who would seek to slow or reverse reform. A free trade agreement with the United States would confer such benefits in spades: Chileans were explicit in stating that an economic alliance with the United States would not only lock in economic reforms but would also enhance Chile's image worldwide.[30] Even if an agreement with the United States would only marginally improve access to the US market for Chilean exports since US trade barriers were already quite low, the seal of approval inherent in a free trade agreement would enhance chances for capturing foreign investment. For Chileans and other Latin Americans considering such agreements with the United States, this search for external capital was at least as compelling a motive as the quest for export markets.[31]

Fear of future US protectionism was another important incentive for countries to seek binding agreements with the United States. Although the US market was then relatively open, protectionism remained an ever-present threat in the US political system. Israel, Canada, and Mexico saw a free trade agreement as insurance against new protectionism in the United States. Just as the United States saw free trade agreements as locking in domestic reforms in developing countries, its trading partners saw them as locking in access to the huge US market.[32] For free trade forces of the United States and its trading partners, free trade agreements promised to keep protectionist forces at bay. These were clear cases of cross-border allies using international agreements to strengthen their hands against domestic opponents.

For Latin Americans, economic reforms and the search for stable access to open markets were symptoms of a more positive attitude toward the international economic system. Statism and protectionism had been rooted partially in the fear that the international economy, over which Latin America had little control, was unstable at best and exploitative at worse. By the early 1990s, many Latin American policymakers and intellectuals increasingly perceived the international economy as, on balance, a benefi-

---

30. For example, see Andrea Butelmann and Patricio Meller, "Evaluation of a Chile-US Free Trade Agreement," in *Trade Liberalization in the Western Hemisphere* (Washington: IDB and ECLAC, 1995), 362-63.

31. This point is argued forcefully in Gary C. Hufbauer and Jeffrey J. Schott, *Western Hemisphere Economic Integration* (Washington: Institute for International Economics, 1994), especially chapters 4 and 7.

32. Howard Rosen, "The US-Israel Free Trade Area Agreement: How Well Is It Working and What Have We Learned?" 104-8; and Richard G. Lipsey and Murray G. Smith, "The Canada-US Free Trade Agreement: Special Case or Wave of the Future?" 317-21, in Schott, *Free Trade Areas.*

cial source of much needed technology, capital, and productivity-enhancing and job-creating trade opportunities. The shift toward more open economies ratified in international agreements represented a sea change in Latin American attitudes toward global economic integration. This shift in economic perspectives toward ideas more consistent with hemispheric cooperation brought with it monumental strategic implications. Whereas in the past politicians feared that close relations with the United States could be the kiss of death, by the 1990s Latin American leaders were openly seeking to sign major economic accords with US presidents.

Early Thinking in the Clinton Camp

During the 1992 campaign, Clinton's Latin American advisers drafted an issues paper on the region that recognized the hemispheric convergence toward democratic political norms and market-oriented economic integration. The advisers supported NAFTA as amended to protect the environment and workers' rights and argued that such a comprehensive trade accord should be open to the rest of the hemisphere. They noted that although competitive elections were now the norm in Latin America, the shallow roots of democracy needed deepening, and poverty and glaring inequalities threatened economic reform and democratic stability. The paper concluded: "We believe that the historic creation of a Western Hemisphere Community of Democracies is within our reach."

As part of a broader exercise considering what initiatives the new president might take in his first 100 days in office, a memorandum was prepared at the Clinton campaign's request proposing steps toward a Western Hemisphere community of democracies that could combine economic integration with political democratization and suggesting that Clinton launch his new policies toward Latin America by convening a summit of the heads of state from Latin America and the Caribbean.[33]

When the new administration took office, it promptly began to review foreign policy issues under the Presidential Review Directive (PRD) process. The review of Latin American policy culminated on 8 September 1994, when the president signed Presidential Decision Directive (PDD) 28, "US Policy Toward Latin America and the Caribbean." A large inter-

---

33. "South America: First 100 Days," unpublished memorandum, Washington, 28 October 1992. During this period, the Cuomo Commission on Competitiveness also proposed a summit of the Americas to draft a social and environmental charter to be incorporated into the NAFTA and future regional trade agreements. See Lee Smith, ed., *America's Agenda: Rebuilding Economic Strength* (Armonk, NY: M. E. Sharpe, 1992), 245-46. Coincidentally, at the outset of the Bush administration, David Rockefeller suggested a hemispheric summit, which he labeled a "Congress of the New World" in "A Partnership for the New World," remarks before the Chairman's International Advisory Council of the Americas Society, Caracas, Venezuela, 16 February 1989.

agency working group completed most of the draft during 1993, and until PDD 28 was signed the draft served as interim policy guidelines. (Disagreements over a few remaining issues, and the lack of urgency felt by key senior officials, delayed the final presentation of the PDD to the president). The PDD was consistent with earlier issue papers prepared by advisers to the Clinton campaign, while adding over eleven and one-half single-spaced pages of programmatic detail. In considering the key elements for a Western Hemisphere community of democracies, the PDD focused on protecting and promoting democracy, strengthening civil society and nongovernmental organizations, promoting economic reform and integration, encouraging sustainable development, fighting drug trafficking and international crime, and monitoring conventional security concerns and weapons of mass destruction. It called for stabilizing and deepening regional democracy through public-sector institution building, good governance, anticorruption reform, and the encouragement of US and indigenous NGOs. Recognizing the links between democratic stability and social equity, the PDD called for investments in human capital such as through health and education. Because USAID's resources were shrinking, the Inter-American Development Bank was cited as a main instrument of social policy.

On trade, the PDD noted that with the passage of NAFTA the president had announced his intention to pursue free trade agreements with eligible countries in the hemisphere. Significantly, the PDD stopped short of endorsing a hemispheric free trade area, stating only that the United States should seize the opportunity to lock in hemispheric reform through continuous trade expansion and that trade should be expanded through sectoral agreements in such areas as investment and intellectual property rights.

Despite US reluctance on trade integration, by late 1993 the essential preconditions for a successful summit meeting were in place. There was an unprecedented degree of convergence between the United States and Latin America on fundamental political and economic matters. The Clinton administration had nearly completed an internal policy review reaffirming this convergence and enumerating specific initiatives, many of which required regional cooperation. All that was lacking was a presidential decision to convene a summit where this convergence could be codified and an ensuing plan of action could be launched.

3

Creating an Initiative

The House of Representatives passed the North American Free Trade Agreement (NAFTA) on the evening of 17 November 1993. It had been a difficult, bruising battle but, in the end, a glorious one. President Clinton was proud to have won a battle of principle, and an upward spike in his public opinion polls suggested that the public responded well to a president demonstrating leadership and standing by his convictions. Clinton had cast the issue as pitting pessimism and retreat against optimism and competitiveness, withdrawal against leadership, the past against the future. The future—and the young president—had won.

Not only was US-Mexico trade policy at stake, but US policy toward the Western Hemisphere also hung in the balance. Had the Congress turned down NAFTA, US policy toward the entire region would probably have been crippled for the remainder of the Clinton presidency. The administration would likely have perceived initiatives that required cooperation with Latin America as political losers, impossible to sell to the Congress or the American people. As it was, many in the administration fretted that the NAFTA battle had divided the Democratic Party and driven a wedge between the president and the party base in the unions and its liberal-left wing. Nevertheless, the victory opened the door to taking the spirit of NAFTA and applying it to the rest of the hemisphere. Such was the hope of the Latin Americanists in the administration.

Vice President Al Gore's CNN face-off against Ross Perot had been a major turning point in the NAFTA debate and overnight made Gore a hero in Mexico.[1] Mexico's trade secretary, Jaime Serra Puche, heaped

1. Gore and Perot debated the NAFTA on "Larry King Live" on Cable Network News, 9 November 1993. Gore traced his own belief in a more open trading system to Secretary of

praise on the US vice president: "For the first time, the distortions and inventions of the opposing group, headed by Mr. Perot, were given correct and specific answers of fact."[2] Immediately after the NAFTA vote, the White House announced that Gore would travel to Mexico City.

Many in the White House saw the Gore trip primarily as an opportunity to underscore the administration's political victory at home. It was also a fence-mending mission to salve the wounds the Mexican ego had suffered during the bruising NAFTA debate, when NAFTA opponents, in the tradition of the no-benefits doctrine described earlier, questioned whether the United States should enter a trade pact with a country characterized as corrupt, drug-ridden, antidemocratic, and socially regressive.[3] But the speech that Gore would deliver in Mexico provided an opportune peg on which to hang a post-NAFTA initiative.

The idea of a post-NAFTA summit was in the air. Within days of the vote in the House of Representatives, two Latin American ambassadors telephoned National Security Council (NSC) staff to suggest a hemispheric summit, and one offered his country as host. Within the State Department, a memo sent to Secretary of State Warren Christopher on possible post-NAFTA initiatives included mention of a summit. So did a memo that circulated within the office of the US Trade Representative (USTR). The idea was emerging spontaneously in many quarters, as if from the collective consciousness of the hemisphere. But the idea could not become reality without the approval of the president of the United States.

The Spark

Leon Fuerth, the vice president's national security adviser, asked for an informal meeting of the National Economic Council to consider ideas for Gore's Mexico City speech. The meeting in the White House Situation Room was attended by, among others, National Economic Council Deputy Director Bowman Cutter, USTR Deputy Charlene Barshefsky, and Department of Commerce Under Secretary Jeffrey Garten. The tenor was decidedly cautious. It was agreed that the vice president would lay out a general vision of post-NAFTA hemispheric relations and that he would not retreat from the president's repeated public calls for freer hemispheric trade. The idea of a summit was mentioned but was as quickly shelved. As one

---

State Cordell Hull, who hailed from his hometown of Carthage, Tennessee: "As the father of GATT, [Hull] inspired my father to enter public service, and in that way is responsible for the inspiration my father passed on to me." Al Gore, remarks at the meeting of the GATT Plenary Committee, Marrakesh, Morocco, 14 April 1994.

2. Tim Golden, "Mexicans Seethe with Anger at Perot's Description of Mexico," *The New York Times*, 11 November 1993, A1.

3. Personal interview with former senior administration official, Washington, 3 May 1996.

participant recalled, "There was no appetite for another summit, in light of the president's existing commitments toward the Asia Pacific Economic Cooperation (APEC) forum and the Group of Seven (G-7).[4] There was no particular animus against the idea, just that there was already too much on the platter."[5] But there was concern that a summit, and the closely associated issue of post-NAFTA trade policy, not be decided upon prematurely. Among officials responsible for trade, many felt that no additional initiatives should be undertaken until the Congress passed the Uruguay Round legislation. Some also thought that if any regional initiatives were undertaken, Asia should take precedence over Latin America. In any case, it was felt the administration should decide such important strategic issues only after careful analysis and orderly deliberation. Some officials also felt that a summit should be announced in the United States by the president.

Shortly after noon on Monday, 29 November, the day before his flight to Mexico City, Gore assembled his staff in his West Wing office to review the draft that his senior speechwriter, Robert Lehrman, had prepared in coordination with the Inter-American Affairs office of the NSC. Gore complained that "there is no there there." He asked one of his advisers, Dana Marshall, for ideas. Marshall ran through a list of possible initiatives, passing quickly over the idea for a summit. The author interrupted and laid out the arguments for a summit: "Sir, calling for a hemispheric summit would serve as a strong centerpiece for your speech. It is a logical next step after NAFTA and will be very well received throughout Latin America . . ." It was obvious that the idea had captured the vice president's imagination. As one participant in the meeting recalled, "The idea immediately recommended itself to the vice president as appropriate to the moment. It was a creative leap."[6] As another participant remembered, a summit announcement would also be newsworthy. When the author pointed out some objections raised at the earlier meeting of deputies, the vice president peremptorily dismissed them. His mind was made up. Further, he had already spoken to the president and said the president had agreed that his speech in Mexico should be a major one.[7]

Gore then summoned National Security Adviser Anthony Lake, who came quickly from his nearby office. Together, they ran through the

---

4. President Clinton had just returned from an APEC summit in Seattle, had already participated in two G-7 summits, and would be expected to continue to attend the annual summit meetings of both groups.

5. Personal interview with participant in the meeting, Washington, spring 1996.

6. Personal interview with Senior White House official, Washington, September 1996.

7. In a press conference the next day, the president said: "The vice president is leaving this afternoon for Mexico where he will deliver a major address on American engagement in Latin America." President Bill Clinton, Press Conference with the leaders of Central America, White House, 30 November 1993.

foreign travel commitments on the president's schedule for the coming year. Three European trips were already planned—the mandatory G-7 and NATO summits and a trip to Russia—but May looked clear. Lake said he would be favorably inclined toward a hemispheric summit but wanted to check the timetable with US Trade Representative Mickey Kantor to be sure that it would not interfere with the congressional vote on the Uruguay Round legislation. Later in the day, Lake reported that Kantor had voiced no objection. Then he tasked the author to draft a memorandum to the president. The memorandum, from the vice president and the National Security Adviser, was to present the arguments for the summit and be forwarded to Lake that evening.

Lake also asked that the memorandum be cleared with the State Department. Lake did not specify with whom at State to clear the memorandum and the author did not ask. To seek the clearance of officials on the seventh floor, at the deputy or under secretary level, might well have stimulated many questions and requests for a formal policy review. Instead, the author telephoned Assistant Secretary for Inter-American Affairs Alexander Watson at home that evening. Watson concurred with forwarding a memorandum to the president recommending that the vice president announce a hemispheric summit in his Mexico City speech. With that, the memorandum went forward.

The memorandum argued the moment was ripe for an historic initiative in inter-American relations and suggested three themes: expanding free trade, strengthening democracy through collective actions and good governance, and exploring global agenda issues such as sustainable development (see full text in appendix B). It proposed that the organizing concept be a hemispheric community of democracies and that the summit issue a declaration of shared principles.

By chance, the next morning the president's schedule included a breakfast with the presidents from Central America. At a prebrief meeting with the president, Gore held a copy of the summit memorandum in his hand, but chose not to broach the topic so it would not be mixed up with the agenda for the Central American meeting. Later in the day, the vice president met with the president in the Oval Office, in the presence of the chief of staff, Thomas "Mack" McLarty III.[8] There, he suggested to the president that a summit would be a logical follow-up to NAFTA and that, moreover, now that most of Latin America was democratic, it deserved more attention. Such an initiative would be fully consistent with the president's policy of global engagement. Gore added a reference to his positive experience at the 1992 Earth Summit in Rio de Janeiro. The president was persuaded.

---

8. Personal interview with Mack McLarty III, Washington, 11 June 1996.

Thus, the bit of folklore that spread around Latin America—that the decision to convene the summit was made on the airplane en route to Mexico City—is incorrect. As with many myths, however, this particular story has a basis in fact. Tony Lake phoned airborne Air Force Two to inform the vice president that the president's schedulers were balking at his making a public commitment to a summit in light of the president's already tight agenda. That night, from the US ambassador's residence in Mexico City, the vice president and McLarty telephoned the chief scheduler, Ricki Seidman. McLarty told her that the president was aware of the planned announcement of the summit and that the speech was important to the vice president. They agreed that the vice president would go ahead and announce the hemispheric summit for 1994 but would avoid public mention of a specific date.

Mexico City

The vice president refined his speech on Air Force Two, line by line, as was his practice. One more important decision was made: to extend the summit invitation to democratically elected leaders. The addition of this modifier was intended to deter would-be coup plotters and their potential co-conspirators (such as the Venezuelan military officers who had recently staged two coup attempts) and also preemptively excluded Fidel Castro.[9]

Before the speech, the vice president met with Mexican President Carlos Salinas de Gortari and informed him of his intention to make public President Clinton's decision to convene a hemispheric summit. After the speech the joint press statement issued by the two governments stated that President Salinas had expressed his support for the summit and his readiness to participate actively in its realization. This was the only consultation with a foreign government that time allowed.

Gore delivered the speech at the Mexico City National Auditorium before an assembly of business executives, students, and media. Gore praised Mexico's "courage and vision," its "willingness to embrace change," and the breaking down of old barriers between the United States and Mexico that the NAFTA symbolized. He referred to the "bruising [NAFTA] debate fueled by lack of information and insensitivity," adding that "this is the time to heal." Gore then turned to the summit.

> The NAFTA debate demonstrated the importance of dispelling myths and stereotypes concerning Latin America. It is clear to us that we must rethink the way we deal with the new Latin America that has emerged. The Clinton administration has undertaken a broad-ranging review of US policy in Latin America as we near the

---

9. Castro, who since 1962 had been a nonparticipant in the inter-American system, had not attended the 1967 summit, although other authoritarian leaders were present.

21st century. As an outgrowth of this review, and because the president believes so strongly that thinking through a new relationship should be a joint enterprise—on his behalf, I wish to announce today that next year the United States will invite—to a Western Hemisphere summit meeting—the democratically elected heads of state of North America, Central America, South America, and the Caribbean. We will seek to make explicit the convergence of values that is now rapidly taking place in a hemispheric community of democracies; a community increasingly integrated by commercial exchange and shared political values.[10] It will be a meeting that we hope will codify our shared principles and set forth a vision of economic and cultural progress that could serve us well in the century ahead.

After a luncheon with Salinas and his chief aides at the presidential mansion, Los Pinos, the vice president and his delegation returned to Washington, the summit announcement a fait accompli.

Deadlines and End Runs

The decision to convene a summit short-circuited the elaborate bureaucratic processes whereby decision memoranda are routinely prepared for the president. It contrasted sharply with the Presidential Review Directive on Latin America, which involved more than 100 people from about 20 agencies and innumerable offices and bureaus who had been laboring since the outset of the administration to define policy toward the region. The interagency working group had produced mounds of background and issue papers, and its members had laboriously and sometimes contentiously negotiated each word of the draft directive. Once the working group had gained approval at the assistant secretary level, drafts had languished for months in the in-boxes of senior policymakers distracted by more pressing business. A region free of major conflict and without large budgetary expenditures or strong constituencies in the bureaucracy, Latin America did not readily command senior-level attention.

For the summit the decision was made quickly (within 36 hours), and the decision chain was very simple: NSC to vice president to the president.

Such end runs are profoundly irritating to those concerned with orderly decision making in which the full range of factors can be carefully weighed.[11] But it is precisely such orderly decision making that enables

---

10. For a contemporaneous elaboration on this concept, see Richard E. Feinberg, "The Hemispheric Community of Democracies: Agenda for Collective Action," address to the Council of the Americas, Miami, 9 December 1993, reproduced in US Department of State, *Dispatch* 5, no. 3, 17 January 1994.

11. On bureaucratic end runs, see Amos Jordan, William Taylor Jr., and Lawrence Korb, *American National Security: Policy and Process*, fourth edition (Baltimore: Johns Hopkins Press, 1993), 225. As Henry Kissinger, an effective practitioner of such tactics, has written of presidential speeches, "Faced with an administrative machine which is both elaborate and fragmented, the executive is forced into essentially lateral means of control," in Henry Kissinger, *American Foreign Policy* (New York: W. W. Norton, 1974), 22. On end runs and access to the president, see Morton Halperin, *Bureaucratic Politics and Foreign Policy* (Washington: Brookings Institution, 1974), 189-218.

established power relations and standing hierarchies of interests to assert themselves, often gives veto power to a series of vested interests, and tends to dilute new ideas and reinforce the status quo.

The existence of a deadline, such as that provided by a major speech, greatly facilitates the end run by narrowing the window in which other bureaucratic players can slow or halt decision making. The tight deadline also gives those initiating an "end run" an excuse for circumventing routine. In this instance, another facilitating factor was the proximity of NSC staff offices to those of the vice president and president. When events are pressing, the White House can make decisions with lightning speed that leaves bureaucratic players at more distant locations in the dark.

As they labored to prepare the summit during the next 12 months, bureaucrats excluded from this decision would question whether the outcome had in fact been in the national interest.

4

US Trade Policy

Bill Clinton believes in the virtues of open international trade. Candidate Clinton supported the North American Free Trade Agreement (NAFTA) negotiations with Mexico, reiterating even in front of blue-collar audiences in Michigan his conviction that trade agreements were good for the US economy. Clinton's campaign advisers, especially those expert in foreign policy, leaned decidedly toward an open and expanding trading system, but Clinton also had to contend with the opinions of the majority leader in the House of Representatives, Richard Gephardt, and other Democrats who wanted to tie NAFTA to provisions advancing worker rights, the environment, and border infrastructure.[1] Clinton mirrored Gephardt's views when he, too, conditioned his support for NAFTA: "I will support a free trade agreement with Mexico so long as it provides adequate protection for workers, farmers, and the environment on both sides of the border."[2] But whereas some Democrats wanted to raise the goalposts on these conditions so high as to preclude agreement with Mexico and Canada, Clinton sought side agreements acceptable to all NAFTA partners.

Less noticed than the NAFTA debate during the 1991-92 campaign was Clinton's broader vision of hemispheric trade. In a November 1991 speech, Clinton expanded on his qualified endorsement of fast-track negotiations with Mexico: "We should seek out similar agreements with all of Latin

1. Richard Gephardt, address on the status of the North American Free Trade Agreement, Institute for International Economics, Washington, 27 July 1992.

2. Governor Bill Clinton, statement, 27 July 1992.

America because rich countries will get richer by helping other countries grow into strong trading partners."[3] The Clinton team advocated expanding NAFTA by proposing "trade agreements with Latin American countries that improve and endorse labor, wage, health, safety, and environmental standards at home and abroad."[4] Clinton expanded on that proposal in an important speech on NAFTA in North Carolina a month before the 1992 elections. "If we can make this agreement work with Canada and Mexico, then we can reach down into other market-oriented economies of Central and South America to expand even further."[5] He justified this hemispheric vision in terms of "positive opportunities" as well as in strategic terms—as a defensive response should the world evolve toward protectionist trading blocs, views that the author heard him articulate repeatedly as president, in public and in private.

President-elect Clinton continued to elaborate on this hemispheric theme. At a press conference two weeks after the election, he reaffirmed President Bush's commitment to negotiating a trade agreement with Chile, expressed interest in increasing trade with Argentina, and added that "a major part of our economic future rests with building up strong two-way trade with Latin America."[6] In teleconference remarks to a meeting of Latin American presidents in Buenos Aires, Clinton supported NAFTA and called for building free trade agreements with other nations in this hemisphere.[7] In the same vein, in remarks broadcast to a Miami gathering of hemispheric political leaders and business executives, Clinton proposed "a genuine hemispheric community of democracies, one where open markets and accountable governments provide the foundations of freedom and prosperity."[8]

---

3. Bill Clinton, address at Georgetown University, 2 November 1991.

4. Bill Clinton for President Committee, "Bill Clinton on Immigration," Little Rock, Arkansas, 1992. The Latin American team that advised the Clinton campaign prepared an issues paper (finalized but never released) proposing NAFTA be open to the rest of the hemisphere. The paper stated, "This regional community of economic partners should be hemispheric in scope, to allow it to pursue common diplomatic and political objectives rooted in geography and shared values. But closer hemispheric economic ties should not translate into a fortress Americas. On the contrary, by uniting the technology, capital, raw materials labor, and talent of two vast continents, Western Hemisphere firms will be better poised to win markets in Europe and Asia."

5. Bill Clinton, remarks, Raleigh, North Carolina, 4 October 1992.

6. President-elect Bill Clinton, press conference in Washington, 19 November 1992, as printed, in "Washington Report" (Council of the Americas, Winter 1993). In these remarks, Clinton linked Latin American growth rates to US exports and employment. His remarks were based on calculations published by the Overseas Development Council, *US Foreign Policy and Developing Countries* (Washington, 1991).

7. Summary of remarks, 1 December 1992, "Washington Report." op. cit.

8. Summary of remarks, 2 December 1992, ibid.

In advocating hemispheric free trade, Clinton was following in the footsteps of his Republican predecessors. His priorities for doing so, however, differed from those articulated by the Bush administration. Bush and the chief spokesman for the Enterprise for the Americas Initiative, US Treasury Under Secretary David Mulford, emphasized that trade agreements would help lock in the free market economic reforms that Latin American leaders had been adopting during the 1980s. When Mexican President Carlos Salinas de Gortari told Bush that a free trade agreement would guarantee Mexico's opening to world market forces, he found a receptive audience.[9] Mulford viewed free trade agreements as a reward to be offered to Latin American nations that agreed to economic liberalization in exchange for debt relief and as a complement to such programs. Bush administration officials mentioned that trade agreements would expand markets for US exports, but their primary theme was systemic. This hierarchy of interests reflected the personal world view of George Bush and other senior officials as well as the bureaucratic fact that the US Treasury, with its systemic view of the global economy, played a lead role in policy formulation and articulation. By contrast, Bill Clinton, while not unaware of these systemic goals, placed greater emphasis on the pragmatic pursuit of market opportunities for US firms. In private but especially in public, Clinton sought to make foreign policy relevant to the immediate interests of everyday Americans, and so he framed US trade with Latin America in terms of more jobs for workers in Peoria.

Presidential Preferences

During 1993 meetings with hemispheric leaders, Clinton regularly referred to his interest in freer trade for the Western Hemisphere. For example, in the press conference following his June meeting with Argentine President Carlos Menem, President Clinton told the press: "I would be prepared to discuss immediately with Argentina, with Chile, and with other appropriate nations the possibility of expanded trade relations along the NAFTA model. I have long thought that NAFTA should be a model for embracing all of Latin America's democracies and free market economies."[10] Over lunch, Clinton told Menem, and repeated at the press conference, that US exports to Argentina had tripled in the last four years, creating 40,000 new American jobs. The president clearly had in mind the linkages between hemispheric trade and the domestic economy.

During the heated NAFTA debates in the fall of 1993, President Clinton continued to place NAFTA in a broader, hemispheric context. On at least

9. Personal interview with senior US Trade Representative official during the Bush administration, September 1996.

10. President Clinton, remarks to the press, White House, 29 June 1993.

11 public occasions during October and November, Clinton revealed his interest in expanding free trade further southward. For example, he told a New York corporate audience that:

> NAFTA could lead the way to a new partnership with Chile, with Argentina, with Colombia, with Venezuela, with a whole range of countries in Latin America who have embraced democracy and market economics. . . . We see this not as an exclusive agreement, but as part of the building block of a framework of continually expanding global trade.[11]

While dedicating the John F. Kennedy Library in Boston, the president painted NAFTA expansion as part of his internationalist vision:

> But there is no better example of what we have tried to do to reach out to the world than our attempt to secure an agreement for a North American Free Trade zone with Canada and Mexico—one that can create 200,000 new jobs for this country by 1995, open a vast new market, make 90 million friends, and set the stage for moving to embrace all of Latin America—700 million people strong—in a trading unit that will bring prosperity to them and to us.[12]

When the president promoted NAFTA at numerous White House events during November, he used those opportunities to hint at a broader vision. On 7 November, he proclaimed that the agreement "will help us to take this kind of deal to the rest of Latin America so we can establish a 700-million-person trading bloc." On 9 November he asserted that NAFTA will enable "us to use the Mexican precedent to go into the whole rest of Latin America, to have a trading bloc of well over 700 million people." On 16 November, he proclaimed that NAFTA "is the gateway to all of Latin America, to 700 million people."[13]

These statements were general and brief but taken together reveal a clear presidential preference and policy direction. A 30 November remark to the press—that the NAFTA expansion was "something I have long supported"—suggested that by repeating the concept so frequently, the president had come to deeply feel it.[14] Largely unnoticed in the US media, these presidential utterances excited the attentive public in Latin America and energized those in the administration working on inter-American affairs. Especially noteworthy were the remarks the president delivered

---

11. President Clinton, remarks to *The Wall Street Journal*'s Second Annual Conference on the Americas, New York, 28 October 1993.

12. President Clinton, remarks at the John F. Kennedy Library, Boston, 29 October 1993.

13. Respectively, remarks by President Clinton in The Oval Office, 7 November 1993; in the Old Executive Office Building, 9 November 1993; and in the West Wing driveway, 16 November 1993.

14. President Clinton, press conference with leaders from Central America, White House, 30 November 1993.

on 17 November, the evening that the House of Representatives passed the NAFTA implementing legislation. He appeared determined to open NAFTA to other Latin American nations:

> Tomorrow I go to Seattle to meet with the leaders of 15 Asia Pacific economies. I will ask them to work toward more open markets for their products. When I return, I'll reach out to the other market-oriented democracies of Latin America, to ask them to join in this great American pact that I believe offers so much hope to our future.[15]

Did all the statements on free trade by Presidents Bush and Clinton cause the executive branch to consider that the United States was committed to hemispheric free trade? Some bureaucrats scoffed at presidential statements as the product of speechwriters and select officials who by dint of their proximity to the speechwriters or the president were sometimes able to insert phrases into presidential remarks without full interagency clearance. Some senior officials were particularly upset when a 4 February 1994 article in *The New York Times* reported, based on background briefings by unidentified administration officials, that the US government intended to make hemispheric free trade the centerpiece of the upcoming summit.[16] From the perspective of the bureaucracy, US trade policy could be made only through a formal interagency process that would culminate in a decision memorandum to the president, complete with individual agency positions and clearly articulated recommendations.

Latin Americans had noticed President Clinton's leanings, but they were also aware of the strong opposition that NAFTA had aroused in the US Congress and the deep splits within the Democratic Party on trade policy toward low-wage areas. They had received mixed signals from US Trade Representative (USTR) officials on the possible nature of post-NAFTA US trade policy. In the wake of the prolonged negotiations over the Uruguay Round and the intensity of the NAFTA debate, there was much talk about trade fatigue and the need for a pause before undertaking new initiatives.

While NAFTA was under consideration, many Latin American diplomats quietly probed for the possibility of accession to the North American accord. Various Latin American countries were jockeying for top positions

15. President Clinton, White House, 17 November 1993.

16. Steven Greenhouse "United States Plans Expanded Trade Zone," *New York Times*, 4 February 1994, D1. The article stated: "With trade rather than aid as the centerpiece of this administration's Latin policy, President Clinton is likely to unveil the free trade plan at a meeting of 34 of the hemisphere's leaders that is tentatively scheduled for the spring, administration officials said. The plan, some officials say, could dominate the hemisphere's economic and political agenda in the next decade."

on the NAFTA accession readiness list.[17] But they lacked the organizational structure and the political solidarity to mount a unified lobbying campaign in Washington. Moreover, without an invitation to membership, the Latin Americans hesitated to push hard for accession for fear of being publicly rebuffed. However interested they were, they were not properly positioned to energize US policy.

As the NAFTA debates came to a close, the future of hemispheric free trade seemed very uncertain. The Latin Americans were expectant but immobile. Much of the US bureaucracy was in no mood to consider an ambitious trade accord with other Latin American states. The political wing of the White House warned against further steps while the anti-NAFTA Democratic constituency, particularly organized labor and its allies in the Congress, was still licking its wounds. Senior executive-branch economic officials were uncertain about what direction trade policy should take. There was a real danger that NAFTA expansion would be placed on the back burner without something to force a decision.

Chilean Accession to NAFTA

Notwithstanding the uncertain political fate of hemispheric free trade, and even before the US Congress passed the NAFTA legislation, the Clinton administration took two steps toward its expansion. First, Clinton reiterated President Bush's pledge to negotiate a free trade agreement with Chile once NAFTA was approved by Congress. Second, Clinton proposed an interim trade agreement with the Caribbean Basin countries that would provide easier access to the US market for certain products covered by NAFTA.

President-elect Clinton had written to Chilean President Patricio Aylwin indicating his interest in pursuing a free trade agreement with Chile. The letter had been sparked by Senator Tom Harkin's visit to Chile. Harkin was a liberal Democrat with protectionist tendencies, but he developed close relations with Chilean political activists during the Pinochet dictatorship. Now that those Chilean activists were in government, Harkin supported them in their desire for closer economic relations with the United States. In signing this letter, Clinton was reaffirming Bush's repeated promises to Chile that once NAFTA was in place Chile was next in line for a free trade accord.

But some economic officials continued to harbor reservations about pursuing bilateral or regional trade negotiations outside the framework of the General Agreement on Tariffs and Trade (GATT) and the World

17. In *Western Hemisphere Economic Integration* (Washington: Institute for International Economics, 1994), 63-96, Gary C. Hufbauer and Jeffrey J. Schott use seven indicators of readiness for economic integration: price stability, budget discipline, external debt, currency stability, market-oriented policies, reliance on trade taxes, and functioning democracy.

Trade Organization (WTO). Others felt that if the United States were to pursue regional trading agreements, the fast-growing newly industrializing economies in Asia deserved priority over South America and certainly over the relatively small Chilean economy. Officials with their eyes on the NAFTA debate worried that mention of additional free trade agreements could cost the support of influential members of Congress on legislation of greater immediate importance to the president, including budget reform.

The March 1993 visit of Chilean Finance Minister Alejandro Foxley compelled the young administration to face the Chile FTA issue. Foxley forcefully presented his case directly to Vice President Gore, Secretary of State Warren Christopher, Treasury Secretary Lloyd Bentsen, USTR Mickey Kantor, and National Security Council (NSC) Deputy Director Samuel "Sandy" Berger. One of Latin America's most respected technopols, Foxley argued that it would be a major setback not only for Chile but for economic reformers and political democrats throughout Latin America if Clinton failed to reaffirm Bush's commitment.

At a National Economic Council (NEC) meeting on 29 March 1993, it was agreed that the president would reaffirm the commitment to seek a free trade area with Chile. There was also general consensus that the administration would request fast-track authority that would cover FTAs and that the administration would explicitly list Chile. This authority would permit trade legislation to proceed through Congress without major procedural delays or amendments that might force the administration to reopen negotiations with trading partners. This request, however, would be decoupled from the more immediate request for renewal of fast-track authority to complete the Uruguay Round. The president would mention his intention to seek this FTA-related authority but without indicating exactly when he would do so. This would keep NAFTA expansion alive and satisfy the Chileans.

The commitment to Chile was sealed in a second Clinton letter to Aylwin and reiterated publicly by the president, at a formal press conference, on 23 April 1993 in response to a question on NAFTA. He said that NAFTA will "lead us from [Mexico] to Chile to other market economies in Latin America."[18]

Caribbean Basin Parity

President Clinton invited the leaders of the five major Caribbean Common Market (Caricom) countries to a luncheon in the White House on 30 August 1993. The NSC staff had conceived of this meeting to focus senior-level—including presidential—attention on the Caribbean. Countries in Central America and the Caribbean were concerned that by granting

18. Federal News Service, "The President's News Conference," 23 April 1993.

traders based in Mexico preferential access to the US market, NAFTA would divert trade and investment toward Mexico and away from their region. In preparing for the meeting, the NSC staff worked with USTR to consider ways of neutralizing trade diversion, especially in the trade-policy-sensitive sector of textiles and apparel. A NAFTA parity bill sponsored by Congressman Sam Gibbons was languishing in the trade subcommittee of the House Ways and Means Committee without much attention from the administration.

At the White House luncheon, the Caribbeans pressed their concern about NAFTA preferences. The NSC had prepared the president, who asked a waiting USTR Mickey Kantor to study the effect of NAFTA on the Caribbean and Central American economies and to consult with them on new measures to increase regional trade. The president repeated this directive in his prepared remarks before the press following the luncheon.[19]

In the following months, Kantor would work with the countries of the Caribbean Basin and the Congress to design the Interim Trade Program, so named to make clear that the United States considered this trade measure a step toward eventual NAFTA accession. Through the interim agreement, the United States would grant qualifying Caribbean Basin Initiative (CBI) countries NAFTA parity on textiles and apparel in return for some reciprocal concessions in textile and apparel trade and progress on protection of intellectual property rights. The vice president announced the Interim Trade Program during a 24 May visit to Tegucigalpa, Honduras, and the administration included it in the congressional trade package implementing the Uruguay Round.

Strong political motives were behind both initiatives to extend NAFTA. Reaffirming Bush's pledge of a free trade area with Chile was primarily a political move—how could a Democratic administration be less favorable than the Republicans to a country synonymous with the struggle for democracy and human rights? The Reagan administration had crafted the CBI trade preferences to bolster the fragile economies of the region and lessen the attractiveness of leftist revolutionaries. By proposing the Interim Trade Program, the Clinton administration appeared to suggest that strategic considerations might play a role in NAFTA expansion.

Together these announcements indicated that the Clinton administration intended to incorporate other countries into its emerging free trade zone. Neither initiative, however, had been taken as the result of an explicit decision by the executive branch to pursue the ultimate goal of a hemispheric free trade area. The decisions on Chilean accession and NAFTA parity had occurred in isolation from any broader strategic framework. Rather, decisions were made incrementally and in response to particular political pressures and situational meetings with foreign officials. The president had frequently signaled his preference for hemispheric

19. Office of the Press Secretary, White House, 30 August 1993.

free trade, but he had not instructed the government to produce plans to carry out those preferences. The decision to proceed toward a Free Trade Area of the Americas would not be made until late 1994, just weeks before the president would host his hemispheric counterparts at the Miami summit.

Division and Delay

There were many reasons to assume that the summit would endorse hemispheric free trade. In his post-NAFTA approval speech in Mexico City, Vice President Gore had proposed generalizing that relationship to the entire hemisphere. Following references to Roosevelt's Good Neighbor policy, Kennedy's Alliance for Progress, and Bolivar's vision of integration, Gore spoke in expansive terms: "We see NAFTA as another such model. We see NAFTA as a starting point for dealing with the common challenges of the Americas."[20]

In March 1993 the president announced his decision to hold the summit in Miami. In earlier eras, American presidents preferred to downplay if not deny economic motives in US hemispheric policy. This former governor suffered from no such complex. As he regularly did in press conferences dealing with Latin America, Clinton talked about the link between expanding export markets and jobs at home. He justified his choice of Miami by noting that Miami's economy was fully integrated with those of Latin America and the Caribbean and that Miami represented "the promise of hemispheric integration": "Our exports to Latin America and the Caribbean have more than doubled in just seven years, rising to nearly $80 billion in 1993. That has generated hundreds of thousands of new jobs for American workers. If we can continue to bring down hemispheric trade barriers, we can create a million new jobs by the turn of the century."[21]

President Clinton's first cabinet and subcabinet were filled with officials whose past experience and philosophical perspectives inclined them toward hemispheric free trade. As a Texan with life-long interests in Mexico, Treasury Secretary Lloyd Bentsen was a leading proponent of more open hemispheric trade.[22] Commerce Secretary Ron Brown and his energetic aides, Jeffrey Garten and David Rothkopf, from the outset were

20. Vice President Al Gore, "Toward a Western Hemisphere Community of Democracies," address to the Mexican, American, and Latin American Chambers of Commerce, Mexico City, 1 December 1993.

21. President Bill Clinton, remarks at the announcement of Summit of Americas, Old Executive Office Building, White House, 11 March 1994.

22. As home to the Enterprise for the Americas Initiative (EAI), the Treasury Department's permanent staff was also strongly in favor of hemispheric free trade.

strong backers of hemispheric free trade; Argentina, Brazil, and Mexico were among the big emerging markets targeted by their export expansion strategy. Secretary of State Warren Christopher and State's Bureau of Inter-American Affairs followed suit. There was some disagreement among USTR officials, but Deputy Charlene Barshefsky had a clear appreciation for the opportunity hemispheric free trade presented.

But some members of the administration had their doubts about regional free trade. As noted above, some senior officials in the White House, USTR, and State, whose portfolios included international trade, preferred a focus on global negotiations or, if regionalism were to be pursued, a focus on the rapidly growing Asian markets. There was also some trade fatigue among negotiators who worked overtime to complete the GATT/WTO and NAFTA negotiations. Although not opposing free trade as such, some senior officials, notably Labor Secretary Robert Reich, were very concerned about the effect of trade on the stagnant, and in some instances declining, real wages of less-skilled workers; they were unhappy that the government programs intended to compensate the losers from free trade were not being given adequate attention and resources. Most important, the political wing of the White House, as well as the vice president and USTR Mickey Kantor, were chary about new trade initiatives while the Uruguay Round legislation was under consideration; moreover, in the immediate aftermath of the bitter NAFTA debate, resentment was still boiling within the defeated constituencies in the Democratic Party—particularly organized labor and its allies in the Congress. An administration decision in favor of "two, three, four NAFTAs would rub salt in those open wounds," one senior official warned.

As a result of these internal divisions and political considerations, as well as other factors considered below, President Clinton would not make the formal decision to seek hemispheric free trade for nearly 11 months after passage of NAFTA and the summit announcement and only a month before the Miami meeting. This delay was costly because it left many in the media and in Latin America fearing that the administration was not taking the summit seriously and had foolishly raised expectations only to leave them unfulfilled.

The lengthy delay in decision making, reflecting the lack of enthusiasm for hemispheric free trade in factions in the administration, suggests serious movement toward an FTAA might never have materialized in the absence of the decision-forcing summit. In the end, the requisites of presidential summitry would be decisive. In this equation, the views of Latin Americans would be critical. Most of Latin America felt strongly that hemispheric free trade was the most critical issue in hemispheric relations and that it had to be the centerpiece of the summit. A summit that skirted the major issue would be a terrible disappointment, a superficial photo opportunity, a lost opportunity in the eyes of most of the other 33 participants.[23] And if the Latin Americans declared the summit a failure, the media would probably follow suit. Thus, the success or failure of the entire enterprise would hinge on its vision of hemispheric trade integration. A senior White House official with experience in summitry recognized this equation early in the summit process: a) presidential summits must be successful—the president's political advisers always see it that way; b) the success of this summit would be defined by free trade; c) hence, the summit would have to endorse free trade.[24] If some White House political advisers preferred to avoid new trade accords with low-wage developing countries, that partisan preoccupation would be trumped by the overriding political requirement that the summit be a success for the president.

The Deputies Committee, composed of subcabinet officers, met for the first time to take up preparations for the summit on 7 February 1994. The deputies were told that the Latin Americans would seek to make reciprocal trade liberalization the central focus of the summit. Understanding that one of the main summit themes should be trade expansion, they set up a working group under USTR to define a trade policy. There seemed to be a general consensus on expansion of free trade, but the discussion was brief and general. There was some sentiment that any NAFTA expansion should be gradual and incremental. Just before the meeting, two well-placed White House economic officials had expressed their opinion that US interests would be better served by gradually expanding NAFTA not only to Latin American countries but also to countries outside the hemisphere.

In the following weeks, the United States began its first round of consultations with summit partners (appendix A gives a chronology of events leading up to the summit). Vice President Gore traveled to Bolivia, Argentina, and Brazil in late March. Under Secretary of State for Economic and Business Affairs Joan Spero led an interagency team to Mexico City in April. Treasury Under Secretary Lawrence Summers and State Assistant Secretary Alexander Watson visited Brasilia in May. During that visit, the delegation also conferred with representatives from Argentina, Chile, and Uruguay. Repeatedly, US officials were told that the Latin Americans hoped that trade would be a centerpiece of the summit, and they agreed that trade should be an important agenda item but avoided any detailed discussions. Meanwhile there were delays in developing the US trade policy. The USTR-led working group failed to circulate the trade policy paper requested by the 7 February deputies' meeting. The deputies met again on 5 May and again asked USTR to draft a trade strategy paper. Again, no paper flowed forth from USTR. On 18 May, the deputies again

23. Interviews with numerous Latin American diplomats, April to May 1996.

24. Interview with former senior White House official, May 1996.

briefly discussed trade policy. Should NAFTA accession be by individual countries or subregional groups of countries? What should be the pace of expansion? To win congressional support for fast-track renewal, should the administration present a full-blown trade strategy to Congress? These issues were not settled. It was possible, however, to agree to delay: USTR need not circulate a trade policy paper until after the administration pinned down congressional support for the Uruguay Round implementing legislation (with fast-track renewal attached). USTR argued that the leakage of a paper on NAFTA expansion could jeopardize that congressional strategy.

On 27 July, the deputies took up the economic part of the summit plan of action but avoided serious discussion of trade. Instead, they agreed that they should be sure to allow adequate time to develop a trade proposal before the summit. On 11 August, the deputies asked USTR, on an expedited basis, to identify trade policy options. Still, no memo surfaced. The administration submitted to Congress its Uruguay Round implementing bill on 27 September. On 30 September the deputies concluded that a trade policy had to be crafted soon to allow time for consultations with the Latin Americans before Miami. In October, with the summit only two months away, USTR, the NEC, and the NSC set about working on a detailed trade policy.

USTR justified its nonresponsiveness to White House coordination in large measure in terms of the legislative calendar. USTR Kantor expressed concern that the Uruguay Round legislation and fast-track renewal would be jeopardized if it leaked that the administration was cooking up a major new trade initiative in Latin America. During NAFTA negotiations, internal USTR memoranda regularly surfaced in private trade publications. (Although once the NEC began to draft trade papers for the summit, they did not leak.) Within the administration, some officials argued that it would not be possible to slide fast-track renewal through the Congress without laying out administration purposes explicitly. Officials at USTR knew that Congress has traditionally granted a fast-track mechanism to the president only after significant discussion and debate about the purposes for which that mechanism will be used.[25]

Action on the GATT bill was delayed until after the mid-term elections and the end of the regular congressional session, and the administration eventually chose to decouple it from fast-track renewal altogether; therefore, 1994 passed without a full debate on fast-track renewal. In 1995 the administration again avoided an open discussion over fast track, despite

25. This point is made in USTR, "Talking Points for Trade Consultations," an October 1993 internal memorandum.

the absence of competing legislation. The administration—or at least USTR with its supporters in the political wing of the White House—did not relish congressional consideration of major new trade initiatives, particularly if they would entail agreements with low-wage countries.[26]

Final Approval

The deputies were the focal point of policymaking on the trade initiative and, as the summit approached, they devoted much more time to it than to any other single initiative (figure 4.1: US Decision Making on Trade Policy). A number of NEC deputies—including Charlene Barshefsky from USTR, Joan Spero and her alternate, Daniel Tarullo, from State, and Robert Kyle from the NEC staff—were experts on trade policy. NEC co-chairs Bowman Cutter and Samuel Berger had considerable trade experience in both the public and private sectors. Barshefsky would be the chief negotiator on the trade initiative, but discussions with summit participants on the other initiatives were generally handled at assistant or deputy assistant secretary levels, where there was more knowledge of social and environmental issues and on Latin American politics (figure 4.1).

Although the deputies were the locus of decision making on hemispheric trade policy, the cabinet did convene on 17 October to consider how the United States would treat trade at the Miami summit and at the upcoming Asia Pacific Economic Cooperation (APEC) forum summit in Bogor, Indonesia. The agency heads debated the value of free trade with low-income countries in general terms. Secretary Bentsen noted that reciprocal trade negotiations with developing countries benefit the United States because its economy is already more open and other countries' markets are more restricted—a point seconded by Samuel Berger and Mickey Kantor. Several participants—including Kantor, Cutter, and Ron Brown, as well as communication adviser David Gergen—underscored that the proposed free trade agreements with Asia and Latin America would cast the United States in leadership positions—as the

26. The story of the nonrenewal of fast-track authority is told in I. M. Destler, *American Trade Politics*, 3d ed. (Washington: Institute for International Economics and the Twentieth Century Fund, 1995), 244-57. Nor would fast-track legislation emerge during the remainder of President Clinton's first term. The administration continued to seek language on labor rights and environmental protection that was unacceptable to congressional Republicans. Some observers within and outside the administration felt that a compromise on these and other fast-track issues would have been achievable had USTR really sought an agreement. Under this theory, USTR, presumably with the backing of the president, did not want to highlight trade issues as the 1996 elections approached because free trade was unpopular with an important Democratic constituency. Thus, whereas it was possible to use the pressures of the summit to persuade an agency such as USTR to negotiate agreements in principle, an agency can drag its feet on implementation that requires major further action. I am indebted to Mac Destler for this insight.

Figure 4.1 US decision making on trade policy

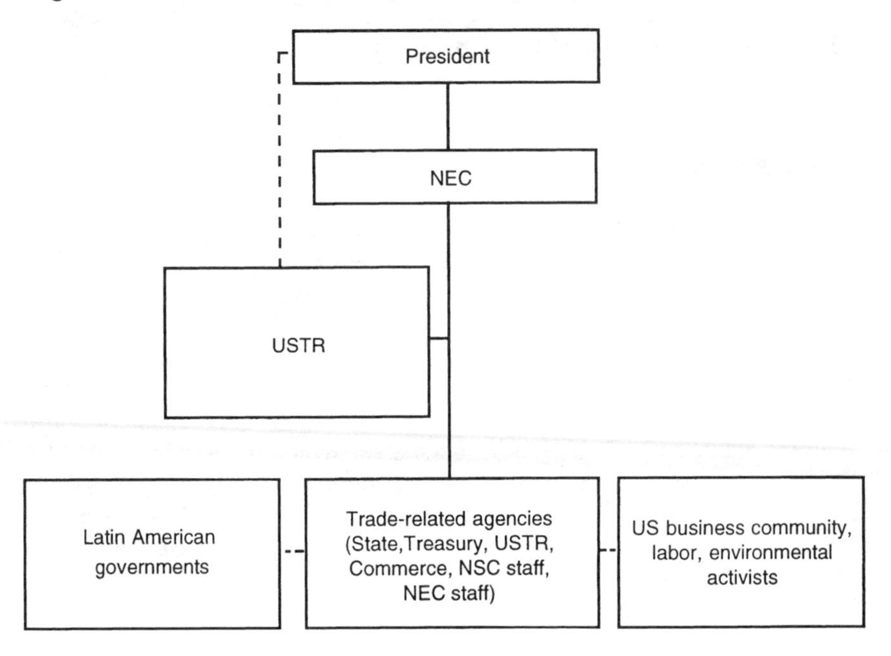

"linchpin" in the words of one principal—in the most dynamic markets of the developing world, thereby not only opening markets to US products but also advancing broader foreign policy goals. George Stephanopoulos focused on media presentation and urged that the administration explain how these trade agreements would make a difference at home. Bentsen and Kantor immediately took up this challenge by citing evidence that trade generated jobs that paid above-average wages.

No principal directly attacked the proposed free trade accords, but thorny issues being raised in the public debate over trade policy found their way onto the table. Secretary Reich raised the issue of the distributional impact of trade on labor markets and added that pursuing a hemispherewide NAFTA could have some negative political implications. One deputy shot back: "Yes, there are implications for 1996—positive ones." Laura Tyson pressed for more attention to compensatory programs for those in adversely affected sectors. The principals also batted about the issues of labor and environmental standards.

Chief of Staff Leon Panetta, who listened silently during most of the meeting, summed it up succinctly: "We have no choice but to move forward on APEC and in Latin America. We are locked in." It was not a ringing endorsement, not a celebratory summation, simply a recognition of political reality. In effect, the principals could consider ancillary issues and attempt to give some direction to speechwriters, but their high-level debate over US trade policy came too late to be decisive. The course of events—in the bureaucracy under them, in negotiations with the Asians and Latin Americans—and the nearness of the summits simply swept them along. The principals were all too experienced in bureaucratic politics to attempt to throw themselves in front of fast-moving trains.

The president was similarly constrained in his choices. By the time he was presented with a decision memorandum on hemispheric free trade in mid-October, he was in the same box as the principals. Moreover, the memorandum (jointly drafted by staff from USTR, NEC, and NSC) noted that agencies were unanimous in recommending that the summit communiqués should advocate a hemispheric free trade area and should establish a work plan and mechanisms to accomplish it. It would be unusual for the president to reject an interagency consensus. The president read the memorandum aboard Air Force One while returning from a campaign swing and made final decisions in the presence of his national security adviser, Anthony Lake. It may well have been that, as the president told the press on the eve of the announcement of the summit, he had "long supported" expansion of free trade throughout the hemisphere, but the presummit decision-making process left him precious little leeway to change his mind.

Setting an End Date

As the summit approached, pressure increased—from the Latin Americans, the media, and US and Latin American business associations—for the trade initiative to contain specifics. The administration's long silence on trade had stirred up doubts about its commitment, so now it was being pressed to demonstrate its bona fides by agreeing to a detailed agenda, plan of action, and timetable for progress. Paradoxically, the collapse of efforts to gain fast-track renewal further upped the ante: as one administration official commented, the administration had to "show more leg" to compensate for congressional wariness. Some officials suggested that the summit itself could be used as a pressure tactic to prompt Capitol Hill to advance, that the summit should be understood not as the culmination of a process but as a springboard to action.

The APEC summit in Bogor added a dimension of "competitive liberalization."[27] APEC was much less advanced in its integration than the Western Hemisphere, so if APEC could agree on a scheme with some details for creating a free trade area—and the explicit end dates of 2010 for industrialized members and 2020 for developing country members endorsed at Bogor—the Western Hemisphere had to do at least as well to be credible. Earlier, the US embrace of APEC had removed many

27. C. Fred Bergsten, "Globalizing Free Trade," *Foreign Affairs* 75, no. 3 (May-June): 105-21.

objections in the trade community to regional integration as a concept, just as the November 1993 APEC summit in Seattle served as a precedent for a regional summit in the Western Hemisphere.

Within the administration, there were two arguments against an end date for the creation of a hemispheric free trade area. First, setting a date would frighten those in Congress and organized labor who opposed NAFTA expansion for precisely those reasons motivating those who favored a date—it would signal administration commitment and establish a marker that would drive future policy. Second, it was argued that a fixed date might undercut US bargaining leverage. As the date approached, the United States would be constrained from simply walking away from the table even if the Latin Americans were withholding important concessions. In mid-October, only the NSC voiced the opinion that US credibility on hemispheric free trade—and the success of the summit—hinged on fixing an end date, and the president accepted the majority view, eschewing a date certain. But the Latin Americans and the media increasingly focused on the issue of a date as indicative of the summit's seriousness of purpose. Fortuitously, passage of the 8 November mid-term elections altered the political calculation and allowed the president more leeway. The Uruguay Round legislation, decoupled from fast-track renewal, was finally passed in a special session of the Congress on 1 December 1994, thereby removing another obstacle to public discussion of hemispheric free trade. Only a few days before the journey to Miami, the president met in the Oval Office with Mack McLarty, Robert Rubin, Bowman Cutter, Samuel Berger, and the vice president's national security adviser, Leon Fuerth. By that time, all those present accepted that the summit's credibility required a date certain and the president concurred.[28]

Only a few days before going to Miami, the president approved the creation of a hemispheric free trade area and by a set date. Without the pressures of the summit, it is unlikely that his senior advisers would have recommended these options and certainly not unanimously. As they did up until the eleventh hour, other pressing global priorities and powerful domestic political considerations would most probably have overridden the president's free trade inclinations. Without the summit, regionwide free trade would probably have remained a vague aspiration, not a hemispheric consensus.

28. Interview with senior White House official present at the meeting, Washington, 3 May 1996.

5

Decision Making and Decentralized Functionalism

The world of today has moved away from big, centralized bureaucracies and top-down solutions—President Bill Clinton[1]

Because of the large number of issues that arise and the many agencies with equities at stake in them, US foreign policy usually is made by interagency committee. But in 1993-94 the Clinton White House had no formal, fixed structure for making decisions on Western Hemisphere affairs. Rather, structures were issue-specific, taking shape to handle problems as they arose. The North American Free Trade Agreement (NAFTA) was managed by the economic agencies, Haiti policy was made by National Security Council (NSC) principals and deputies and by a shifting series of smaller cabals, and most political issues were handled by mid-level officials at the State Department and White House. The State Department's assistant secretary for inter-American affairs chaired a broad interagency working group (IWG) on Latin America, but it met infrequently and was not convened when important issues arose. A State-chaired IWG on economic issues convened monthly, but it served only to exchange information, not to make decisions or even to recommend courses of action to more senior officials. There was no NSC subcommittee, no standing cabinet-level group, no Deputies Committee (DC) dedicated to hemispheric affairs. However, this very lack of focus and coordination had made it possible for a few individuals to circumvent bureaucratic proce-

1. Commencement address, Pennsylvania State University, University Park, Pennsylvania, 10 May 1996.

dures and gain presidential approval of the summit. Formalized rules probably would have blocked the end run that led to presidential approval of the summit.

Administration officials realized that a massive undertaking like the summit would require more formal interagency coordination. The State Department proposed that it coordinate preparation, but the White House decided that the summit was a presidential event and that it should maintain control through the NSC, National Economic Council (NEC), and other coordinating committees. At the suggestion of the State Department, a large summit IWG was established at the assistant secretary level, co-chaired by State and NSC. This IWG would make sure that appropriate agencies had a voice in policy preparation, but the IWG reported to the White House-chaired Deputies Committee.

There were good reasons for not giving State the lead. State's operational responsibilities typically leave it little time for longer-term policy initiatives, and many foreign service officers are more adept at process than policy.[2] State also has difficulty coordinating other agencies when functional issues—trade, finance, environment, and narcotics—are at stake; the specialized agencies house more expertise and control most budgets and programs. Conversely, other agencies recognize the White House's jurisdiction over presidential events.

The Deputies Committee

Deputy National Security Adviser Samuel Berger convened the first DC on the summit on 7 February 1994 to discuss summit themes. Deputies present included Leon Fuerth (Office of the Vice President), Bowman Cutter (NEC), Joan Spero (State), Lawrence Summers (Treasury), Charlene Barshefsky (USTR), Carol Lancaster (USAID), and Frank Wisner (Defense). Commerce, US Mission to the United Nations, the Environmental Protection Agency (EPA), Joint Chiefs of Staff (JCS), and NSC were also represented. The ornate Cordell Hull room in the Old Executive Office Building was packed with deputies and their aides. Never before during the Clinton administration had such a collection of senior officials and their immediate subordinates met to consider the breadth of hemispheric affairs. The Presidential Decision Directive (PDD) on hemispheric affairs, which set the framework for administration policy and would be signed by the president, was drafted at middle and working levels with senior-level clearances obtained by NSC staff by telephone. Not once had the principals or deputies met to consider the PDD. The PDD was not sufficiently important or controversial, or perhaps it was a case of the

---

2. Leslie Gelb, "Why Not the State Department," *Washington Quarterly* (Autumn 1980). Gelb wrote this piece shortly after retiring from State.

urgent driving out the important. But on 7 February 1994 the prospects of a presidential event immediately attracted senior-level participation.

This first DC meeting considered the broad themes of the summit. As was standard operating procedure for a DC meeting, the NSC staff circulated a background paper. The paper was prepared with input from the summit IWG, which began work in early January. The deputies generally agreed that the summit should approve a declaration of principles and an associated work plan focused on a few major issues. The summit should seek to strengthen democratic government and expand free trade. There was some concern that treating social policy as a main agenda item could be inflammatory in Latin America, so the social issues were placed under a broader economic umbrella that would include trade and investment.[3] The simple symmetry of two themes—one political, one economic—was also attractive. The DC tasked the summit IWG to consider further actions and to develop a plan for consultations with the other countries participating in the summit.

The DC would remain the ultimate interagency authority on summit policy.[4] The venue was moved to the Situation Room in the West Wing of the White House to limit attendance and facilitate discussion and decision making. The "Sit Room" table accommodates twelve officials, and another dozen or so aides can sit in the outer circle of chairs against the wall. This tight architecture made it easier for Berger and Cutter to justify saying "no" to the many bureaucrats seeking entrance to the White House's inner chamber. Often the most important decision, which would predictably determine a meeting's outcomes, was made before the meeting—NSC-NEC selection of who would attend. A core group of agencies was routinely invited: State, Treasury, US Trade Representative (USTR), Office of the Vice President, NSC, and NEC. Other agencies were included depending on the topics at hand.

At the initial meetings of the committee, the national security agencies were invited, including the Department of Defense (DOD), JCS, and Central Intelligence Agency (CIA). But traditional security issues, especially military issues, were not prominent on the summit agenda. Political, economic, and social issues had largely replaced traditional security issues on the US hemispheric agenda; implicitly, the United States had redefined hemispheric security as democratic stability, economic progress, and social integration.[5] Nor were CIA threat assessments relevant to summit

3. This concern regarding the social agenda proved unfounded because the Latin Americans would insist that poverty be a key agenda item.

4. As the summit approached and the trade issue took center stage, the DC gradually evolved from an NSC-chaired committee to a joint NSC-NEC committee, co-chaired by Samuel Berger and Bowman Cutter.

5. To be sure, during 1993-94, aside from NAFTA, Haiti policy, which presented a unique mixture of traditional and new security issues, was by far the most salient issue in the Western Hemisphere for senior policymakers.

preparation. As time went on, the seats formerly allocated to the defense and intelligence chiefs were occupied by representatives from such agencies as Commerce, EPA, and the agency most directly focused on the new security issues of international crime, the Department of Justice.

That foreign policy is economic policy is not a new finding.[6] In preparing an important foreign policy initiative such as the Summit of the Americas, the greater novelty was involving many agencies whose primary jurisdiction is domestic. Agencies such as Interior, EPA, Transportation, Education, Labor, and Justice have developed international sections with interests in Latin America and the Caribbean. In general terms, these agencies view international diplomacy as a means to agreements where international collective action is necessary for the successful pursuit of their functions, or as territory where they can reproduce themselves through technical assistance to counterpart agencies abroad.

Policy Formulation and Coordination

In making foreign policy, the DC generally initiates and coordinates policies across agencies, sets priorities, and, when an issue is sufficiently important or controversial, molds options for decisions by cabinet officials and the president. In the case of the Summit of the Americas, the committee depended on working groups to suggest policies and agenda initiatives outside the committee's trade expertise. The deputies would meet approximately seven times before the United States would circulate its first draft agenda to the hemisphere in mid-August 1994, and while these meetings served to educate the deputies, they were not frequent enough to allow the deputies command of the process. Generally chaired by an assistant secretary and dominated by powerful lead agencies or strong individuals, the working groups became the main locus of power for the design of US proposals for the summit's substantive agenda. The deputies reacted to proposals passed up to it by the lower rungs of the decision-making ladder. It was a classic case of bottom-up policymaking.

Although not presuming to originate policy, the deputies might have attempted to set priorities. However, the DC had difficulty containing the size of the agenda, as pressures from the many bureaucracies, the activist nongovernmental sector, and other governments overwhelmed efforts to keep the agenda tight.[7] Deputies repeatedly directed the subordi-

6. For an early treatment of this theme, see Richard N. Cooper, "Trade Policy is Foreign Policy," *Foreign Policy* 9 (Winter), 1972-73, 18-36.

7. Agenda crowding can sometimes be avoided when an assertive actor in a lead agency imposes order on the proliferation of ideas, as Under Secretary of State Robert Zoellick reportedly did for the US-Japan Structural Impediments Initiative (SII) talks. Michael Armacost, *Friends or Rivals* (New York: Columbia University Press, 1996), 50-51.

nate structure to reduce the number of proposed initiatives, even as they mostly left the choices to the agency-dominated working groups. In one deputies meeting in July, State's Summit Coordinating Office (an executive secretariat that coordinated and collated paper flow) presented an unwieldy chart with 30-odd proposed initiatives. The overwhelmed deputies directed the three main working groups to lay aside bureaucratic agendas, trim their wish lists, and focus on making the summit event a success.

The deputies also coordinated policy. For example, agencies should be aware of how impending actions by other parts of the bureaucracy might affect their interests so they can register their concerns. The Defense Department wanted the summit to bless a meeting of ministers of defense—no such meeting had ever been held before in the Western Hemisphere. The State Department was leery of an initiative that they saw as potentially tilting the still delicate civilian-military balance in Latin America back toward the armed forces. State reported that a number of Latin governments opposed the initiative for the same reason and that it was generating broad suspicions about US intentions and a possible hidden agenda for the summit. The deputies resolved the dispute by persuading DOD to remove the proposal from the summit agenda in return for agreement that it would be addressed after the summit. Seven months after Miami, Defense hosted the first-ever hemispheric conference of ministers of defense in Williamsburg, Virginia.

In the role of policy coordination, the deputies were a court of last resort to which an agency could appeal a decision of the working groups. The chair, as honest broker, could assure a form of due process, correcting possible imbalances in the competition of ideas that occurred at lower bureaucratic levels.[8] For example, USAID, overpowered in the Treasury-dominated economics working group, sometimes successfully appealed to the deputies. USAID sought and won greater emphasis on issues of poverty and equity. In response to appeals by representatives from the White House counternarcotics office (ONDCP) and the Department of Justice, the deputies also may have placed more emphasis on counternarcotics than did the democracy working group.

Because most deputies are noncareer political appointees, they are interested in blending policy and political concerns. When meeting in the Situation Room in the basement of the West Wing, they were conscious of the proximity of the Oval Office. In preparing the summit's trade initiative, they were acutely aware of the president's political interests, as well as the congressional agenda.[9]

---

8. For a discussion of the "honest broker" and "due process" roles in White House decision making, see Roger B. Porter, *Presidential Decision Making: The Economic Policy Board* (New York: Cambridge University Press, 1980), 25-29.

9. The deputies did not, however, handle the sensitive Cuba issue, of great concern to the Cuban-American community in Miami. Instead, decisions on how to address Cuba policy

Sustained senior-level attention to an issue sometimes leads to more money, but the DC did not garner additional financial resources for summit initiatives. "Trade not aid" was a slogan appropriate for the times, and Treasury noted that the Inter-American Development Bank (IDB) had recently received a major injection of new capital, some of which could be aimed at summit objectives. Nevertheless, the working groups believed that a modest amount of fresh, targeted resources would facilitate implementation of many summit action items. Therefore, they drew up a modest budget of under $100 million to support select initiatives; however, the deputies were not willing to go to battle with the Office of Management and Budget (OMB) and Congress to support it.

These DC meetings also helped to inform the deputies themselves about hemispheric affairs. None were specialists in Latin America, and some had come to the table with almost no knowledge of the region. Even USTR Deputy Barshefsky, whose portfolio included the region, had been much more deeply involved in negotiations with China and Japan than with Latin America. Muted and on the back benches, aides specializing in Latin America were appalled at the superficialities and misconceptions voiced at the initial deputies meetings. But the ongoing DC process gradually educated the deputies. The deputies also benefited from summit-related travels in the region and from conversations with the stream of dignitaries who journeyed to Washington in the months before Miami.

In sum, the deputies pressed the working groups to narrow their agendas, sorted out some interagency disputes, handled the politically sensitive trade issue, and were educated in the process. They were the final, authoritative rung on a ladder of bottom-up policy process. At the same time, they lacked the expertise and intensity to fulfill the strategic planning role. After some posturing and declarative statements, the deputies rubber-stamped most of what the working groups presented.[10] They judged that creating a free trade area was sufficient to make the summit a success and therefore were not compelled to seek additional financial resources to support other initiatives.

Working Groups and the New Agenda

The impulse behind creating and expanding the NSC system had been the growth of the military and intelligence services during World War II and the ensuing Cold War.[11] For four decades, the central tasks of US

in the summit context were made altogether outside deputy and IWG channels, by a rump assembly of State, NSC, and other White House officials.

10. Interviews with present and former administration officials, Washington, April-May 1996.

11. Karl F. Inderfurth and Loch K. Johnson, eds., *Decisions of the Highest Order: Perspectives on the National Security Council* (Pacific Grove, CA: Brookings-Cole Publishing, 1988). See

foreign policy were deterring the military power of the Soviet Union and containing communism. Responsibility rested primarily with State, Defense, and the intelligence agencies, and it seemed feasible for a few senior officials in these agencies to dominate these narrowly bounded issues, to discuss them intelligently, and to decide them, if necessary, with the president.[12] Cold War security policy, therefore, lent itself to centralized policymaking.

By 1994, the Soviet Union and the communist threat no longer existed. The agenda facing the hemispheric summit was different and much broader and broached a range of issues under the jurisdiction of over a dozen agencies—trade, investment, capital markets, external debt, energy, biodiversity, pollution, education, health, labor absorption, women's rights, indigenous peoples, modernization of the state, democratic reform, and many other topics of interest to developing countries. No matter how well educated, no matter now quick a study, no presidential adviser or cabinet official could possibly have sufficient understanding of this vast array of issues to formulate an informed opinion. In the post-Cold War world, this gap between responsibility and knowledge is one of the great dilemmas and challenges to policymaking today.[13]

The summit preparatory process found a solution to the authority-expertise gap in what might be termed decentralized functionalism. The deputies created three broad IWGs to design the US summit agenda: democracy and effective government, economics, and sustainable development (later broken into separate working groups for social and environmental issues; figure 5.1). These in turn created at least ten subgroups. These IWGs were composed of representatives from agencies with relevant functional responsibilities and expertise. Hence, the political working group included NSC, State, Treasury, DOD, Commerce, JCS, USTR, USAID, Justice, Labor, ONDCP, and CIA. (Within State, Bureau of Economic and Business Affairs [EB], Nicaraguan Institute for Women [INM], US office of the Organization of American States [USOAS], Policy Planning, and the Inter-American Affairs Bureau [ARA] and its Summit Coordinating Office were also represented). Economic initiatives were

---

also Christopher C. Shoemaker, *The NSC Staff: Counseling the Council* (Boulder, CO: Westview Press, 1991), and Amy Zegart, *In Whose Interest?: The Making of American National Security Agencies*, Ph.D. dissertation, forthcoming, Stanford University.

12. Even so, decisions about developing areas were often made with inadequate knowledge and understanding. See Richard E. Feinberg, *The Intemperate Zone: The Third World Challenge to US Foreign Policy* (New York: W. W. Norton, 1983). For a relevant case study, see Robert S. McNamara with Brian VanDeMark, *In Retrospect: The Tragedy and Lessons of Vietnam*, 1st ed. (New York: Times Books, 1995).

13. For a discussion of "asymmetric information," in which the agents in an organization know more about the business at hand than the principals, see John J. Dilute Jr., Gerald Garvey, and Donald F. Kettl, *Improving Government Performance: An Owner's Manual* (Washington: Brookings Institution, 1993), 24-28.

Figure 5.1 US government policy planning

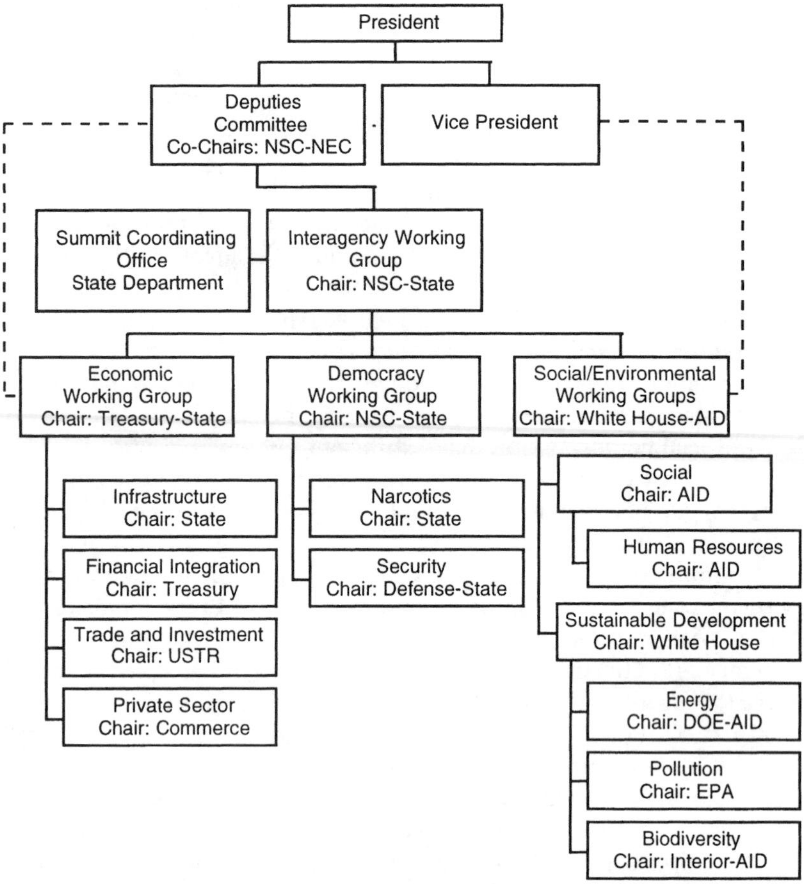

- President
  - Deputies Committee — Co-Chairs: NSC-NEC
  - Vice President
    - Summit Coordinating Office — State Department
    - Interagency Working Group — Chair: NSC-State
      - Economic Working Group — Chair: Treasury-State
        - Infrastructure — Chair: State
        - Financial Integration — Chair: Treasury
        - Trade and Investment — Chair: USTR
        - Private Sector — Chair: Commerce
      - Democracy Working Group — Chair: NSC-State
        - Narcotics — Chair: State
        - Security — Chair: Defense-State
      - Social/Environmental Working Groups — Chair: White House-AID
        - Social — Chair: AID
          - Human Resources — Chair: AID
        - Sustainable Development — Chair: White House
          - Energy — Chair: DOE-AID
          - Pollution — Chair: EPA
          - Biodiversity — Chair: Interior-AID

Source: Summit of the Americas News, August 1994, 6, and personal interviews.

designed in working groups chaired by Treasury and State's economic bureau and included representatives from Commerce, USTR, USAID, Labor, Education, and Health and Human Services (HHS). Environmental initiatives were produced by the White Houses's Office of Environmental Policy, NSC, State, Treasury, USAID, EPA, Interior, Energy, and OMB.

Decentralized functionalism located authority closer to expertise. It also facilitated access to nongovernmental expertise and provided mechanisms for negotiating with other countries. And it gave birth to potentially powerful mechanisms for carrying out the Miami accords.

Many middle-level officials at the various functional agencies enjoyed regular contact with nongovernmental actors, or NGAs (the private sector, nongovernmental organizations, think tanks and academics, and professional associations). As representatives of constituencies and often fountains of expertise and innovative ideas, NGAs can be useful components of the policy process for many functional issues. The structure of decentralized functionalism provided open channels of communication that enabled the nongovernmental sector to play important roles in forging the summit agenda.[14]

Decentralized functionalism readily produced the instructions, monitoring, and personnel for the US teams that negotiated most of the summit agenda. Working group chairs or their immediate subordinates had the expertise as well as the time to attend the many meetings in Washington and throughout Latin America and the Caribbean that were required to build support for and negotiate the summit proposals. International discussions at this expert level are often more fluid and flexible than when issues are elevated to more senior levels, where the stakes seem to increase and talks occur under the scrutiny of the media and the political opposition.

After Miami, as the bureaucracy turned its attention to carrying out summit agreements, decentralized functionalism would transform itself into cabinet diplomacy. Agencies heavily involved in designing and negotiating summit initiatives would become committed to seeing them put in place. As soon as the president departed Miami, the crisis-driven DC moved on to other problems, and it fell largely to the individual agencies to seek to transform the summit texts into realities. The structure created to organize the summit was well suited to building the engagement and sense of ownership that would translate into postsummit action, agency by agency.

In retrospect, a core IWG of the assistant secretaries of the crucial agencies would have been a more efficient locus for formal decision making than the DC on most substantive matters. The summit IWG served for information sharing and gave all the agencies and working-level personnel the sense of participation and inclusion, but the more than 50 people in attendance were far too many to permit frank discussion and effective decision making. A core group of 5 to 10 key individuals met

---

14. For a collection of proposals from outside governments, see Robin Rosenberg and Stephen Stein, eds., *Advancing the Miami Process: Civil Society and the Summit of the Americas* (Miami: North-South Center Press, 1995). In contrast, in preparing for the 1967 summits, the United States had largely circumscribed consultations outside official circles to meetings with a narrow spectrum of senior leaders such as David Rockefeller, the leadership of the AFL-CIO, and a few academics. Assistant Secretary for Inter-American Affairs Lincoln Gordon convened a half-day consultation with a half dozen academics, including Alfred Hirschman, Joseph Grunwald, Theodore Schultz, and Raymond Vernon. Secretary of State Dean Rusk met with a small group of private citizens, including (in addition to David Rockefeller) Douglas Dillon, Theodore Hesburgh, Adolf Berle, Robert Nathan, and George Harrar (president of the Rockefeller Foundation). Rusk also met with Andrew McClellan and Ernest Lee of the AFL-CIO. See NSF, NSC History, OAS Summit Meeting, Box 12, memoranda of 21 May 1966 and 6 February 1967, Lyndon Baines Johnson Library.

from time to time but did not have formal decision-making authority. A more formal core working group at the assistant secretary level would have gathered sufficient expertise and representation to make most important decisions legitimately and intelligently. Most summit-related policy issues were resolvable in the working groups, and the DC could have been reserved for any remaining arguments.

Because only senior officials can make decisions on resources and gain access to the president (although in this case the deputies provided little of each) some engagement of the deputies and agency heads will always be desirable when planning hemispheric summits. Occasional public statements by senior officials, and the president, are also important to give the public and other countries the clear sense of policy direction and coherence. Senior officials can also review other policy initiatives affecting hemispheric relations, possibly impinging on the summit process, even when these matters are not strictly on the summit agenda.

In sum, if security issues were predominant during the Cold War, traditional security threats (encroachment by external powers, civil wars, or territorial conflicts) have diminished sharply and were virtually absent at the Summit of the Americas. Political, economic, and social issues are now paramount. Hence, decentralized functionalism is the appropriate bureaucratic approach for the United States to take toward hemispheric affairs.[15]

Working Groups: A Closer Look

The working groups combined political appointees and career civil servants, many of whom had considerable expertise. State Department representatives and some of the functionalists were familiar with hemispheric diplomacy. Many in the group had participated in the long-gestating Presidential Review Directive (PRD) reassessment of hemispheric policy, which had helped build an interagency consensus on many of the major issues. Here was an opportunity to gain greater visibility for those policies and, most important, to transform an intragovernmental consensus into a ratified inter-American plan of action.

Many participants were content to table proposals already included in the PRD or otherwise approved. Veterans of bureaucratic battles knew that efforts to go beyond boilerplate would encounter resistance and that, with so many players at the table, it would be difficult to advance fresh ideas. Nevertheless, in each working group one or more energetic individuals seized the opportunity to push the envelope. As one ambitious par-

---

15. More generally, I. M. Destler similarly concluded that we should accept the inevitability of decentralized foreign economic policymaking in *Making Foreign Economic Policy* (Washington: Brookings Institution, 1980), 227.

ticipant said, "we did not want to lose this once-in-a-generation opportunity. We purposefully decided to take risks, to advance ideas which were new to the bureaucracy, and would invite debate in Latin America." Leading voices in the democracy working group advanced innovative anticorruption initiatives, the economics working group designed new approaches to foster direct investment, and the sustainable development working group crafted three new partnerships for environmental protection.[16]

Another important inspiration and source of new ideas was the nongovernmental sector. The democracy and environmental working groups met repeatedly with people and organizations outside the government and digested their publications. For example, the Inter-American Dialogue provided valuable input on ways to strengthen the prodemocracy programs of the Organization of American States (OAS).[17] Transparency International brought anticorruption expertise. A broad coalition of environmental groups was instrumental in designing the three sustainable development partnerships.[18] NGAs were included in some working group meetings and participated in certain official US delegations to consult with other hemispheric governments on summit initiatives.[19]

Throughout the spring and into early summer, the working groups vetted initiatives proposed by various agencies, solicited input from NGAs, sounded out other countries (as described in chapter 6), and received feedback from the deputies and the vice president. The summit IWG pushed the agencies to prepare concrete, realistic, and presidential initiatives to delineate mechanisms and institutions responsible for implementation, and to provide a negotiating strategy to build sufficient support within a cluster of potentially interested countries. By August, the United States was prepared to circulate to the other governments in the hemisphere 14 initiatives (appendix C).[20] What follows is an overview of

---

16. Even if other countries rejected an innovative US initiative, some US policymakers felt all would not be lost: the Latin American sense of participation in the process would be enhanced. I am indebted to Alexander Watson for this point.

17. Inter-American Dialogue, *Advancing Democracy and Human Rights in the Americas: What Role for the OAS?* (Washington, May 1994).

18. After the summit, the environmental nongovernmental organizations (NGOs) wrote a letter to Vice President Gore expressing appreciation for the access they had enjoyed, noting that "the role played by NGOs in the preparations for the summit was unprecedented for this type of presidential-level meeting. . . ." Rosenberg and Stein, *Advancing the Miami Process,* 413-14.

19. For an excellent account of how the US government worked with NGAs and encouraged other governments to do so as well, see Cathryn Thorup, "Building Community Through Participation: The Role of Non-Governmental Actors in the Summit of the Americas," in Rosenberg and Stein, *Advancing the Miami Process,* xiii-xxvi.

20. The initiatives are reproduced in "Fourteen Summit Agenda Initiatives Presented by the United States to Governments of the Hemisphere," in Rosenberg and Stein, *Advancing the Miami Process,* 3-7.

how the three working groups, as an exercise in decentralized functionalism, formulated this menu of ideas.

Democracy

Of all the summit issues, democracy was probably the least determined by bureaucratic interests and most driven by individual initiative. There is no agency in the US government whose primary function is to promote democracy abroad. There is no Department for Democracy Promotion, not even a deputy for democracy. The democracy offices at the NSC and State were not heavily involved in summit preparation. Rather, individuals at the NSC, State, and DOD with personal interests in democracy saw the summit as a splendid opportunity to promote the consolidation of democracy and to promote trust in public institutions by making democratic governments more effective and responsive.[21]

During 1993, the NSC staff and the Inter-American Affairs Bureau of the State Department had been developing an anticorruption initiative out of concern that authoritarians in Latin America might seize the populist anticorruption banner. To preempt this danger, it was critical to identify democracy with anticorruption. The summit provided the perfect multilateral launching pad for an initiative that would associate the assembled democracies with good governance. The Clinton administration could legitimately promote good governance, not as a paternalistic US criticism of Latin America but as a problem common to the entire hemisphere since its own reinventing government initiative was a self-critique of American democracy. Moreover, corruption had become a cause célèbre in several Latin countries, and a number of presidents were seeking to carry out anticorruption pledges made during their campaigns. For the United States, the summit was also an opportunity to gain hemispheric support for the Foreign Corrupt Practices Act (which makes it illegal for US businesses to bribe foreign officials) and to level the playing field by calling for other governments (read the Europeans and Japanese) to require equally honorable behavior of their private sectors.

Some leaders in the democracy working group were also concerned with the wide gap in many Latin American nations between the state and the individual, a theme many working group members had grappled with in developing the administration's policy for the region. The democracy working group decided that the summit offered a chance to strengthen civil society. In the 1980s in many Latin American countries grassroots community organizations had mushroomed, and the summit

21. Notably, Assistant Secretary of State Alexander Watson, Deputy Assistant Secretary of State Michael Skol, Legal Adviser Fay Armstrong, and US Ambassador to the OAS Harriet Babbitt.

could identify measures to create a more favorable climate for their development. One such measure was a planned USAID project to help NGOs build networks among themselves. The Commerce Department promoted its partnerships between the public sector and business under the civil society aegis.

The Reagan-Bush years had seen the growth of a large counternarcotics complex throughout the executive branch. Members of the complex seized on the summit as an avenue to regain some of the influence they felt they had lost under the Clinton administration. Some of the counternarcotics officials wanted their issue to be a stand-alone item, equal to democracy and sustainable development, but the IWG filed counternarcotics under the democracy umbrella, where drugs were but one of several threats to democratic stability. The counternarcotics offices sought to fashion an initiative that would reiterate a hemispheric commitment to combat drugs and do battle against the cartels, including an endorsement of the administration's kingpin strategy aimed at cartel leaders and the slogan "nowhere to hide"—a pledge to prosecute people accused of serious crimes, including narcotics trafficking, either through extradition or domestic justice. In addition, they sought a commitment by governments to establish goals for a significant reduction of illicit coca cultivation by the year 2000.

The summit was a perfect venue to reaffirm and strengthen the OAS's capacity to defend democracy. The democracy working group proposed creating an OAS mediation and reconciliation service and an operations center for crisis management. The service would consist of a small professional staff tied into a wider network of experts around the hemisphere to foster constitutional outcomes to brewing crises. The operations center would enhance the OAS's administrative capacity to cope with political crises in member countries.

Not all of these initiatives prospered. Some were deemed worthwhile but not sufficiently presidential, and some were postponed because the timing was not yet right. Some proposals would make it into the 14 initiatives that the United States circulated throughout the hemisphere in August but would be diluted or even eliminated on the way to Miami (for example, measures to enhance the OAS's capacity to defend democracy). But an impressive number of these proposals would survive.

Economics

The Treasury Department dominated the economics working group. Traditionally, the Treasury sought to maintain control over international economic policy and looked with suspicion on White House coordinating bodies such as the National Economic Council that threatened its relative autonomy.[22] As an interagency process, summit preparations might also impinge on Treasury's turf. Treasury successfully struggled to circumvent the IWG, co-chaired by the NSC and State, by having the economics working group report directly to the deputies, where Treasury representatives, with their close allies in the economic cone of the State Department, could seek to control the discussion.

Initially, Treasury wanted the summit to reiterate the fundamentals of macroeconomic and structural reform, but the Latin foreign ministries indicated in early consultations that they considered such language both self-evident and preachy, so Treasury settled for a phrase in the summit declaration of principles. Treasury also sought to advance another long-standing institutional interest: liberalization of capital markets. Modeled on the Organization for Economic Cooperation and Development (OECD) capital movements code, the Treasury proposed a hemispheric code that would commit countries to facilitating freer capital flows, bolstering transparency, and adopting comparable financial standards. A committee on hemispheric capital markets, modeled after the OECD capital markets committee, would promote the code and examine other issues related to cross-border capital flows. This new committee would comprise senior financial officials (since the United States is the dominant hemispheric actor in international capital markets, the Treasury safely assumed it would lead). To further promote regulatory reform of financial markets, Treasury offered technical assistance through the Council of Security Regulators of the Americas (COSRA) and the Internal Revenue Service and Customs.

The economics working group also promoted private-sector financing of infrastructure. Rita Rodriguez, a director of the Export-Import Bank, proposed a hemispheric infrastructure protocol that would provide political risk coverage to private investors. The protocol would standardize treatment of private investors in such infrastructure as telecommunications, transportation, and energy. The fourteen initiatives circulated by the United States sought to promote both capital market liberalization and private investment infrastructure, and both initiatives would find a place in the summit communiqués.

Treasury also sought to further its standing objective of having all countries sign bilateral investment treaties, which provide protection against expropriation, by asking all current signatories to make their commitments multilateral and invite others to join or simply to sign a single hemispheric investment protocol. This gambit failed for lack of interest in Latin America.

22. I. M. Destler, *The National Economic Council: A Work in Progress* (Washington: Institute for International Economics, 1996). Also see his *Making Foreign Economic Policy*.

Environmental and Social Issues

The PDD on Latin American policy had contained only a brief section on environment, so the sustainable development working group did not begin with an interagency consensus on what mattered most for the United States. Existing international conventions, including the Climate Change and Biodiversity Conventions and Agenda 21 from the 1992 Rio Earth Summit, provided some guidelines. Coordinated by the White House's Office of Environmental Policy, the working group relied on the expertise of EPA, the Department of Energy (DOE), the Department of the Interior, USAID, and staff from the Treasury Department's international affairs office. Eventually, three initiatives emerged: energy conservation, natural resource management, and environmental protection.

DOE and USAID crafted an energy initiative emphasizing renewable energy and energy efficiency. Summit leaders would agree to begin carrying out programs to promote sustainable energy use based on integrated resource planning by 1998. Interior took the lead in developing the conservation initiative, which would focus on enhancing scientific and management capacity in forests, coral reefs, and reserves. EPA drafted an environmental protection initiative that would strengthen environmental standards, beginning with sectors critically important to human health, including lead and pesticides. The working group proposed that funding for the three environmental initiatives come from the multilateral development banks and that public-private sector partnerships involving business and NGOs would promote their implementation.

Within the working group, USAID had responsibility for social issues and fought hard for its policies on investing in people, defined primarily in terms of education and health. The agency sought a summit endorsement of its planned project, Partnership in Educational Reform in the Americas, aimed at improving the quality of education. In addition, countries would commit to the goals of 100 percent primary school completion rates and 75 percent secondary school enrollment by the year 2000. The health initiative would also set targets: countries would pledge to reduce child mortality rates by one-third and maternal mortality rates by one-half by the same deadline. These quantitative targets would make it into the final summit texts. USAID also sought to advance an initiative to make gender equality a policy objective in development, but some US officials did not want to begin to include initiatives targeted at special groups. Instead, the interagency process accepted a microenterprise initiative whose primary beneficiary would be poor women.

Policy

Under pressure from the deputies and the IWG, the subgroups shaved and reformatted their proposals until the number of initiatives stood at 14. In reality, many of the 14 were composites, blended to fit under the ceilings imposed by higher authorities, so that the number of actionable items far exceeded 14. The working groups did some heroic pruning but at times found it easier and less conflictive to sum together rather than weed out, reflecting the same tendencies of bureaucratic decision making that would reappear in intergovernmental diplomacy. The deputies generally accepted the final recommendations of the working groups. The IWG was not empowered to overrule agencies and hence could make cuts only if its arguments persuaded those with bureaucratic interests at risk. Within the working groups, each agency naturally pushed its own agenda and programs: Treasury protected its capital market liberalization initiative, USAID guarded its core interests in basic poverty alleviation programs in health and education, and DOE promoted energy conservation. Meanwhile, the decentralized, accessible policy process offered committed officials and outside experts room to inject their proposals.

Over the next three months, the 14-initiative draft would be altered and further expanded by successive rounds of intergovernmental discussions, but many of the core ideas would survive. The working groups would provide the teams of expert negotiators that would transverse the hemisphere to build support for their proposals.

Operations, Logistics, Media

As host to the summit, the United States not only had the lead in preparing the agenda but also had to organize the three-day meeting in Miami. The State Department's Bureau of Administration managed everything from the selection of summit sites to the care and feeding of the media to the schedule of the leaders' limousines. It worked closely with the Miami Host Committee, a 100-plus member group of influential locals, whose tasks included fundraising for the event. The administrative office reached a maximum of 47 personnel at the summit and was assisted by nearly 500 local volunteers. Within the State Department's Bureau for Inter-American Affairs, the Summit Coordinating Office under Tony Gillespie housed about 30 people by the time of the summit.[23] The main function of this office was to manage paper flow: to collate the proposals emerging from the working groups, to communicate by cable and fax with other countries, and to assist in negotiating the summit texts.

In late summer, the president asked his former chief of staff, Mack McLarty, and former deputy secretary of the Treasury, Roger Altman, to oversee summit preparation, including logistics, public affairs, and the Miami budget. They established an Operations Committee that included

23. Bureau of Inter-American Affairs, Department of State, Summit Coordinating Office, photocopy, "After Action Report on the Summit of the Americas," 1995.

the various branches of the White House and State Department concerned with Miami meeting logistics. McLarty and Altman worked closely with the leadership of the Miami Host Committee and succeeded in making their budget more realistic. The Operations Committee also coordinated the activities of the cabinet officials who would be giving speeches before and during Miami, as well as hosting official events at the summit. The committee provided them with a briefing book, prepared by the NSC staff and summarized on a 3½ × 7-inch note card (appendix F: Summit of the Americas note card). The committee shared with the DC oversight for public affairs planning, occasionally including senior White House and State Department officials such as George Stephanopoulos, David Gergen, and Tom Donilon. As early as 10 August a senior-level meeting in the Situation Room that combined communicators and policy officials considered US objectives for the summit and how they could best be presented to the media. An interagency Summit of the Americas Communications Group coordinated public affairs at the working level. In the final days of summit preparation, a senior-level steering committee was established, including McLarty, Altman, and the co-chairs of the DC, Berger and Cutter. It resolved some last-minute problems, particularly cabinet officials scheduling and public affairs. Notwithstanding this proliferation of committees, the DC remained in charge of substantive summit preparation, including negotiations on summit texts and planning for the leaders' private discussions.[24]

The Vice President

The formal DC-led bureaucratic structure omitted an individual who could exert decisive influence whenever he felt so inclined. Having announced the summit, Vice President Gore felt a certain ownership and asserted that the president had asked him to act on his behalf to assure that the summit was a success. From time to time the vice president convened deputy-level meetings to be briefed on summit preparations and to make known his views on issues of special interest to him. Two issues that he cared passionately about were reinventing government and protecting the environment.[25] At one DC meeting, an official reported that

---

24. In her description of the summit preparatory process, Margaret Daly Hays overstates the policy role of the steering committee. Margaret Daly Hays, "Building the Hemisphere Community: Lessons from the Summit of the Americas Process, No. 3," (*Occasional Papers in Western Hemisphere Governance*, Washington: Inter-American Dialogue, July 1996), 5.

25. For example, see Report of the National Performance Review, *Red Tape to Results: Creating a Government that Works Better and Costs Less* (Washington: Government Printing Office, 1993) led by Vice President Al Gore; and Al Gore, *Earth in the Balance: Ecology and the Human Spirit* (Boston: Houghton Mifflin Co., 1992).

some Latin Americans were uncomfortable with the good governance theme. Gore closed the issue by underscoring that corruption was perhaps the greatest threat to democracy in the hemisphere and that the summit should not back off from it.

Gore understood how to use public addresses to set international agendas. For example, as the hemisphere was reviewing the US-circulated 14 points, the vice president projected his reinventing government campaign into the hemispheric arena in a speech delivered at the Inter-American Development Bank:

> For much of the hemisphere, the challenge of the '70s was the protection of basic human rights. The triumph of the '80s was the rejection of authoritarian regimes and the transition to free elections. To redeem the promise of self-government and to ensure the progress of democracy in the hemisphere, the challenge of the 1990s is the creation of an effective, efficient, and transparent state.[26]

By late May, the vice president felt the deputies were paying insufficient attention to sustainable development. He sharply criticized the NSC staff for clearing remarks he was to make to an assembly of hemispheric ambassadors that in his view gave insufficient attention to sustainable development. Immediately afterwards, his assistant for National Security Affairs, Leon Fuerth, convened a meeting with key officials to register his boss's anger. The vice president asked the Deputies Committee to give sustainable development more attention, and as a result the United States pressed to make sustainable development a major summit theme. The vice president personally selected the summit logo—a green hemisphere against a blue background. Gore also championed the telecommunications initiative.[27]

At the initiative of the US Information Agency (USIA), Gore hosted some 30 hemispheric cultural leaders of diverse political backgrounds at his Washington residence on 11 November to begin a weekend conference on "A New Moment in the Americas?"[28] The cultural leaders did not debate the summit's plan of action; instead, the meeting offered the "consultation" of nongovernmental leaders and gave an intellectual dimension to the Miami process. After cocktails, the vice president organized the group in tight circles in the living room. The guests were asked to introduce themselves and to answer whether it was, indeed, a new moment in the Americas. Amidst a flood of prohemispheric sentiments, participants

---

26. Al Gore, remarks to the Inter-American Development Bank, 16 September 1994.

27. Gore was less firm on hemispheric free trade: while a supporter in principle, he reflected the conflicts in the Democratic Party and advocated caution on its political timing.

28. Robert S. Leiken, ed., *A New Moment in the Americas* (Miami: North-South Center Press, 1994). This volume contains a discussion of the meeting with the vice president, the conference papers, and a foreword by the vice president.

generally agreed there was a convergence of values around democracy and a new trust and openness in the Americas. The fluidity of the exchange, the optimistic tone of most participants, and the general atmosphere of good will was a positive omen for the upcoming Miami event.

The President

No discussion of presidential summit decision making would be complete without analyzing the role of the chief executive. The president delegated preparations for the summit to subordinates—the vice president, the NSC-NEC, McLarty, and Altman. However, he personally made the key decisions in consultations with his senior advisers. It was the president who had decided to convene the summit. He participated actively in selecting Miami as the site. He approved the US initiative to seek a free trade area in the Americas, a formal decision preceded by many public statements in favor of expanding free trade in the hemisphere. He wrote other hemispheric leaders at important junctures. President Clinton was the central figure at the summit itself, delivering a speech that defined the summit themes, chairing the leaders' meetings, orchestrating the final plenary, and addressing the media. In Miami, Clinton eschewed bilaterals, using the social occasion to build personal relations with his hemispheric counterparts.

At the same time, the president had not sweated the details or wrestled with questions of tactics and strategy as the agenda evolved and summit texts were negotiated. Unlike prolonged crises such as Haiti, Bosnia, and the Middle East, where President Clinton developed in-depth knowledge and personal commitments, the Summit of the Americas did not so profoundly engage him. This would create problems during implementation in the second half of his first term because other issues would divert his attention from the hemisphere, and political trade-offs would slow progress on achieving the summit's central agreement on free trade.

6

Hemispheric Diplomacy

US policymakers had to contend with a multitude of bureaucratic entities and societal interests as they struggled to formulate a coherent agenda for the summit. At times this intramural struggle was so consuming that officials seemed to forget that Miami was not another interagency meeting and that the interests of 34 countries would be represented at the summit table. US officials knew exactly what to do when faced with preparing a presidential event—call an interagency meeting. When the US government turned its attention to the diplomacy for the upcoming hemispheric summit, it had no ready-made blueprint from which to work. After all, the last such event had been held in 1967.

US officials carefully studied the two previous hemispheric summits, largely as examples of what not to do. As discussed in chapter 1, both the 1956 Panama summit and the 1967 Punta del Este summits had little effect on hemispheric affairs.[1] Leaders of 19 countries met in Panama in July 1956, under the auspices of the Organization of American States (OAS). In the absence of a significant preparatory process to design a substantive agenda, the meeting was characterized by its "distinct protocolary and bilateral overtones."[2] The leaders made few specific commitments for future action, instead establishing committees to study critical

1. The Clinton administration's view of past hemispheric summits can be found in *Building a Partnership for Prosperity: White House Report on the Summit of the Americas* (Washington: White House, 1995), 7-11.

2. Samuel Eaton, "The Inter-American Meeting of Presidents: Punta del Este, April 12-14, 1967," unclassified State Department memorandum, 19 June 1967, 8.

problems. These committees then faded into oblivion. The most that could be said for the Panama summit was that it—and the Cuban revolution of 1959—suggested possible future directions for President Kennedy's Alliance for Progress.[3] The next hemispheric gathering took place in April 1967 in Punta del Este, Uruguay, at the request of the Latin American governments to strengthen what by then was a floundering Alliance for Progress. Again the OAS co-hosted the event with Uruguay, but preparations were much more extensive than for the Panama meeting, and the summit communiqué covered a variety of important economic and social issues.[4] Because the OAS was unable to bring focus to the preparations or adequate expertise to the more technical issues, governments, with the assistance of experts drawn mainly from regional institutions, intervened to help draft the Punta del Este agenda. That summit's most salient regional initiative—free trade within Latin America—would founder, as would many of its ambitious proposals, unaccompanied as they were by adequate implementation mechanisms, financial resources, or political will. Whatever impetus to closer US-Latin American economic cooperation might have come out of the Punta del Este meeting was lost with the withdrawal of Lyndon Johnson from the 1968 presidential campaign and the decision of President Richard Nixon to abandon Kennedy's Alliance.[5] The failure of the 1967 summit to fulfill its goals was such a disappointment that 27 years would elapse before the hemisphere would try again.

Clinton administration officials drew several lessons from these previous endeavors. First, the Western Hemisphere of 1994 differed greatly from that of the Alliance for Progress era, when roughly half of the leaders attending the summits owed their power not to popular sovereignty as expressed at the ballot box but to the power of their armed forces. Then the critical summit issue was the amount the United States would pledge in foreign assistance. At Punta del Este, Ecuador abstained from signing the declaration to demonstrate its dissatisfaction over US conditions on foreign aid. The Punta del Este Declaration called for creation of a common market encompassing all of Latin America but excluding the United States. It was an era of North-South division, of industrial countries subsidizing the economies of developing areas primarily out of security concerns rather than out of a vision of mutual economic benefits. It was a time

3. On the alliance, see Jerome Levinson and Juan de Onís, *The Alliance That Lost Its Way: A Critical Report on the Alliance for Progress* (Chicago: Quadrangle Books, 1970).

4. See Eaton, "The Inter-American Meeting of Presidents: Punta del Este, April 12-14, 1967."

5. This is the assessment of Lincoln Gordon, one of the summit's organizers, as expressed in "Finally Talking About Cuba," *The Washington Post*, 28 March 1994, A20. Similarly, Joseph Grunwald noted that the hopes of the 1967 summit soon "fizzled," in Joseph Grunwald, Miguel S. Wionczek, and Martin Carnoy, *Latin American Economic Integration and US Policy* (Washington: Brookings Institution, 1972). For a discussion of the 1967 summit written at the time, see Lincoln Gordon, "Punta del Este Revisited," *Foreign Affairs* 45, no. 4 (July 1967).

when political institutions could not be discussed in any depth (other than to condemn the common enemy of communism) because the divisions between the military *caudillos* and the civilian democrats were too wide. In contrast, by 1994 the intellectual and political climates were much more conducive to a hemispheric summit: the hemisphere had become overwhelmingly democratic, conflicts over bilateral aid flows had faded along with the aid itself, the North-South conflict had diminished, and the North American Free Trade Agreement (NAFTA) was opening the door to economic integration that transcended old divisions. Clinton administration officials reasoned that in this more favorable environment, the Miami summit could aspire to accomplish much more.

The Clinton administration also concluded that the OAS should not be entrusted with this summit.[6] With its stylized debates and culture of gaining a consensus by accepting the least common denominator, it was feared the OAS would produce a high-sounding document with a long list of desirable ends but with few realistic goals.[7] Moreover, the ambassadors to the OAS, who make up its Permanent Council, were mostly generalists with limited knowledge about the new, more technical issues confronting the hemisphere in the mid-1990s.

The OAS was also poorly suited for taking advantage of one of the new strengths of the hemisphere—the growth of civil society and the organized nongovernmental sector. Unlike the United Nations, the OAS had not granted nongovernmental actors (NGAs) official observer status and was not prepared to incorporate them into summit consultations. By the mid-1990s, civil society was far better developed and organized than it had been in 1967, demanding a much more elaborate and open process.

The White House had its own bureaucratic reason for wanting to circumvent the OAS. Foreign ministries control the OAS and staff its day-to-day governing body, the Permanent Council. For example, the United States' representative to the Permanent Council is a State Department official housed in the Inter-American Affairs bureau. If the OAS orchestrated summit preparation, leadership within the US government would likely fall, inconveniently, to the State Department.

In preparing for the Miami summit, Clinton administration officials perused texts from earlier summits and noted that inadequate attention had been paid to implementation mechanisms. High-sounding goals, especially those of the 1967 declaration and action program, were often

6. The United States was not alone in this assessment. A Central American diplomat told the author, "If the OAS had run the summit, it would have sunk." Personal interview, Washington, April 1996.

7. A participant in the Panama and Punta del Este summits commented that for the diplomats who negotiated the communiqués, "the summit declarations were ends in themselves, not means intended for future action." Personal interview, 1996.

left unattached to procedures or institutions capable of transforming them into deeds.[8]

Based on this reading of history, the Clinton administration decided to erect a structure of hemispheric consultations outside the traditional OAS framework. It would seek summit agreements appropriate to the mid-1990s based not on North-South inequalities but on mutual interests. It would seek to avoid a laundry list of elegant but empty promises and instead craft a shorter list of results-oriented initiatives. It would draw on experts' recommendations and gain legitimacy from extensive consultations with civil society. Within the summit texts, it would embed viable mechanisms for implementation that would burnish the summit with an atmosphere of serious intent.

Forging Bonds

When the summit was announced in December 1993, White House officials had the following May in mind as a possible date. But as President Clinton's schedulers delayed a final decision, and other "must" events were recorded on his calendar, the only time available was the first half of December, a full year after Vice President Gore's Mexico City speech. That left plenty of time for summit preparation—perhaps too much, since a bureaucracy with a distant deadline will typically be unresponsive and lackadaisical, with working groups adopting a leisurely pace. Other countries faced the same quandary of the urgent driving out the important. The low temperature of summit preparations resulted in a buzz in diplomatic circles and the media that the United States was not giving the summit sufficient attention. In fact, it was predictable that intensive preparations would not begin until nearer the summit deadline.

The long lead time, however, allowed time for extensive consultations among the nations of the hemisphere and made it possible for the nongovernmental sector to be engaged in the summit process. During the course of dozens of meetings held over a nine-month period, North American and Latin American diplomats developed an esprit de corps. Unlike most diplomatic exchanges, which focus on immediate, narrow issues, summit preparations placed the most profound themes in hemispheric affairs on the table. What is the definition of democracy? What is the legitimate scope for collective action in defense of democratic institutions? How far and how fast should the hemisphere integrate its economies? What are the region's social priorities, and what is the role of government in poverty

8. Declaration of Panama, signed by the presidents of the American republics, Panama City, 22 July 1956. Cited in Department of State, *Bulletin*, 6 August 1956, 220. Declaration of the presidents of America, signed at the American Chiefs of State Conference, Punta del Este, 14 April 1967. Cited in Department of State, *Bulletin*, 8 May 1967, 712-21.

alleviation and environmental protection? Should all nations be held to the same duties and obligations, or should the hemisphere differentiate among its members by size or wealth?

The long lead time also gave the nongovernmental sector time to mobilize constituencies, draft policy proposals, and lobby governments to reflect their preferences in the summit texts. Their participation—in what people began to refer to as "the Miami process"—would give greater social depth and political legitimacy to the summit.

Cascading Modular Multilateralism

The United States arrived at a strategy for negotiating a consensual text only gradually. The first impulse of the Deputies Committee was to go out into the hemisphere to consult on broad themes themselves. Intended to demonstrate that the United States was listening to the opinions of the hemisphere, this first round of talks left the impression that the United States had announced an event without a clear agenda. But this first burst of activity gave birth to consultations with the hemisphere's natural subregional groupings—the Caribbean, Central America, and South America—in addition to meetings with individual countries. Geographic divisions, however, did not necessarily correspond to functional interests. Countries from throughout the region might be interested, for example, in combating corruption. So the United States encouraged meetings among countries that expressed interest in particular issues. Countries concerned with combating corruption would meet together, with or without the United States, to draw up an initiative. The United States calculated that such a self-motivated modular group would likely craft an initiative with innovation and bite. Moreover, so long as the module included countries with recognized expertise and leadership on the given issue, it would be well placed to win hemispheric support for its handiwork. And it would be hard for other Latin American countries to resist such self-selected coalitions with their technical know-how and political legitimacy—more difficult than to nay-say only the United States. Once several of these issue-specific coalitions had their initiatives in hand, countries would be more likely to support each other—to back scratch—than to criticize others involved in the same process and risk retaliation.[9]

Together, these three strategies—bilateralism, geography-based plurilateralism, and issue-specific coalition building—gradually came together in what might be labeled "cascading modular multilateralism" (CMM).[10]

---

9. On "back scratching," see Kenneth Oye, *Economic Discrimination and Political Exchange: World Political Economy in the 1930s and 1980s* (Princeton, NJ: Princeton University Press, 1992).

10. I defined modular multilateralism in an earlier work thus: "The system we present in this paper—modular multilateralism—is a pattern of decision making among groups of nations, North and South, that share a common problem and need to come to an agreement.

Figure 6.1 The Miami process

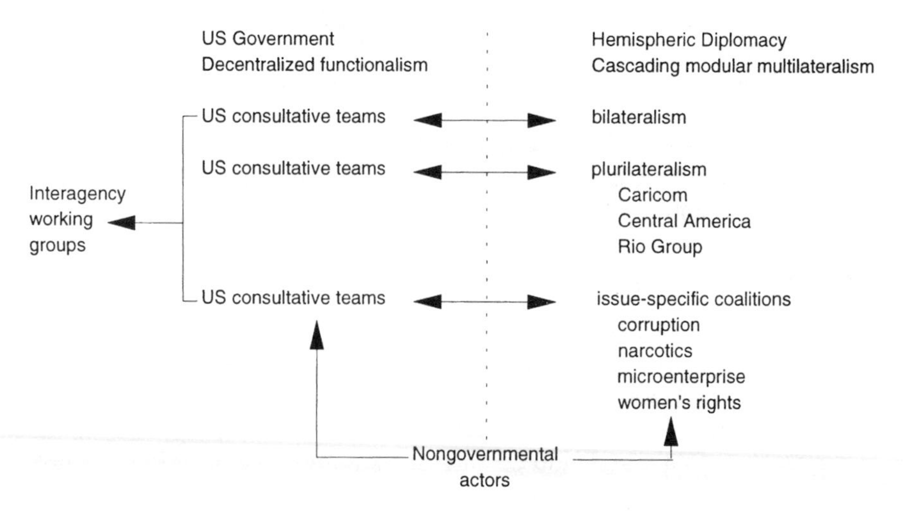

For example, the United States might discuss an initiative bilaterally with a country that would then discuss it within a subregional group, some of whose members might attend an issue-specific forum. Not a few diplomats found all of this confusing and disorganized, and complained that it was hard to keep abreast of the many meetings.[11] But in the end, CMM produced expertly crafted initiatives that had the support of a winning coalition of states and NGAs and would culminate in the cascade of consensus initiatives that would be approved at the final, traditional all-parties meeting of vice foreign ministers at Airlie House in the suburbs of Washington two weeks before Miami.

This new, decentralized, multilayered diplomatic process dovetailed nicely with the internal structure that the United States had adopted for summit preparation (figure 6.1). The various expert-level working groups staffed the US summit consultation teams to fit each meeting. A single working group might staff a team attending an issue-specific forum. Bilateral and plurilateral consultations, which would typically cover a range of issues, required an interagency team with experts from each of the three main working groups. The results of all consultations would be reported back to the full working groups and, if the consultations were held overseas, to the entire government through embassy cables. It was the interaction between the process of decentralized functionalism internal

It is *multilateral* in that it involves many players coming to the table at the same time, and *modular* in that particular actors at the table at any one time will vary according to the issue at hand.'' Richard Feinberg and Delia Boylan, *Modular Multilateralism: North-South Economic Relations in the 1990s* (Washington: Overseas Development Council, 1991), 7.

11. Personal interview with senior Chilean diplomat, Santiago, Chile, September 1996.

to the United States and the diplomacy of cascading modular multilateralism that ultimately produced the summit texts.

Latin American Reactions to the Summit

Gore's announcement in Mexico City of President Clinton's intent to convene a summit had caught the hemisphere by surprise. Certainly, a summit was a logical follow-up to NAFTA, and more than one diplomat had informally suggested to the US government that a summit would be timely. But there had been no warning before Gore's speech, and no time for prior consultations or trial balloons in the media. Nor did the announcement itself receive much media attention.

As awareness of the summit spread in the new year, many in the hemisphere welcomed this new indication of US interest in the region. Pablo Tattemanti, an Argentine career diplomat, recalled that "Argentina felt that the United States was still redefining its post-Cold War agenda and that Latin America was not at the top of that agenda. The summit could be Latin America's moment."[12] A senior Brazilian diplomat noted that "it was time for a US initiative toward Latin America. We were not bothered by the unilateralism of the announcement."[13]

But not all the reactions were favorable. There were concerns that the United States, having unilaterally convened the summit, might seek to impose an agenda. Gore's speech had mentioned possible summit themes only in very general terms, allowing those who were deeply suspicious of US motives to imagine a hidden agenda, even if it was impossible to fathom what those secret motives might be.[14] Other cynics anticipated another cycle of raised expectations, possibly fed by US promises, followed by inaction and disillusionment. A senior Brazilian diplomat recalled, "In the beginning, there were questions as to the depth of the event. Every US president needs a new initiative toward Latin America. We recalled previous US initiatives that produced very modest results, such as Kissinger's New Dialogue and Bush's Enterprise for the Americas."[15] Announced in early March, the decision by the Clinton administra-

---

12. Personal interview with Pablo Tattemanti, Washington, 22 April 1996.

13. Personal interview with a senior Brazilian diplomat, May 1996.

14. Personal interview with senior Chilean diplomat, Santiago, Chile, September 1996.

15. Personal interview with senior Brazilian diplomat, May 1996. In February 1974, Secretary of State Henry Kissinger met with Latin American foreign ministers in Mexico City to sustain a new dialogue. The Latin American agenda was typical of the period's new international economic order themes while Kissinger's agenda included international security themes. There was little dialogue and much frustration, and the Declaration of Tlatelolco yielded few concrete results. Kissinger caught the antagonistic mood of the conference when he listed the concerns of the Latin Americans: "You are concerned that the United States has abandoned its special commitment to the hemisphere; that we have left unresolved old

tion to host the summit in Miami added to this skepticism. Many Latin Americans would have preferred Washington, the hemisphere's most powerful political city. The selection of Miami pointed more to Clinton's interest in domestic politics than to engagement in relations with Latin America.

As Jorge Pinto, then vice minister in the Mexican foreign ministry, explained, "In Mexico, many saw the summit as a positive follow-up to NAFTA, to tightening links between the United States and Latin America through free trade arrangements. On the other side was the omnipresent predisposition of the pessimists, the negative thinkers, who saw anything coming from the United States as a problem. They thought it would be hard to reach consensus."[16] In other words, those with the ascendent prohemispheric attitudes (chapter 1) responded favorably while those with antihemispheric dispositions worried about US intentions.[17]

An Argentine diplomat saw another cleavage, between those who saw an opportunity for Latin American initiative and those who preferred to wait passively or even suspiciously for whatever the United States would put forward. "When you are invited to a party, you don't ask first to see the menu. You arrive at the party and then you see," is how some Latin Americans excused their passive posture.[18] At the outset, some countries recognized that the summit might advance their free trade objectives, although very few saw clearly how the Miami conclave would force the United States to define its trade agenda in very ambitious terms. A few countries, including Argentina, correctly foresaw that the summit would provide a new vehicle to advance their own foreign policy objectives.

---

problems while new ones arise; that we do not seek community but hegemony; that our relationship does not adequately contribute to the social welfare of the hemisphere; that this relationship is frequently alien to your needs and constitutes an obstacle to their satisfaction." Henry Kissinger, speech before the Conference of Tlatelolco, Mexico City, 21 February 1974. For the declaration, see Ministry of Foreign Relations of Mexico, *Conferencia de Tlatelolco entre Cancilleres de América Latina y el Secretario de Estado de los Estados Unidos de América* (Mexico: Mexico City, February 1974).

16. Personal interview with Jorge Pinto, New York City, 9 April 1996.

17. Latin Americans had registered similar reactions before the 1967 Punta del Este summit, according to a US State Department participant: "The predominant Latin American attitude at the beginning of the preparatory process for the summit meeting can best be summed up as, on the one hand, a strong desire for action that would give the Alliance for Progress a new push but, on the other hand, considerable skepticism about the possibility of achieving that push through a summit meeting at this time. The skepticism derived from memories of the 1956 summit meeting, when little of substance was accomplished; the recognized difficulty of the integration process in Latin America; and uncertainty regarding United States motives, particularly at a time that its resources were under strain from other demands." Sam Eaton, "The Inter-American Meeting of Presidents: Punta del Este, April 12-14, 1967."

18. Personal interview with Argentine diplomat, April 1996.

It was against this backdrop of hesitant hopes, lingering suspicions, and general uncertainty that the United States and the rest of the Western Hemisphere began to add definition to the Clinton-Gore initiative. Summit texts were negotiated in three rounds. First, senior US emissaries discussed possible summit themes in general terms with senior Latin American and Caribbean officials, including presidents and cabinet officials. A trip to South America by the vice president was the first and most important of these consultations. Then from August through mid-October intensive expert-level consultations hammered out a short draft declaration of principles as well as an associated and more detailed plan of action. Two weeks before Miami, vice foreign ministers came together at Airlie House to reach final agreement on the summit texts.

The Vice President in South America

Vice President Gore's trip to South America in late March initiated the first round of consultations. As with many other events during 1994, its original purpose was not summit-related, but it nevertheless served as an opportunity for summit consultations. Gore had agreed to attend the World Telecommunications Union meeting in Buenos Aires to deliver a keynote address that would link the Clinton administration's national telecommunications policy and international development. Gore also wanted to stop off in Bolivia to visit President Gonzalo "Goni" Sánchez de Lozada. Gore had earlier received the Bolivian president and the two politicians shared interests in reinventing government and sustainable development. Gore had also received the Bolivian vice president, indigenous leader Víctor Hugo Cárdenas, and had accepted his invitation to visit his childhood home on the Altiplano. After Bolivia and Argentina, Gore stopped in Brazil to make sure the Brazilians would feel engaged in the summit.

The three-country trip to South America allowed Gore to explore several of his interests. In Bolivia, Gore the spiritual environmentalist spoke of his profound respect for indigenous peoples and their intuitive stewardship of the earth. In his meetings with Argentine officials, he focused on commercial interests and pushed for passage of legislation that would require Argentine firms to make royalty payments to US pharmaceutical companies, and he told the telecommunications conference that developing countries should open their markets to foreign telecommunications firms. In Brasilia, the vice president held a televised town meeting in which he talked with an assembly of Brazilian citizens. At each stop, Gore was able to relate his long-standing interests and political values to themes for the upcoming summit.

The Bolivian Altiplano

The venue of Gore's brief visit to Bolivia was the windswept Altiplano. The vice president's delegation drove directly from the La Paz airport to Huatajata, the childhood home of Víctor Hugo Cárdenas.

Gore and Sánchez de Lozada later flew down from La Paz to tropical Santa Cruz, the city in which the Bolivian president wanted to host a major conference on sustainable development after the Miami summit. Addressing other possible summit themes, Sánchez de Lozada pushed for a major trade initiative that would open the way for early Bolivian accession to NAFTA. Gore responded that the administration favored expansion of a free trade area to encompass all of the hemisphere, but cautioned that it was a question of politics and timing. Sánchez de Lozada also spoke of his efforts to reinvent the government since he was submitting the Bolivian state to a sweeping reorganization. (As economic minister in the mid-1980s, Sánchez de Lozada had slain the inflation monster. He had run for the presidency on an anticorruption platform, quipping that corruption was like inflation: a little was tolerable but too much could kill you.) Sánchez de Lozada thought good governance should be a summit theme and Gore agreed, adding that since corruption was a sensitive issue it would be better if the initiative came from Latin America rather than the United States.

Sánchez de Lozada was interested in having the summit address good governance, trade integration, and sustainable development. These were issues that Gore had on his list, and they were very much at the core of the Bolivian president's own political agenda. If anything, as an enterprising leader with one term in which to work, Sánchez de Lozada wanted to establish more ambitious goals and to achieve them sooner. Later, Bolivia would be among those countries to push for the year 2000 as the target date for hemispheric free trade, five years sooner than would be agreed on in Miami.

Buenos Aires

The Gore delegation arrived in Buenos Aires late in the evening. At a post-midnight dinner at Olivos, the presidential palace, Carlos Menem urged that poverty be a central summit theme. Gore concurred and proposed that the summit consider sustainable development, economics, and trade so that the hemisphere could preserve the environment and pursue growth simultaneously. Menem added drugs, education, and telecommunications. Gore agreed and, in his address on telecommunications, would tie information technology to education.

Menem expressed interest in NAFTA accession, urging the United States to decide as soon as possible which countries were ready for admission. Gore affirmed US interest in hemispheric free trade—this time more assertively than in his earlier discussion with Bolivian President Sánchez de Lozada, perhaps responding to the drumbeat of interest in NAFTA accession that he was hearing from one Latin American interlocutor after another. Gore again cautioned, however, that the pace of trade liberalization should be such as to not arouse a domestic political backlash. "Our labor unions choked on NAFTA and almost choked me after my debate with Ross Perot," a grinning Gore told Menem.

The Argentines raised Menem's pet idea of creating "White Helmets," a rapid-reaction international assistance corps. It was unclear whether Menem had in mind long-term development assistance or emergency aid in the wake of natural disasters or civil strife, but Gore offered US backing if Argentina put forward the initiative for summit consideration. He suggested that Argentina link the White Helmets proposal to sustainable development.

During the Buenos Aires visit, a member of Gore's party met with 10 leaders from civic groups advocating good governance, including Poder Ciudadano (Citizen Power) and Conciencia (Consciousness). These leaders wondered if the summit might be an opportunity to press their cause, and the US representative encouraged them to organize with like-minded groups in the hemisphere—as well as with groups in their own country and with their government. Later that day, the US adviser relayed this discussion to the Argentine foreign minister, Guido di Tella (who had once directed a major public policy institute), and he agreed to be in touch with the groups.[19]

Brasilia

The brief Brasilia stop consisted of a town meeting and a 45-minute meeting with President Itamar Franco.[20] There was little discussion of the summit agenda as such. Rather, Gore's primary purpose was to reassure the Brazilians that the United States recognized their stature in hemispheric affairs. After Franco made brief opening remarks, Gore, who was seated next to the shy, visibly nervous Brazilian president, looked Franco directly in the eye, and in his strong, forthright voice said that President Clinton and he had tremendous respect for the role that he was playing in stabilizing democracy and that Brazilian historians would recognize the leadership President Franco had provided during a period of turmoil. Franco beamed as his head cabinet ministers all agreed with the American

19. During a subsequent round of consultations, the Argentine government invited two of the nongovernmental organizations to sit at the table with the official US and Argentine delegations.

20. The meeting with Franco was also attended by then-Finance Minister Fernando Henrique Cardoso, who would later accompany Franco to the summit as president-elect.

vice president. Gore's words instantly dissipated the tension in the room. Gore then said that President Clinton had asked him to extend his personal invitation to attend the summit, and Franco immediately accepted.

Returning to Washington, the US delegation felt satisfied that their original themes of good governance and sustainable development reflected Latin American interests as well. The Latin Americans had broached more specific issues including education, narcotics, telecommunications, and trade.

Mexico

By the time a US consultations team—led by Under Secretary of State Joan Spero—traveled to Mexico City on 21 April, the interagency process had developed ideas ready to test with the other countries. The ideas would later be circulated in modified, written form as the menu of 14 initiatives (appendix C). In Mexico, the US team met separately with President Carlos Salinas's chief of staff and other senior members of his government. In these meetings, the US team talked about trade, good governance, and economic initiatives. For their part, the Mexicans, reeling from repeated political shocks and focused on their presidential elections that August, had not yet given the summit serious thought.[21]

Mexico's Chief of Staff Santiago Oñate seemed ambivalent about the summit. He welcomed US leadership and saw an opportunity to create a new hemispheric agenda. But he opined that the most recent US policy initiative, the Bush administration's Enterprise for the Americas Initiative (EAI), "lacked coherence and was a bad precedent." He noted that Mexico would only be able to seriously focus on the event after its 21 August elections. Specifically, Onate noted that it was Mexico's official position to open NAFTA to other countries, but that the NAFTA countries still needed to determine the modalities of accession. He proposed the environmental protection of border areas as a possible summit item. On democracy promotion, Onate said it would be possible for the summit to ascribe to common goals but felt that an agreement on common actions would be more difficult.

French-educated diplomat Andrés Rosenthal, who embodied many antihemispheric attitudes, was even more prickly. He pointed out that the next Mexican president would take office on 1 December and there was no precedent for the head of state to leave the country so soon after his inauguration. He denigrated the choice of Miami as a venue and

---

21. During this period, Mexican Foreign Minister Manuel Tello visited Washington, and the Clinton administration urged him to allow international observers, including those from the United States, to monitor the August elections. The Salinas administration did so, setting a precedent for Mexico and facilitating summit agreement on international monitoring of elections.

expressed concern that the Cuban-Americans might cause trouble. Rosenthal also summarized the three areas he saw as US interests: regional economic integration, social progress "so that social fabrics don't tear," and the strengthening of "democratic tendencies." He recalled—with evident preference for an event that excludes the United States—that the Ibero-American summits also treat democracy and the social agenda, but not economic integration because of Spain and Portugal.[22] Nevertheless, Rosenthal did offer some constructive thoughts on procedure. He suggested the formation of a core group of countries at the vice ministerial level to prepare the summit, with themes farmed out to various countries for elaboration. These procedural ideas were consistent with the cascading modular multilateralism schema that the United States was gradually organizing though the United States did not wish to share the responsibility for the overall effort with a collective core group.

Trade Vice Minister Herminio Blanco was characteristically direct in his assessments: countries had high expectations that the summit would include a strong free trade initiative and "everyone [would] want to be on the list" for NAFTA accession. Blanco demonstrated his sophisticated knowledge of US politics by noting a gap between hemispheric expectations and realities in the US Congress. Spero remarked that the Clinton administration was not yet seeking congressional authority to proceed with hemispheric trade integration because of pending Uruguay Round legislation and disinclination to reopen NAFTA wounds so soon. Blanco also discussed various modalities for hemispheric trade integration and Spero had to concede that the United States lacked a specific integration plan.

Finance Ministry Under Secretary Guillermo Ortiz responded positively to the US team's sketch of a hemispheric code on portfolio capital flows. However, in a private meeting afterwards, Ortiz warned the author that it would be difficult to gain a hemispheric consensus on such a code. Ortiz's appreciation for the perspectives of his fellow Latin Americans would prove to be on the mark.

All in all, the Mexicans harbored modest expectations about the summit. They did not doubt that the hemisphere could draft a document of general principles but cited political realities in the United States and elsewhere as reasons to question whether meaningful progress could be made on core trade and investment issues. There was an undercurrent of irritation, even antagonism, toward the Miami event, in part because the timing was insensitive to the Mexican political calendar, in part because of Mexican

22. The annual Ibero-American summits bring together the Latin American countries of the Western Hemisphere with Spain and Portugal. Unlike the Miami summit, they exclude the United States, Canada, and the Caribbean (with the exception of the Dominican Republic) and include Cuba. They began as part of a celebration of the 500th anniversary of Columbus' voyage and became annual affairs.

suspicion that the United States might not be able to fulfill its promises, and in part because of deep-seated Mexican distrust of US intentions.[23]

The Vice President in Central America

On 24 May Vice President Gore flew to Tegucigalpa, Honduras, for a one-day summit consultation with the seven Central American leaders.[24] The Central Americans strongly endorsed the good governance and sustainable development themes.

Honduran President Carlos Roberto Reina had won office promising a "moral revolution" against illicit enrichment in public office. Other presidents spoke of corruption as the greatest enemy of democracy and social progress. Not only was there no resistance to the good governance theme, but the Central Americans embraced it. Their domestic political postures would be fortified if the entire hemisphere included an anticorruption plank in its agenda.

By chance, the day that Gore had flown to Mexico to announce the summit, President Clinton had entertained the Central American leaders in the White House. They had proposed a regional initiative on sustainable development. In Tegucigalpa, the Central Americans spoke of a regional alliance for sustainable development and proposed establishing a joint US-Central American working group to flesh out the idea. The vice president agreed and urged that the alliance be ready for signing in Miami.

At that White House luncheon, the president had promised the Central Americans that he would seek to protect them against spillovers from NAFTA that might divert trade and investment flows from their region toward Mexico.[25] In Tegucigalpa, Gore announced a legislative initiative that would partially fulfill the president's pledge: the Interim Trade Program granting duty-free access to the US market for textiles and apparel to qualifying Central American and Caribbean countries.

The Tegucigalpa meeting also gave Gore a forum to expound on nongovernmental participation in international agenda building. He informed the Central Americans that his government was consulting broadly with

23. As late as August, Onate told a senior US official that Mexico would prefer that the summit be postponed. He dropped the proposal when he was told that the summit was important to President Clinton. Personal interview with senior administration official, Washington, 11 June 1996.

24. The presidential participants were José María Figueres of Costa Rica, Alfredo Cristiani of El Salvador, Ramiro de Léon Carpio of Guatemala, Carlos Roberto Reina of Honduras, Violeta Chamorro of Nicaragua, and Guillermo Endara of Panama. Also present was Prime Minister Manuel Esquivel of Belize.

25. Press conference by President Clinton and the leaders of Central America, White House, Washington, 30 November 1993.

NGAs: "We mark this summit as a new point of departure, where all governments are open to expressions by nongovernmental organizations in the appropriate way. It is not for me to say just how other governments pursue this, but we do want to be able to say at the summit that we benefited from disagreement."

The Tegucigalpa exchange was relaxed and consensual. The Central Americans welcomed signs of renewed US attention to the region. The vice president signaled to them that he was open to their ideas and willing to support their initiatives. The end of the Cold War and the winding down of the Central American civil wars had significantly reduced tensions in the region and between the region and the United States. The Tegucigalpa session suggested new themes for US-Central American relations that were convergent with the emerging summit agenda.

The Caribbean

On 31 May Joan Spero led a summit consultations team to the English-speaking Caribbean. In Barbados, she met with Prime Minister Erskine Sandiford and with officials from the bureau of the English-speaking Caribbean Common Market (Caricom). She flew on to Trinidad and Tobago to meet with Prime Minister Patrick Manning. From the outset, the consultations with Caricom, while generally cordial, would prove to be less than fruitful. Some in the Caribbean would come to see the summit process as helping to integrate the English-speaking Caribbean into hemispheric diplomacy, but many doubted the relevance of the summit to Caricom concerns.[26] The Caribbean was still relatively new to the inter-American system and was neither economically nor culturally integrated with Latin America. The region already boasted long-standing, relatively uncorrupt democracies modeled on the Westminster system and disdained Latin American political instability. The islands questioned their capacity to benefit from the Interim Trade Program and were disappointed that the United States was not offering more foreign aid as part of the summit package. They resented industrial-country pressures to graduate them as middle-income countries from concessional assistance programs, but the summit was not addressing those concerns. More broadly, the Caribbean was suffering from the profound anxiety that their geographic area, which from time to time had been an important crossroads in world history, was now being relegated to the backwaters of time. Caricom leaders could not see how the summit would provide a means of escaping that depressing destiny.

---

26. Personal interview with a senior Caribbean diplomat, Washington, 22 April 1996. At the 1967 Punta del Este summit, Eric Williams of Trinidad and Tobago, as the only Caricom member of the OAS, was the sole representative of the English-speaking Caribbean.

At the Caricom consultations, many of the comments focused on income transfers or existing trade disputes—items not on the US summit agenda. Prime Minister Mitchell from Saint Vincent and the Grenadines responded favorably to the US initiative for a stronger OAS but reformulated that expansion to provide more scholarships. Caribbean leaders spoke of the growing use of their islands as transit points by international drug traffickers and pleaded for more equipment and training. They talked about immigration, their opposition to graduation, and the threat to marine life posed by spear guns. They pleaded for special attention to the problems of small island developing states. They also railed against US opposition to the European Union's scheme for providing their bananas with preferential access to European markets and pushed for revisions in US sugar quotas. In Trinidad and Tobago, Finance Minister Wendell Mottley suggested that the summit take on the problem of the unequal distribution of income in the hemisphere.

Despite their concerns regarding the substantive agenda, Caricom leaders suggested that the summit be seen as an ongoing process and that internationally approved action plans be subject to periodic review. Prime Minister Patrick Manning offered his country as a site for a summit preparatory conference, and Spero suggested that it focus on employment creation and small business. This eventually evolved into a workshop on microenterprises that drafted the summit initiative on that subject.

South America Again

In early June, on his way down to represent the United States at the OAS General Assembly in Belem, Brazil, Deputy Secretary of State Strobe Talbott stopped in Caracas, Venezuela, to consult with President Rafael Caldera and Foreign Minister Miguel Angel Burelli about the summit and about Haiti. Caldera expressed his support for initiatives that would strengthen democracy, foster trade integration, and combat poverty. The Venezuelans underscored their special interest in developing anticorruption proposals that would address the issue of illicit fortunes gained in government service. Talbott said that the United States would look to Venezuela for advice on developing a proposal for the summit agenda. In a separate meeting, one of Caldera's cabinet officers asked the US delegation if a free trade agreement with the United States might be possible. Afterward, in public remarks, Talbott affirmed that President Clinton strongly favored expansion of the free trade community in the Western Hemisphere.

At the OAS General Assembly, Talbott's delegation held separate summit consultations with several delegations, among them Argentina, Chile, and Brazil. The Argentine vice foreign minister, Fernando Petrella, made clear his enthusiasm for Wilsonian themes that would strengthen democracy within countries. Similarly, Chilean Foreign Minister Figueroa noted that the summit could internationalize domestic policies and signal that the international community could help solve the daily problems of people. He also urged that the United States seize the opportunity of the summit to project a clear message of US commitment to Latin America, including a vision of an inclusive hemispheric free trade area. But the Brazilian foreign minister, Celso Amorim, warned that the region had overly high expectations of the summit and there was a danger that the Latin American public could read the summit as prescriptions from the United States. At the same time, Amorim sought to strike a constructive tone. He urged that the summit agree on cooperative actions to advance human rights, including prison and judicial reform and proposed international cooperation to combat corruption, for example through agreements to provide access to bank accounts. The US delegation noted Amorim's statement that Brazil was interested in joining NAFTA but would wait for an invitation before knocking. Amorim proposed that the Inter-American Development Bank (IDB) consider opening a window to support regional integration efforts, including assistance to retrain and relocate displaced workers (a creative idea that failed to win support in the US government or elsewhere).

Canada

The Canadians had taken a keen interest in the summit. Miami would be the first summit for Canada, which had not been a member of the OAS at the time of the first two. Canada also had a special interest in multilateral diplomacy as well as NAFTA. Vice President Gore traveled to Ottawa on 19 July for consultations with Prime Minister Jean Chrétien. Canada was growing more interested in Latin America, and the prime minister was planning to visit the region early in 1995. The Canadians said that they strongly favored initiatives that would strengthen the OAS, especially in the collective defense of democracy. They were also favorably inclined toward initiatives that would strengthen civil society. Canada felt it was important to discuss free trade and preferred NAFTA expansion to a collection of bilateral free trade agreements. Finally, the Canadians warned against a proliferation of proposals and urged the hemisphere to set priorities in negotiating the summit agenda.

Conclusions from Round One

The first round of consultations, while excessively relaxed in time and overly general in scope, gave the United States a clearer understanding of the attitudes of its summit partners. The deputies grasped that poverty was an important theme in Latin American political discourse and that the Latin Americans assumed it would be addressed in Miami. Fears within the US government that the anticorruption theme would alienate Latin Americans were also allayed. Most important, the consultations made it clear that the Latin Americans and Caribbeans wanted guaranteed access to the US market and that the sine qua non for a successful summit was a US commitment to expanding free trade.

Along the way, the United States became committed to several Latin American initiatives. Gore signaled the US willingness to support Menem's White Helmet initiative, offered to showcase the Central Americans' sustainable development alliance in Miami, and expressed interest in Sánchez de Lozada's proposed Santa Cruz conference on sustainable development.

Through these consultations, the Latin Americans significantly influenced the first draft of the plan of action. The deputies approved these 14 initiatives for circulation in mid-August to governments throughout the hemisphere. Now the task in the second round of consultations was to reach consensus on specific initiatives with detailed action plans.

Round Two

The United States gathered reactions to its 14 points through various channels. It sent out interagency teams to hold intensive consultations around the hemisphere (appendix A). US ambassadors visited the governments of their host countries. Hemispheric governments wrote directly to the Summit Coordinating Office at the State Department. A copy of the initiatives soon leaked into the NGA world, increasing the transparent nature of the summit preparatory process.[27]

Predictably, other countries treated the 14 initiatives as a skeleton on which to hang more proposals. The 14 were fattened, and others were added. The second set of proposals, which the United States circulated in October, had grown to 17 initiatives. The text circulated just before Airlie House had expanded to 19 initiatives. The final plan of action totaled 23 separate initiatives with more than 150 action items among them. The search for consensus and inclusion explained this process of elongation. The multitiered consultations process of cascading modular multilateralism did, however, help the United States resist the tendency toward least-common-denominator blandness. The final text would suffer some dilution, but many specific action items would survive.

---

27. The 14 initiatives were published in their entirety in a special newsletter prepared by the Inter-American Dialogue and the North-South Center, *Summit of the Americas News* (Miami: North-South Center Press, September 1994), 4-6.

As described earlier, Round Two consultations (from August through mid-October) could be divided into three overlapping types: plurilateral, bilateral, and issue-specific coalitions. The following case studies, drawn from each of the major issue areas in the summit's plan of action, illustrate these consultative processes and their intensity. The initiatives can also be arranged on an intensity continuum in accordance with the quantity and depth of the consultations. The corruption and women's rights initiatives exemplify coalition building; the energy and education initiatives illustrate bilateral-plurilateral-multilateral combinations (corruption and energy being more intensive than education and women's rights); the US government marketed the infrastructure initiative in bilateral and plurilateral consultations (but not intensively); and the microenterprise initiative derived from yet another process—a unique multilateral public-private forum. Trade, which is discussed at length in chapter 7, is another example of the intensive, bilateral-plurilateral method.

Anticorruption

Negotiation of the anticorruption initiative provided a prime example of intensive, issue-specific coalition building (or modular plurilateralism). Several countries with special interests in the subject worked together to draft the initiative and then market it to the rest of the hemisphere. The process was notable on several counts. First, it placed a new, critically important subject on the hemispheric agenda. Never before in a hemispheric multilateral forum had corruption—so deeply rooted in the political culture of many countries—been addressed in such a straightforward way. Second, the countries involved brought specific concerns and expert knowledge to the task. The initiative contained several innovative and workable action items. Third, the country groupings provided sufficient political authority to win the support of other nations.

During 1993, the Inter-American Directorate of the National Security Council (NSC) had created an interagency working group (IWG) within the US government to consider the problem of corruption. The NSC staff feared that the rising outcry against political corruption in Latin America, while without doubt healthy in the long run, could in the short run undermine the legitimacy of democracy itself and open the door to authoritarian populists. After the working group had surveyed ongoing programs that fit under the umbrella of good governance and anticorruption, and sketched several further possible initiatives, the chair of the group passed to the State Department for implementation. In addition, the Presidential Decision Directive on US-Latin American relations had codified the US government consensus that corruption was a threat to the legitimacy of democracy and deserved the attention of US policymakers. But the anticorruption IWG was unable to launch its mission, in part because of resistance from some foreign service officers and officials responsible for economic issues who feared that the United States could come across as preachy and gratuitously quarrelsome. The summit provided the missing policy hook and the necessary senior leadership in the person of the vice president.

Deputy Assistant Secretary Michael Skol returned to the Inter-American Affairs Bureau at the State Department in late 1993 after having served as ambassador to Venezuela. In Caracas he witnessed a series of corruption scandals that culminated in the impeachment and eventual conviction of former president Carlos Andrés Pérez. Skol saw the anticorruption issue as one that could enjoy wide political appeal in Venezuela: regime opponents could use it to hammer the government, it fit neatly into the political left's moral critique, and business was attracted to reforms that would lead to a more reliable, fair, and efficient legal climate. Skol took over leadership of the anticorruption working group, which once summit preparation got under way blended into the democracy IWG.[28] Skol met with many in the NGAs, including the National Endowment for Democracy, human rights groups such as the Washington Office on Latin America and the Lawyers' Committee for Human Rights, the Council of the Americas, the US Chamber of Commerce and, most important, Transparency International, which specialized in fighting corruption.

The first round of diplomatic consultations allayed fears among some deputies that the anticorruption theme would irritate the Latin Americans. On the contrary, many Latin leaders had gained elective office by decrying the corruption of their predecessors and opponents and welcomed the opportunity to elevate their cause to the hemispheric level. Some foreign ministries were apprehensive, however, and, although they could not deny the legitimacy of the issue, wanted to keep any initiative very general.

The United States built consensus in several ways. It met frequently in Washington with a coalition of representatives from embassies of interested countries—including Chile, Ecuador, Honduras, and Venezuela—at first discussing general principles and then exchanging drafts.[29] The United States also pressed the initiative during bilateral and plurilateral consultations, which helped to familiarize negotiators with the general theme as well as the action items. In addition, Skol traveled to Quito to attend a conference on ethics co-sponsored by the US Information Agency (USIA) where he met with President Sixto Durán Bállen and Vice President

---

28. The author is indebted to Michael Skol for much of this account of US government actions. Personal interview, 24 April 1996.

29. The Washington embassies of these countries were being responsive to their senior leadership. Venezuelan President Rafael Caldera and Honduran President Roberto Reina had run on anticorruption platforms, Chilean President Eduardo Frei had formed a blue-ribbon Commission on Public Ethics, and Ecuadorian Vice President Alberto Dahik was a supporter of Transparency International.

Alberto Dahik before flying directly to Caracas to confer with President Rafael Caldera. During this trip, Skol struck an important compromise: the United States would support Caldera's plank that would tie extradition to corruption crimes, and Venezuela would support the internationalization of the US Foreign Corrupt Practices Act, which criminalizes bribery in international commerce. Skol also met with Honduran President Reina in Washington. Meanwhile, at the initiative of the Chileans, in June 1994 the OAS General Assembly in Belem, Brazil, established a Working Group on Probity and Public Ethics, chaired by the Chilean lawyer Edmundo Vargas Carreno. The OAS committee kept in close contact with the Washington embassy working group, and its working drafts paralleled theirs in most respects.

The anticorruption language in the 14-initiative draft also responded to the US agenda. It sought to multilateralize the Foreign Corrupt Practices Act (but without mentioning the US legislation by name) by criminalizing bribery in international business, and proposed participation in an Organization for Economic Cooperation and Development (OECD) working group on bribery in international business that had recently recommended criminalizing bribery in international transactions.[30] Inspired by a Chilean national commission on corruption, this first draft initiative also proposed national action plans to review various laws and practices relating to the management of public funds.

After the second round of consultations, the United States circulated a revised draft plan of action in early October. Several Latin American countries had proposed that corruption be explicitly linked to democracy, so an introductory chapter was added, decrying corruption as a threat to democracy, efficient economy, and social progress. Also in response to Latin American concerns, the October draft downplayed the OECD working group. Only Mexico was an OECD member, and the Latin Americans feared it was a rich man's club whose policies might not be tailored to their realities and which might introduce an element of North-South finger pointing.[31] Instead, they preferred that the OAS Working Group on Public Ethics create a liaison with the OECD working group. The October draft made explicit reference to national commissions on public ethics—although this reference would eventually be deleted by the Brazilians as being too interventionist. The October draft contained another important addition: at the initiative of the Venezuelans, the draft stated that "governments will cooperate in criminal investigations and proceedings related

---

30. See Organization for Economic Cooperation and Development Press Release, "Recommendation of the Council of the OECD on Bribery in International Business Transactions," (Paris, 27 May 1994).

31. US government document (unclassified), "Responses to Phase II Consultations," 6 October 1994, and personal interviews with senior Latin American diplomats, Washington, April-May 1996.

to corruption, including extradition. . . ." Caldera was keen on seeking the extradition of Venezuelans accused of illicit enrichment who had fled to Miami and elsewhere.

The October draft contained all the important elements of the final document. At Airlie House, an effort by the Rio Group (under strong Brazilian influence) to introduce diluted language was deflected, chiefly by Venezuela. The Latin Americans working in the informal issue-specific coalition on corruption found that the Rio Group was less conducive to structuring a strong initiative with a detailed work plan. Instead, the coalition countries focused their efforts on their joint work and on the US-circulated draft.[32] The draft the United States proposed at Airlie House (which formed the basis for the final text) was very similar to the October draft, picking up one idea from the Rio Group that Brazil had proposed: a commitment to develop mechanisms in the judicial and banking areas to facilitate international investigation of corruption cases. At Airlie House, the anticorruption initiative sailed through with little controversy.

Women's Rights

The women's initiative is a fascinating study of how the nongovernmental sector and small countries can alter the hemispheric agenda. Early in US interagency planning, the US Agency for International Development (USAID) had proposed an initiative on women, but it was blocked by those who feared a proliferation of special interest items.[33] The October draft plan of action contained several references to women within other initiatives: the education initiative lamented that "large segments of society, including women, minorities and indigenous peoples, have not been equipped to participate fully in economic life"; the health initiative focused attention on maternal mortality rates; and the initiative on microenterprise noted its special relevance to women. But there was no separate initiative on women.

Early during summit preparations, NSC and State Department officials addressed the Washington Liaison Committee on Latin America, a loose coalition of Washington-based organizations interested in Latin America, to solicit their input for the summit agenda. After this meeting, the International Center for Research on Women (ICRW) and the Inter-American Dialogue decided to convene a conference of women leaders to focus on the summit.[34] On 6 May 1994 representatives from ICRW, the Inter-

32. Personal interviews with senior Latin American diplomats, Washington, April-May 1996. The Rio Group is a caucus of the South American countries (exclusive of Guyana and Suriname) plus Mexico and Panama, with representatives from the Caribbean and Central America.

33. Personal interview with senior USAID official, Washington, 24 April 1996.

34. This account relies heavily on International Center for Research on Women and Inter-American Dialogue, *Strengthening the Role of Women in Society* (Miami: North-South Center Press, 1996).

American Dialogue, and other nongovernmental groups met with US government officials and representatives from private philanthropic organizations in New York City to explore ways to incorporate nongovernmental participation more effectively in the summit. At this meeting, Ford Foundation representatives discussed the ICRW-Inter-American Dialogue proposal for a women's roundtable and later agreed to fund it. Nancy Birdsall, IDB executive vice president and board member of ICRW, offered the IDB facilities to host the October roundtable. The roundtable of more than 30 prominent women leaders from the private sector, academia, nongovernmental organizations, and government hammered out a communiqué on women's rights, which they circulated to foreign ministries and heads of state, urging them to incorporate women's issues at the summit.

Nicaraguan Ambassador to the United States Roberto Mayorga arrived at Airlie House with a draft initiative on women's rights. Sonia Picado, the Costa Rican ambassador to the United States, brought copies of the roundtable communiqué for distribution to delegations. Speaking on behalf of his widely respected president "Doña Violeta" Chamorro, there was no opposition to Mayorga's initiative, which was incorporated into the final summit text without major modification.[35]

The final text of the women's rights initiative mirrors important points in the roundtable communiqué: full respect for all rights of women, promotion of the participation of women in decision making, a call for measures to reduce violence against women, measures to improve women's ability to earn income, and an appeal to international financial organizations to intensify programs in favor of women. The final text also included references to various international agreements and agencies, but it omitted several of the more demanding items of the roundtable communiqué, such as the call for tracking progress through existing institutions and by publishing data disaggregated by gender. The communiqué also called on multilateral institutions to set targets for recruiting and promoting female staff and funding research. But the summit plan of action set no targets and established no monitors, nor did it ensure women's reproductive rights.

Notwithstanding the dilutions, ICRW and other nongovernmental organizations that had lobbied hard for the women's rights initiative were generally satisfied with their success. Previous hemispheric summits and communiqués from other hemispheric gatherings typically contained no more than passing references to women's rights. This time, NGAs, Central American governments, and an informal network of politically powerful

35. Mayorga had approached Chamorro and proposed that he, in her name, sponsor a women's initiative. Mayorga had been influenced by the roundtable communiqué and by preparations for the upcoming UN World Conference on Women in Beijing as well as by his conversations with Nancy Birdsall of the IDB and the Nicaraguan Institute on Women. Personal interview with Roberto Mayorga, Washington, 25 April 1996.

women (including the moral authority of a female head of state) were able to bypass virtually the entire process of governmental negotiations and insert a women's rights initiative into the Miami Plan of Action.

Energy

The 14 initiatives circulated by the US government in mid-August contained three under the heading "alliance with nature," including one on energy drafted primarily by the Department of Energy (DOE). It emphasized sustainable—nonconventional, renewable, and efficient energy—use.[36] The draft initiative called on countries to develop national energy work programs based on integrated resource planning that would be ready for implementation by 1998. The multilateral development banks would increase their financing of identified sustainable energy projects.

Controversy over the energy initiative arose in part because it appeared in the 14 points with little prior consultation on major details. North-South fault lines also began to reappear: the United States was pushing for conservation while the Latin Americans wanted to emphasize production, marketing, and official resource transfers to help them develop their energy resources. The US-circulated October draft was more responsive to Latin concerns. It contained three separate references to external finance, calling for the multilateral development banks to increase financing of energy projects substantially.[37] At the insistence of Brazil, the redraft called for governments to ratify the Convention on Climate Change but omitted the Brazilian proposal for language referring to excess production and consumption of energy by industrial countries.[38] The October initiative also included three new items that bore a US stamp: encouraging private-sector investment, identifying at least one model project in each country by November 1995, and convening a ministerial meeting in April 1995 "to address the entire range of hemispheric strategies for the future."

The United States sponsored a conference on the sustainable development initiatives in Quito, Ecuador, in late October. Attended by represen-

36. The US government consulted closely on the energy initiative with environmental nongovernmental organizations, including the Natural Resources Defense Council (NRDC), the International Fund for Renewable Energy Efficiency, and the US Export Council for Renewable Energy. During the second round of consultations, the US delegation often contained two or three representatives from environmental NGAs with expertise on energy, who were in constant contact with the sustainable development working group. Personal interviews with participants in the Department of Energy and NRDC, spring and summer 1996.

37. The US Treasury, which is responsible for the international financial institutions within the US government, vetoed a Department of Energy proposal that the Inter-American Development Bank increase lending for energy to 25 percent of its total lending. Personal interview with US government official, Washington, 24 April 1996.

38. "Responses to Phase II Consultations."

tatives from energy and foreign ministries and local embassy officers, the conference reviewed the October draft Plan of Action. Some of the debates on the biodiversity and pollution prevention initiatives reignited old North-South divisions, including calls by the Latin Americans for cost-free technology transfer and accusations that due regard was not given to national sovereignty. The discussion on energy, however, was more technical and less confrontational.

At Airlie House, the US-drafted initiative included due dates and a calendar of future meetings for least-cost national energy strategies, as well as action items calling for identification of model projects, increases in official lending, reports by energy ministers, and sustainable energy forums. Responsive to Latin American interests, the draft also contained language calling for the promotion of energy services to meet environmental and developmental requirements. References to additional official and private finance were retained.

During the Airlie House debates, all the due dates and reporting requirements were deleted by the Latin Americans, significantly weakening the initiative's urgency. But the biggest development was a new energy initiative by Venezuela that emphasized energy cooperation and production to promote economic growth that directly countered the US-inspired conservationist initiative. There was no time at Airlie House to meld the two initiatives, so they remained separate. The Airlie House wordsmiths sought to render the two initiatives compatible by introducing the word "sustainable" into the Venezuelan initiative. Although the final text called for more World Bank and IDB financing of efficient and renewable energy, omission of quantitative targets or due dates left the initiative without certain sources of finance—a critical component in an area requiring massive capital investments. Nevertheless, the final text retained significant substantive language that both DOE and environmental NGAs could support.[39] Pledges to attend a sustainable energy symposium provided the beginnings of a follow-up.

The United States had problems negotiating the energy initiative because it began late, failed to build strong allies elsewhere in the hemisphere, was unable to gain the full support of the two countries with the clearest interest in the subject (Venezuela and Mexico), and failed to use the Quito preparatory meeting to flesh out differences and build a durable consensus among key players. The early US-inspired drafts may have been too ambitious in the absence of significant new funding, and the Department of Energy was unable to persuade the US Treasury to press the multilateral development banks on its behalf. Without such funding, the United States lacked leverage with the Latin Americans.

---

39. For example, NRDC concluded that "important policy and conceptual breakthroughs are found in the Miami summit's Partnership for Sustainable Energy Use." See Justin Ward et al., *Implementing the Summit of the Americas: Building Sustainable Development Partnerships* (Coral Gables: North-South Center, 1995), 3.

The consultations did seem, however, to focus the US Department of Energy on the hemisphere, engage the nongovernmental sector, and provide an avenue for Venezuela to emerge as a leader. Other energy ministries that had been involved in the consultations were prepared to consider seriously those recommendations that survived. Preparations for the summit established a hemispheric agenda on energy conservation and production with elements of a work plan that would carry on beyond Miami.

Education

The Latin Americans insisted that the social agenda be an important part of the summit text.[40] In response, the United States first separated sustainable development from economic prosperity and then gave both environment and poverty their own chapters. Mark Schneider, the assistant administrator of USAID for Latin America and the Caribbean, chaired the US interagency working group on social issues. USAID had long focused on health and education, had gained interagency agreement that the Clinton administration should promote social equity through investments in health and education, and from the outset sought to place those core institutional issues on the summit agenda.

With social issues a part of the 14 initiatives, hemispheric consultations on education and health initiatives proceeded smoothly. The United States was able to work with experts and officials and rely on previously negotiated hemispheric and global agreements. USAID in-country missions built support for draft initiatives through the functional ministries, which in turn could influence the lead negotiators in their foreign ministries.

The initial US draft of the education initiative was primarily the work of USAID, with input from the US Department of Education and conversations with IDB experts. USAID officials were influenced by the 1994 Narino Accords (which set goals and timetables for improving the quality of life for children) to be reached by 1995 and by a Nancy Birdsall article that attributed part of East Asia's development successes to the emphasis on primary and secondary education.[41] The core ideas in the draft were in the final summit text: commitment to 100 percent primary school completion rates and 75 percent secondary school completion rates by a fixed date (2000 in the 14 initiatives and 2010 in the final text); decentralized decision making with greater civic participation; and creation of a partner-

---

40. Information on US policy in this section is based in large part on a personal interview with a senior Clinton administration official, June 1996.

41. Nancy Birdsall and Richard Sabot, "Inequality, Exports and Human Capital in East Asia: Lessons for Latin America," in *Rethinking the State in Latin America*, ed. Colin I. Bradford Jr. (Paris: OECD, 1994).

ship for educational reform based on consultations within countries among officials and NGAs interested in education.

But hemispheric consultations diluted the initiative in two important respects. First, the higher-income Caribbeans, who already enjoyed high primary school completion rates, inserted items promoting technical and professional training, and Latin Americans—led by Brazil—added an item for strengthening the quality of higher education and for promoting cooperation to produce scientific and technical knowledge. US language calling for governments to invest an increased proportion of their budgets in primary education was deleted, even if target completion rates remained. So the focus of the initiative was blurred, and no financing was identified. Second, USAID had proposed that the educational reform partnership, which it intended to fund, monitor progress toward an agreed-upon action plan. At Brazilian insistence, the monitoring task was deleted, and the hemispheric partnership was reduced to being a "consultative forum."[42]

Together with those on health, women, and microenterprise, the education initiative defined the summit texts' chapter on poverty eradication. Clear targets with end dates were set for primary and secondary school completion rates, even if their importance was downgraded by addition of other objectives and subtraction of a monitoring requirement. The initiative approved USAID's partnership for educational reform. But the low intensity of education initiative negotiations failed to ignite new interest in an old subject and did not build new coalitions, engage the NGAs, or catalyze additional finance.

Infrastructure

Many of the US-inspired initiatives grew from bureaucratic imperatives as agencies pressed for attention to their interests. In contrast, the infrastructure initiative demonstrates that a lone individual without strong bureaucratic backing is able to present a novel idea and place it on the agenda.

During her long tenure as a member of the board of directors of the US Export-Import Bank, Rita Rodriguez realized that the international community had focused inadequate attention on the special problems facing private foreign investors in infrastructure projects.[43] Unlike many traditional projects whose foreign exchange earnings provide security to the foreign investor, infrastructure projects—especially public utilities and transportation—often generate revenues primarily in local currency.

---

42. "Responses to Phase II Consultations."

43. Personal interview with Rita Rodriguez, 24 June 1996.

Politically sensitive, such projects are often subject to government regulators who have the power to alter the rules of the game at any time. At the Eximbank, Rodriguez had witnessed efforts to structure individual deals that provided more certainty to investors and long-term lenders in infrastructure projects. She saw the summit as an opportunity to develop rules that would cover the entire hemisphere. She drew up a draft initiative and succeeded in gaining the support of the NSC staff, the Treasury, and the State Department. Rodriguez herself discussed the initiative with senior officials at the IDB and with acquaintances in finance ministries around the hemisphere.

The final text, however, was but a shadow of Rodriguez's brainchild. Initiative 8 of the 14 initiatives proposed that countries agree to develop a protocol to facilitate financing for private infrastructure projects. The protocol could set policies and procedures for the regulatory regimes governing infrastructure and provide for compensation to investors against political risk. But several Latin governments, especially Brazil, objected to the emphasis on private as opposed to official capital and did not want to commit to a protocol, even if it would stop considerably short of being a formal treaty obligation.[44] Argentina, Mexico, and other countries balked at guarantees of compensation to private investors hurt by regulatory actions over which central governments might have little control. So the final text allowed simply that "governments that so wish will develop suitable mechanisms, including multilateral and bilateral commitments on regulatory and legal rules and practices, to encourage private investment" in infrastructure projects. The IDB was asked to work with governments to develop such mechanisms. The final text could be seen as a platform, albeit a shaky one, from which to later launch hemispheric negotiations. But the IDB could be excused if it chose to wait for a firmer signal of widespread interest before it pushed for implementation.

Rodriguez had successfully built her alliances within the US government, but her government did not garner strong allies that would resist predictable Latin efforts to water down the binding aspects of the proposal. Nor was she able to catalyze active IDB involvement or engender sufficient interest among private investors. As of this writing, there was no postsummit implementation.

Microenterprise

The microenterprise initiative drew support from several quarters within the US government. As expected, USAID was interested because it had long offered assistance to artisans and mom-and-pop businesses. From within the US Treasury, the office responsible for the multilateral banks

---

44. "Responses to Phase II Consultations."

was interested because the IDB had a long history of assisting microenterprises. Less predictable was support from within the Council of Economic Advisers, where economist Constance Dunham had a personal interest in the subject.[45]

But it was the 31 October-2 November conference held in Trinidad and Tobago that gave the initiative its final definition and its winning coalition. Prime Minister Patrick Manning had offered Trinidad as a site for a pre-Miami conference, and USAID, IDB (through its multilateral investment facility), and the Ford Foundation funded it. Joan Spero responded in favor of a conference on a more limited topic, suggesting that small business might be a good subject to discuss in the small island states of the Caribbean.

What was unique about the Trinidad conference was the presence of large numbers of NGOs from throughout the hemisphere. With their in-depth knowledge of the needs of microenterprises developed from their hands-on experience, NGOs contributed valuable input. During much of the conference, public- and private-sector members intermingled and forged consensus around specific measures. It was a degree of public-private sector partnership rarely seen in hemispheric diplomacy. The consensus reached at Trinidad was incorporated largely verbatim into the texts prepared for Airlie House by both the US government and the Rio Group. With some editing, the basic concepts and much of the wording agreed to were forwarded to the leaders for signature in Miami.

Nearly two years later, individuals working at IDB, the US government, and at NGOs still felt that the Trinidad conference and the subsequent summit endorsement had significantly enhanced the credibility and stature of microenterprises.[46]

The Emerging Hemispheric System: First Assessment

No preconceived plan accounted for the varied ways summit initiatives were negotiated. On the contrary, they arose piecemeal in response to the emerging forces at play in hemispheric relations and to the enterprise of ambitious, well-placed individuals. Precisely because of its spontaneity, in many ways cascading modular multilaterialism more truly reflected the current configuration of hemispheric society than would any design based on traditional blueprints. By opening space for cabinet diplomacy, this issue-driven multilateralism made it possible for ministries to bring

45. Interview with Constance Dunham, Washington, 12 August 1996. Others involved were Sherman Boone at Treasury and Ramon Daubon at USAID.

46. Interviews with officials at IDB, USAID, and Acción, Washington, summer 1996.

their knowledge and energy—and sometimes financial resources—to the process. Similarly, the involvement of NGAs brought practical expertise and passionate commitment, and, in the eyes of some, enhanced legitimacy to the table. Out of this unplanned experiment would emerge a new, much richer, and deeper inter-American system that was more representative of the contemporary forms of governance and social relations in the Western Hemisphere.

This approach allowed the US government to penetrate counterpart ministries while NGAs enabled US society to delve deeply into Latin American societies. The United States succeeded in gaining the endorsement of many measures in its own agenda as codified in Presidential Decision Directive 28 on Latin America. In turn, exposure to Latin American and Caribbean ideas and policies was especially significant for senior-level US officials. The entire process enhanced convergence across an array of issues and actors.

Nevertheless, case studies presented in this chapter reveal serious flaws in the pre-Miami negotiations and suggest several other assessments of the value of cascading modular multilateralism and its optimum use:

- Major players should be consulted early and intensively. Venezuela was deeply involved in the anticorruption initiative and became a team player, but neither Venezuela nor Mexico ever felt ownership of the energy initiative.
- Repeated, frank discussions of broad themes as well as detailed action items can help reduce the fear of new ideas, build greater trust, and create the sense of common purpose. The most important outcome may be not in the wording of the texts but rather in the appreciation of common concerns. Even though the wording for the common defense of democracy was diluted, the Miami process increased countries' comfort in mutual assistance should their political institutions be threatened (as would become manifest in the successful collective defense of democracy in Paraguay in April 1996).
- Heads of state should be kept informed of the progress of negotiations and should be more actively engaged if their officials become too wedded to narrow bureaucratic notions and interests. Because cumulative modular multilateralism relies on middle-level officials in decentralized agencies, the risk arises that these actors may adopt overly rigid postures that prejudice international progress. During preparations for the summit, discussions between Vice President Gore, Mack McLarty, and Brazilian leaders helped soften Brazilian resistance to new ideas. More intensive communications between President Clinton and leaders from other nations might have paid even bigger dividends.

As practiced during the Miami process, this approach suffered from these flaws as well:

- The pre-Miami process was too anarchic. Its openness to new ideas from a wide variety of sources was healthy and accounted for much of the summit's energy and high spirit. Indeed, such openness was appropriate for the first summit in a generation when a new hemispheric agenda was being defined. Still, some greater degree of organization and planning would have been useful in setting priorities and delineating the breadth of the agenda. More rigorous first round consultations might have allowed for a more orderly and disciplined second round.

- Information exchanges were inadequate. Governments had difficulty tracking the many meetings. As organizer and host, the United States could have mounted a comprehensive reporting system and made its product available to other countries.

- Involvement of NGAs was irregular. Their participation was too novel for a clear consensus on governing rules. There was great unevenness in the degree to which governments consulted these organizations at home—just as NGA involvement varied tremendously across initiatives.

- Rules were not explicitly set for such critical policymaking matters as timetables for implementation, budgetary sufficiency, and monitoring. The United States tended to write such measures into draft initiatives, but Brazil and some other Latin American countries sought to delete them. Inadequate attention was paid to establishing clear rules for these matters, which would prove to be critical in the post-Miami implementation stage.

Notwithstanding these flaws, the Miami process produced major advances in hemispheric diplomacy. The value of cascading modular multilaterialism lies in its potential to capture the energies of the international agencies, functional ministries, and organized civil society. It also fosters mutual understanding and convergence.

7

Free Trade Area of the Americas

With little more than a month left before the summit, the US government convened consultations on the trade initiative. These consultations were structured entirely differently from the more informal, decentralized, and iterative processes through which the other initiatives were being cobbled together. For other initiatives, the United States sent delegations abroad or participated in multilateral gatherings; for the trade initiative, the United States convened meetings in Washington. For most other discussions, the United States was represented at the assistant secretary level or below; on trade, the United States sent Deputy US Trade Representative (USTR) Charlene Barshefsky. Of all the presummit sessions other than the final Airlie House conference, the trade sessions most resembled traditional diplomatic negotiations.

The trade discussions themselves were unusual because the United States met with the various subregional groups in succession. Separate sessions were held with the members of the Caribbean Common Market (Caricom), the Central American Common Market, the Andean Pact, and the Southern Cone Common Market (Mercosur), and individually with Canada and Mexico. This hub-and-spoke approach, which took advantage of the existing architecture of subregional integration pacts, may have enhanced the US bargaining position. Certainly, it gave the United States the opportunity to absorb the views of one subgroup at a time and to incorporate that new knowledge into its stance in subsequent meetings. The United States also avoided the large-group dynamic wherein the most disruptive element sometimes captures a meeting and in which there are strong tendencies toward finding a consensus through the least common denominator.

Of all the presummit meetings, these were the riskiest for the United States. Among the Latin Americans and Caribbeans there was considerable resentment that the United States had delayed the discussions on trade for so long. That USTR had just withdrawn legislation for fast-track renewal and for the Interim Trade Program for the Caribbean basin countries seriously undercut US credibility. The United States was assuming the position of convener and chair and was adopting a format that many Latin Americans saw as a divide-and-conquer tactic. Nevertheless, the meetings succeeded for two main reasons. The United States gave the Latin Americans what they most wanted—credible commitment to a hemispheric free trade area. And Charlene Barshefsky performed brilliantly, controlling the debate while persuading the Latin Americans that she was genuinely taking their concerns into account. Latin American answers to her questions did inform US thinking and affect the final outcome.

The United States went into the talks with three main objectives.[1] The main point was for the leaders in Miami to adopt the objective of a hemispheric free trade area (FTA). This was very much pushing on an open door, a truth that not all the members of the Deputies Committee or even the USTR players seemed fully aware of. Second, USTR wanted to establish the scope and disciplines of the North American Free Trade Agreement (NAFTA) as the benchmarks for hemispheric integration. Third, future trade talks would proceed on two tracks: existing forums such as the Organization of American States (OAS) and the US-led bilateral and subregional trade and investment councils would serve to discuss principles and to ensure transparency and convergence as subregional integration proceeded, but the actual trade negotiations would occur outside these forums. Multilateral negotiations might well be a useful supplement, but the main action would be NAFTA accession. The rough analogy, Barshefsky told the Canadians, was to the Organization for Economic Cooperation and Development (OECD) versus the General Agreement on Tariffs and Trade (GATT).

The first session began on 21 October with the Canadians, and emphasis was on NAFTA expansion and the value of establishing NAFTA-like standards for hemispheric trade integration. The delegates also analyzed the intentions and solidity of Mercosur and the future of NAFTA-Mercosur interaction. Neither delegation seemed to have given much thought to the structure or functions of the mechanism whereby trade agreements would be negotiated other than to convene a trade ministerial shortly after Miami.

---

1. USTR, briefing materials for trade consultations, 21-28 October 1993; interviews with participants.

Designing Procedures

After the meeting with the Canadians, Barshefsky asked the author to work with her staff and the NEC to consider procedural mechanisms for trade integration. In drafting the memo, the author drew on an excellent paper prepared jointly by the OAS, Inter-American Development Bank (IDB), and UN Economic Commission for Latin America and the Caribbean (ECLAC), as well as on the astute advice of NEC Deputy Bowman Cutter, who reflected on his APEC experience. The memo recommended five integration mechanisms:[2]

- *NAFTA Enlargement Working Groups.* NAFTA partners would form expert-level working groups to clarify their positions on a series of issues related to NAFTA accession, including definition of readiness criteria and negotiation procedures.
- *OAS-IDB Americas Commission.*[3] The OAS and IDB would jointly staff a committee to promote transparency and convergence among the subregional trading blocs. It would serve as a secretariat to the OAS Special Committee on Trade. The commission could also serve to tie IDB and World Bank sector loans to NAFTA standards.
- *Revitalized Trade and Investment Councils.* The councils, created as part of the Bush administration's Enterprise for the Americas Initiative, had lost momentum because they did not appear to be leading toward the ultimate prize of a free trade agreement. The Latin Americans had seen the councils as requiring concessions without offering adequate reciprocal rewards. Tied now to NAFTA enlargement, they could promote GATT-consistent readiness for comprehensive trade agreements. Revitalized councils would keep those countries not ready for NAFTA accession involved in integration and avoid dividing the hemisphere into NAFTA-ready and NAFTA-nots.
- *Trade Ministerials.* Periodic trade ministerial meetings would maintain political control and provide continuing impetus to integration. The

2. Organization of American States, Inter-American Development Bank, UN Economic Commission for Latin America and the Caribbean, "Towards Free Trade in the Western Hemisphere" (Washington, 15 September 1994). This publication recommended annual meetings of trade ministers with preparatory subministerials and that the OAS Special Committee on Trade, with technical support from the IDB and ECLAC, promote free trade, facilitate the convergence of the subregional groups, and provide support to the ministerials. See also "Free Trade Area in the Americas: Procedural Mechanisms: Concept Paper," unsigned and undated draft US government memorandum.

3. A similar "Americas Commission" was proposed earlier in Richard Feinberg and Peter Hakim, *New Direction in US-Latin American Relations* (Washington: Overseas Development Council-Inter-American Dialogue, 1991).

proposed Americas Commission and revitalized trade and investment councils would report to the ministerials.

- *Trade and Commercial Forum.* To build political support for hemispheric integration, stakeholders should be given a voice in the process. A hemispheric forum was needed to bring together government trade officials and private business.

Submitted to the NEC Deputies Committee on Monday morning, 24 October, the recommendations on integration helped frame the discussion within the US government and, ultimately, the summit texts, which incorporated the basic thrusts of all five points (although the texts contained no explicit reference to NAFTA working groups).

Intensive Consultations

After the Canadians Barshefsky entertained the Chileans, led by the economist Andrea Butelmann. These discussions raised several interesting theoretical questions, such as whether the hemispheric free trade area should be open to Asians (Bowman Cutter's response: that's a problem for a later period but let's not close the door). Given Chile's status as next in line, the main focus was on the conditions the United States would set for NAFTA accession. Roger Altman assured the Chileans that fast-track renewal would be a top administration priority in 1995 and the odds for passage were reasonably good. The Chileans asserted that US commitment to a date certain for NAFTA accession would help overcome the US credibility problem.

In the talks with Caricom, the Caribbean delegates focused on the special problems of the Caribbean Basin and of small states. They complained bitterly about the recent administration decision to delete the Interim Trade Program from the 1994 legislative agenda and US opposition to the European Commission's banana regime, which gave preference to Caribbean producers. Jamaican Ambassador Richard Bernal proposed preferential treatment for smaller economies that would allow them to phase in concessions more gradually, noting that the APEC blueprint differentiates among countries by income levels. Barshefsky agreed that countries would be free to decide on their own timing for trade liberalization but demurred on the request for nonreciprocal granting of NAFTA parity. The Caribbeans also proposed that an existing multilateral organ such as the OAS be energized to foster a multilateral dialogue on trade integration.

Next came the Central Americans, who raised the idea of associate membership in NAFTA. Barshefsky offered to study the concept more closely after the summit. Some Central American delegates expressed caution over a much enhanced OAS role, and Barshefsky assured them that the United States would not multilateralize negotiations on NAFTA accession. She added that the United States would like the summit texts to mention NAFTA accession if other countries would agree.

The Mexican delegation agreed that NAFTA accession should be the core of hemispheric integration and that the NAFTA partners needed to design accession mechanisms. They expressed reservations about an enhanced OAS role and about a set date and suggested flexibility for small states.

When their turn came, the Andeans voiced a more widespread concern: that the US demand that labor and environment be on the integration agenda was thinly disguised protectionism. Like Caricom and the Central Americans, the Andeans also requested preferential treatment and gradual implementation of trade liberalization. Barshefsky responded firmly that the United States could not commit to asymmetrical treatment while noting that in a negotiation, phasing naturally arises. She stated her surprise at the differing views that countries held about the OAS and continued to probe for ideas on mechanisms. What role might the OAS and its Special Committee on Trade play? Could the trade and investment councils define readiness criteria (implicitly, for NAFTA accession) and advance liberalization toward convergence on functional issues? How could these be linked to a political process such as periodic ministerials? She posed questions about future summits, creation of an executive committee of countries, and even whether a new institution was needed (while underscoring that no multilateral forum would be the locus of negotiations).

The final session was with Mercosur. The Brazilians, who occupied the Mercosur chair during this period, opened with a statement of support for a hemispheric free trade zone but as a long-term objective and emphasized that it should build on subregional schemes. Fernando Petrella, the Argentine deputy foreign minister, also endorsed a hemispheric free trade zone, adding that Argentina's commitment to Mercosur did not exclude participation in other initiatives. Argentina offered a paper proposing exact dates—that a formal agreement be reached not later than the year 2000 and that free trade be achieved by 2015. Argentina felt that it was a basic bureaucratic rule that serious initiatives need timetables and did not shrink from the discipline implied by a set date.[4] Brazil and its close ally Uruguay expressed reservations about hard dates, suggesting it was preferable to allow NAFTA and Mercosur to mature at their own pace. Brazil feared that too much focus on hemispheric trade could detract from Mercosur.

4. Interview with Argentine Ambassador Fernando Petrella, 10 May 1996.

The Brazilians and Argentines enjoyed tweaking the United States. Reflecting what she had heard in earlier sessions, Barshefsky proposed that the summit texts pay homage to national sovereignty and the right of each nation to make its own decisions on trade. Brazilian delegation leader José Artur Denot Medeiros answered that Brazil had no problem with a mention of sovereignty, even if it would seem implicit. Barshefsky retorted that other countries had raised the issue, not the United States. "I didn't think you would have," the Brazilian mocked. Later, Barshefsky feigned shock that some countries were expressing opposition to an expanded OAS role. Brazil seized the opportunity to note that unlike in the past it now favored a stronger OAS role in trade policy. Ever fleet of foot, Barshefsky concurred that all must show confidence in the OAS. In a final note of levity, when Barshefsky queried whether democracy should be a precondition for participation in a hemispheric trade accord, Petrella wryly responded, "Why, is the US planning to relinquish democracy?"

Two weeks after these talks, the American people elected a Republican majority to both houses of Congress and sent to Washington a class of freshmen seemingly skeptical of international engagements and of free trade. But this looming cloud did not deter the administration from pursuing the course it had set out on toward free trade at the Asia Pacific Economic Cooperation (APEC) forum and the Summit of the Americas. The momentum of events carried the United States forward, irrespective of the shoals that lay ahead.

The outcome of the October trade discussions at the State Department was a new USTR draft trade initiative that was circulated throughout the hemisphere. It contained most of the concepts and even much of the language of the final summit texts. It endorsed a trade area in the Americas, called for comprehensive agreements, listed the NAFTA disciplines, and established a follow-up process consisting of ministerial meetings, an active OAS Special Committee on Trade fortified by the IDB and ECLAC, and reports from trade and investment forums (a reference to the USTR-led trade and investment councils). In deference to the Caribbean and Central American countries, the USTR draft recognized different levels of development and allowed for technical assistance to smaller economies. To accommodate Brazil and Mercosur, there were no direct references to NAFTA, and the draft referred to reaching "high levels" of disciplines rather than "highest levels," which would have been perceived as promoting NAFTA standards.

Some contentious points remained, however, and would be settled at a second round of consultations between Barshefsky and the subregional groups from 21 to 23 November and at a final all-parties negotiating session on 2 December. Brazil fought for and won several significant changes in the text aimed at lessening future US influence and leaving the integration process less carefully scripted (or more realistic and flexible, depending on one's point of view). Brazil deleted language that called for "improving disciplines" in subregional trade arrangements, which would be seen as a criticism of Mercosur standards. Brazil objected to USTR-proposed language that said, "We appreciate the United States' willingness to coordinate these (future) hemispheric meetings," and succeeded in inserting language directing the OAS to assist the host country in arranging the ministerial meetings. Brazil also deleted language that would have directed ministers to "determine the means of monitoring progress." But Brazil failed to gain support for its argument that it was premature to define the coverage and extent of commitments to be included in the free trade agreement; instead the Latin Americans added to the USTR-proposed list of disciplines areas in which the United States was seen as an offender of free trade precepts: agriculture, subsidies, safeguards, rules of origin and antidumping, and countervailing duties.

Just prior to this final round of negotiations, APEC had announced its 2020 free trade date. Argentina sent a strongly worded note to the US Department of State urging reconsideration of a date certain—an issue omitted from the USTR draft. Argentina warned that "If the APEC declaration is not balanced with a similar commitment by America, we will have surrendered the priority of US trade initiative to the Pacific."[5] Brazil was forced to accede to the Latin American majority and accept a date certain. As described in chapter 4, the US government also reconsidered when it became apparent that the success and credibility of the summit hinged on announcement of a date certain. The United States and other countries felt that the Argentine proposal of 2000 was too ambitious but agreed that credibility required early results and therefore concurred on language calling for "concrete progress . . . by the end of this century." The final Miami text called for the conclusion of negotiations for the Free Trade Area of the Americas (FTAA) no later than 2005.[6]

The remaining contentious issues of labor and the environment would keep negotiators at the State Department until 2 a.m. 3 December. The Latin Americans felt strongly that the United States was playing to its domestic political audience, and some questioned the very legitimacy of linking these issues with international trade. Whereas throughout earlier discussions the Latin Americans were often divided and coalitions shifted, here traditional battle lines were drawn. In the end, the United States held firm in its demand that the summit tie trade to labor and the environment, but the Latin Americans would accept only very watered-down

---

5. Letter from Ambassador Raul Granillo Ocampo to Charles Gillespie, US Department of State, 18 November 1994.

6. The FTAA acronym was selected because an earlier proposal, AFTA (American Free Trade Area), means "the sore in the mouth of cattle suffering from *aftosa*, or hoof-and-mouth disease," in Spanish.

language. The final text simply notes that free trade and economic integration "are key factors for raising standards of living, improving the working conditions of people in the Americas, and better protecting the environment." Countries agreed "to make our trade liberalization and environmental policies mutually supportive. . . . As economic integration in the hemisphere proceeds, we will further secure the observance and promotion of worker rights, as defined by appropriate international conventions." The Latin Americans made clear their distrust of US motives by demanding a pledge to "avoid disguised restrictions on trade."

In the end, the final text satisfied all parties. The Latin Americans and Caribbeans got what they most wanted from the entire summit process—promise of continued and expanded access to the US market as well as to the markets of their other hemispheric neighbors. The United States felt that the text had enough specificity to be credible and to make Miami a success for the president. The Brazilians were pleased that sufficient homage was paid to subregional accords, and any language smacking of US hegemony had been excised. An Argentine diplomat summed it up: "The trade initiative promised to create a network of discussions, to promote convergence, to initiate a process to bring the subregional blocs together, with modalities, an agenda, a schedule, a date. That was a great achievement."[7]

---

7. Interview with Argentine diplomat, 22 April 1996.

8

The Spirit of Airlie House

In early October 1994 the United States circulated to governments throughout the region a new composite draft declaration of principles and a plan of action with 17 initiatives and asked for comments by 21 October, promising to prepare and circulate fresh drafts in early November. If the original 14 initiatives were embryonic, the October and November drafts had assumed the shape and proportions of the future newborn. With each iteration, the draft was taking on the composite features of its many parents. Each participant could recognize some of its own traits and hence claim parentage. A consensual document was emerging.

An important problem remained, however: how to obtain the final approvals of governments. The United States considered having its ambassadors present texts directly to heads of state but concluded that presidents would demur and turn the texts over to their foreign ministries for comments. In the end, the United States accepted that it had no alternative but to bow to the long-standing desire of the Latin American foreign ministries to convene a traditional, all-parties conference. Experienced State Department diplomats had recognized early on that the Latin Americans would eventually insist on an all-parties preparatory conference to negotiate the final texts and included such a plenipotentiary meeting on internal planning charts. But the United States had feared that a 34-nation assembly, if convened prematurely, would incubate a nebulous, weak text. Now, after the innumerable rounds of consultations, conferences, and expert meetings, the well-formed offspring of months of consultations was beyond danger. All that was needed was the official blessing of legitimacy.

So the United States convened an all-parties meeting for 27-29 November at Airlie House, a conference center in Warrenton, Virginia, about 75 minutes outside of Washington. The site was conveniently close to the capital, but out of the glare of the media. Located in the rolling green hills of horse country, the center could be reached only by a narrow, rural road. The sleeping quarters were simple, even spartan, and the food was standard American fare. There was nothing to distract the conferees from their deliberations.

Some senior US policymakers were worried by intelligence reports focusing on the remaining complaints of some Latin Americans and Caribbeans, the purposeful posturing intended to wring last-minute concessions. The intelligence bulletins suffered from their usual bias: better to overemphasize the bad news than be caught napping and be accused of an intelligence failure. The result of this inherent bias in intelligence reporting was to spook some senior policymakers who were too removed from actual negotiations to place the alarmist intelligence reports in context and balance them with their own opinions. So some anxious senior administration officials were more prone to compromise to reach a consensus, fearful that the success of a presidential event hung in the balance. President Clinton, however, remained confident that "it will come together."[1]

Pre-Airlie Consultations

As the Airlie House finale approached, senior-level missions were dispatched to head off potential problems with Peru, Brazil, and the Caribbean Common Market (Caricom). Alexander Watson and Tony Gillespie traveled to Lima on 7-8 November. Peruvian President Alberto Fujimori's government, still isolated from hemispheric diplomacy after Fujimori assumed extraconstitutional powers in April 1992, had been a marginal participant in summit preparations. But Fujimori, at a mini-summit with President Bush in San Antonio in 1992, demonstrated that he could cause trouble when he loudly denounced US drug policy at a press conference. Watson, a former ambassador to Peru and extremely popular in Lima, listened carefully to Fujimori's concerns and assured him that the Peruvian point of view was being taken into account, including the sensitive counternarcotics issue, in which the United States was prepared to recognize that drug trafficking was a problem not only of Latin American supply but also of US consumer demand.[2]

Another US delegation flew to Brasilia to massage Itamaraty (the Brazilian foreign ministry) and President Itamar Franco.[3] Mack McLarty gained

1. Personal interview with Mack McLarty, Washington, 11 June 1996.

2. Personal interview with Alexander Watson, Washington, 3 June 1996.

3. Earlier pilgrimages to Brasilia are outlined in appendix A.

a firm commitment from Franco that he would include President-elect Fernando Henrique Cardoso in his Miami delegation.

On 17 November McLarty led a delegation to Jamaica to confer with the Caricom leaders. Once again, the English-speaking Caribbean focused more on their own problems than on broad summit themes. Some leaders chastised the United States for giving short shrift to the problems of small island states. At the time, McLarty felt sandbagged but in retrospect would recognize that the encounter served to give the Caribbeans the opportunity to blow off steam. Their mood would be more positive at Airlie House.

On 21-23 November Deputy US Trade Representative (USTR) Charlene Barshefsky held her second round of consultations with all the subregional groups in Washington and made it clear that the Clinton administration was prepared to commit to hemispheric free trade (chapter 7). The United States shifted from being a reluctant player to an aggressive advocate of a strong trade initiative.[4] Thus, before Airlie House commenced, Latin America had already obtained its principal summit objective: a US commitment to a preferential trading and investment arrangement with the Western Hemisphere. The US commitment generated goodwill that would grease discussions on the rest of the agenda at Airlie House.

The Final Offensive of the Rio Group

A week before the Airlie House conference was to begin, the Brazilians transmitted a Rio Group draft plan of action to the US government. Although resembling the latest US composite draft in structure and themes, it lacked much of its specificity. Short on specific action items, firm commitments, and accountable mechanisms for implementation, the Rio Group draft presented precisely the outcome that the United States had been working to circumvent and that cascading modular multilateralism intended to surpass.

The Airlie House conference was set to begin on Sunday evening, 27 November. The preceding Saturday morning, the shrewd head of the Brazilian delegation, Vice Minister Roberto Abdenur, invited a US team to the Brazilian embassy.[5] Abdenur proposed melding the US and Rio Group texts. He also wanted another conference, a full-blown ministerial, to review the handiwork of Airlie House and to deal with any remaining disputed language. Abdenur reassured the US team that he believed that

4. Similarly, Brazil, which at the beginning of summit preparation argued within the councils of the Rio Group that it was premature to consider hemispherewide measures and that nothing should be done that might divert energy from Mercosur, was also now a willing player. Brazil, too, had been boxed in by the other Latin American countries and dragged along by the quickening pace of summit preparations.

5. The US team included Alexander Watson, Tony Gillespie, and the author.

the Miami Summit was the first expression of a new, cooperative spirit of an emerging community of nations and that Miami would be part of an ongoing dialogue. The US delegation was not mollified. It was offended by Abdenur's preachy, paternalistic presentation, even as it respected his negotiating tactics—Abdenur cleverly positioned Brazil to be South America's chief interlocutor with the conference hosts. Tony Gillespie responded firmly to the Brazilian gambit: the United States would view an effort to put forth a subregional draft at this late date as decidedly not helpful. He also pointed out that the US text was a composite, printed in a variety of fonts, thereby identifying the source of the highlighted phrases by country and group of countries.

On Sunday morning, McLarty invited to breakfast Abdenur and the Brazilian ambassador to Washington, Paulo Tarso Flecha de Lima. Abdenur proudly cabled back to Itamaraty that McLarty said he had "great respect for Brazilian diplomacy."[6] Abdenur went directly from breakfast with McLarty to a Rio Group conclave where the Brazilians sought to stir up latent resentments against the United States, to foster fears that Washington would use the summit agreements to monitor their activities and intervene in their domestic affairs.[7]

On Sunday evening, 27 November, the delegations assembled in plenary session. As host of the conference and the summit, the United States assumed the chair (alternating between McLarty and Gillespie) and armed the secretariat with computers and printers capable of providing delegates with timely text revisions. Separately, Joan Spero headed the eight-member US delegation.[8] Only the Brazilian delegation was as large.

The declaration of principles was tackled first, and the review of the US-prepared composite text proceeded without major incident. But the critical question—Brazil's desire to meld the US and Rio Group composite texts of the more controversial plan of action—remained unresolved. McLarty sent a note to Abdenur reminding him that the United States and Brazil had to resolve key issues before the upcoming deadline. The upshot was a late night big-power parley between the Brazilian delegation and Alexander Watson and the author.

The midnight bilateral meeting focused on the economic initiatives in the US composite plan of action. The Brazilians pressed to make the text less binding, for example by altering some verbs from "commit" to "consider." The Brazilians dwelled on the nuances of each word, working

---

6. Personal interview with Brazilian diplomat, Washington, spring 1996.

7. Personal interviews with Latin American participants in that meeting, Washington, spring-summer 1996.

8. The US delegation included Alexander Watson, Bowman Cutter, Jeffrey Shafer, Mark Schneider, Kathleen McGinty, Harriet Babbitt, and the author. In addition, the United States fielded a support staff of at least 14 while the US-staffed secretariat numbered about 20.

hard to twist the Plan of Action in the direction of the Itamaraty world view. Yet as the conversation proceeded, Abdenur turned on one of his colleagues, the Brazilian liaison to the Rio Group, and criticized him for seeking a vague text. That signaled a turning point. The mood lifted further when Abdenur discovered his signature hat was missing. "Watson is too much of a gentleman to be culpable," the Brazilian diplomat said with a sly smile, "but Feinberg is another matter." The author quipped that he would return the hat when they had reached agreement on the texts.

The mini-summit adjourned at 2 a.m. Abdenur cabled Itamaraty that the "atmosphere between the United States and Brazil could not have been better."[9] Both sides had come to understand, Abdenur informed his colleagues in Brasilia, that the United States and Brazil were working together to ensure the success of the enterprise, a fact he took great pleasure in being able to report. The following morning, Abdenur told the other Rio Group countries that the United States was showing respect for the Rio Group text—taking a constructive attitude, and the Latin Americans could respond in kind. As the instigator of conflict, and having attained the respect and leadership role they had sought with such tenacity, the Brazilian diplomats could now play peacemaker.

On Monday morning, in accordance with understandings struck the night before, the Brazilians acquiesced and allowed the US-circulated draft to be the working document that guided the conference. In return, the chair allowed Brazil to circulate a document that displayed the US composite and Rio Group texts side by side. During the discussions, the United States also accepted three important stylistic suggestions of the Rio Group. The Latin Americans preferred to place the democracy sections of the texts up front, before the economic sections. Trade might be the single most important initiative, but for the Latin American diplomats politics would always trump economics: as one Latin American diplomat phrased it, the "more noble" concept should occupy the lead. The United States also agreed to group many of the points relating to follow-up mechanisms and events in an appendix. The Latin Americans felt this made the main body of the text cleaner and more presidential. From the US perspective, this appendix would underscore the importance that the summit leaders were giving to implementation.

The third Latin American concern grew out of a misunderstanding. The US composite text divided the action items under each initiative between those actions that were the responsibility of the international community and those under the aegis of individual governments. Inter-American Development Bank (IDB) President Enrique Iglesias had originally suggested this bifurcation, and the United States had accepted it in part because it assumed that Iglesias usually presented Latin American

9. Personal interview with Brazilian diplomat, Washington, spring 1996.

perspectives accurately. But some Latin Americans feared the United States would use the national actions category as an excuse to hold individual governments accountable and to monitor their behavior.[10] Because the summit texts were vastly expanding the scope of activities subject to collective action, the Latin Americans' fear of US meddling in their domestic affairs was heightened. For its part, the United States had seen the international-national categorization as a concession to Latin American opinion and so agreed readily to erase the subheadings.

With these matters addressed, the conference settled down to reviewing the US composite texts, each country spoke for itself, and each initiative was refined and approved in working groups and plenary sessions. Brazil had obtained US recognition of its status as a leader in South America and an effective chair of the Rio Group. The United States also preserved its primary objectives: the Airlie House conference was on track, much of the plan of action's specificity was intact, and the congenial atmosphere boded well for Miami.

The Triumph of Cascading Modular Multilateralism

The plenary sessions reviewed the US-circulated draft initiative by initiative. On any particular issue, leadership tended to devolve onto those countries with recognized authority and expertise. For example, delegates were aware that certain countries had been working on the anticorruption initiative and deferred to them on that issue. The anticorruption coalition was sufficiently large and representative of the various subregional groups to maintain plenary discussion momentum, discourage dissonance, and even strengthen the paragraphs on corruption.

The US composite draft declaration of principles mentioned corruption only briefly, as one item in a list of propositions to be undertaken to ensure continuing faith in democratic institutions. The anticorruption coalition—primarily Venezuela, Ecuador, Honduras, and Chile, strongly supported by Argentina and Colombia—successfully pressed for a full sentence and then proposed that sentence be set apart as a separate paragraph. The assembly concurred that corruption should be framed as not only undermining the legitimacy of political democracy but also as fostering social disintegration and distorting economic decisions. Coalition members asked and obtained support for a comprehensive attack on corruption (appendix D).

For the plan of action, the Rio Group text had subsumed corruption within a broader, more vaguely defined initiative on modernization of

10. Personal interview with Latin American diplomat, Washington, May 1996.

the state. The delegates agreed to lift some language from the Rio Group text but to subsume it under the umbrella of the corruption initiative: modernization of the state—that is, deregulation, privatization, and the simplification of government procedures—reduces the opportunities for corruption.

The conference strengthened the anticorruption initiative in two other respects. Both the US and Rio Group drafts implicitly targeted public corruption. Caricom advocated adding the problem of private-sector malfeasance. Language broadening the scope of the initiative was inserted: "Corruption in both the public and private sectors weakens democracy. . . ." Second, the US-circulated draft had simply tasked the Organization of American States (OAS) with developing a normative framework. The assembly crafted language that charged the OAS with negotiating a new hemispheric agreement on corruption that should include the extradition of individuals charged with corruption. Airlie House paved the way for the anticorruption convention that the OAS would complete in early 1996.

There were other examples of issue-specific coalitions defending their initiatives. When the plenary formed smaller working groups to redraft initiatives, the membership invariably included countries that played lead roles in developing those initiatives. A working group on the controversial civil society initiative was chaired by Trinidad and Tobago, in recognition of Caricom's leading role in placing the issue on the summit agenda. The English-speaking Caribbean was proud of its democratic tradition and was drafting its own Charter for Civil Society. However, for those Latin Americans rooted in more authoritarian or corporativist traditions, civil society smacked of political liberalism peculiar to the United States. Some Latin Americans feared civil society was merely code for those nongovernmental organizations, direct descendants of the old left, that claimed to represent the people and had no respect for constituted authority.[11] In the most paranoid Latin American formulation, US-based nongovernmental organizations (NGOs) were the latest incarnation of US interventionism.

The author sustained several long conversations in the spring of 1996 with the lead Mexican summiteer, Jorge Pinto, over the definition and political significance of civil society. Because of his personal interest in the topic, Pinto became the lead negotiator on the subject for the Rio Group.[12] Based on these bilaterals, Pinto and the author were able to reach agreement on the key issues confronting the working group, including a definition of civil society that included not only NGOs but also the private

11. This was Itamaraty's view. However, Brazilian foreign policy became more supportive of the civil society concept upon the election of Fernando Henrique Cardoso, because he and his wife had a long history of deep involvement in civil society organizations.

12. Personal interview with Jorge Pinto, New York, 9 April 1996.

sector, labor, and political parties.[13] The Latin Americans insisted that civil society associations had responsibilities as well as rights and that their activities should be transparent and accountable. Finally, Pinto and the author struck a deal: the author would sacrifice one of his pet projects—an action item in the US-circulated draft endorsing "the establishment of an OAS annual prize for democracy, governance, and civil society to recognize the outstanding contributions of individuals or groups"—in return for retaining consideration of a new IDB civil society program. The recommendations of the working group were promptly adopted by the plenary.

Coalitions broke down the North-South wall and allowed differences among Latin Americans to surface. The increasingly collegial atmosphere also contributed to frank discussion. For example, the energy initiative gave rise to intense intra-Latin American debate. Mexico fought hard for deletion of an item calling for regulatory reform to promote competitive energy development capable of attracting private investment because it would affect its own statist policies. Chile, with strong Central American support, temporarily persuaded the Mexican delegation to permit a reference to private-sector energy development, but higher authorities in Mexico City directed the Mexican delegation to revert to its hard line posture. The Chilean representative stated that if Mexico wasn't prepared to privatize its energy sector now, surely it would do so in the future.[14]

Compromise and Consensus

The US-circulated composite draft plan of action represented the maximal US position. The United States had no new initiatives to add and did not intend to seek to reinsert ideas from earlier drafts that had met resistance. For each initiative, the US interagency working groups had decided what was essential and what could be deleted under pressure.[15] The working groups also identified allies who could be relied upon to defend the draft initiatives.

The Brazilians and some other Latin Americans were intent on using the conference to render the plan of action more modest in its ambitions, less exact in its objectives, less specific in its timetables, and less accountable in its implementation. For example, the draft initiative on capital markets liberalization proposed consideration of a "Hemispheric Capital Movements Code" to provide for progressive liberalization of capital

13. Pinto also insisted that the disaggregated list include individuals.

14. Personal interview with a senior Chilean diplomat, Santiago, Chile, September 1996.

15. US Summit Consulting Office, "Airlie House Consultations: Executive Briefing Book (unclassified)," 25 November 1994.

restrictions. Brazil succeeded in deleting reference to a "code," replacing it with the softer "common guidelines."

Several countries took advantage of the conference to bring up ideas, slightly repackaged, that the United States or other countries had resisted earlier or to float new ones. Caricom overcame US resistance and inserted a sentence in the initiative on capital markets calling for a review of external debt problems. Argentina successfully advanced a separate initiative on confidence-building measures that essentially endorsed ongoing efforts in the OAS, spearheaded by Argentina, to reduce military tensions. Anodyne initiatives on promoting cultural values and stimulating tourism were proposed and adopted without fanfare. (Because their preparations scored very low on the "intensivity" continuum, it was predictable that little would be done to promote their implementation after Miami.) The total number of initiatives grew from 19 to 23. Given the large-group tendency toward laundry lists, it was remarkable that the number of initiatives grew by only 21 percent. The self-disciplined delegates realized that they were drafting a historic document.[16]

During those two days, the workmanlike atmosphere was interrupted only once by a vociferous outbreak against a US position, and this occurred on a purely stylistic matter: the title of the document. The United States had originally proposed "Partnership for Prosperity: Democracy, Free Trade and Sustainable Development in the Americas." The United States thought Partnership for Prosperity was a succinct sound bite with an upbeat, contemporary flavor. Brazil, however, wanted the more traditional "development" in the main title. They compromised on "Partnership for Prosperity: Democracy, Free Trade, Development, and Environmental Protection in the Americas." Unfortunately, the secretariat failed to incorporate this agreement in the next revision circulated to the plenary, leaving the delegates thinking that the debate over the title was still unresolved. This opened the way for a Caribbean delegate to insist that "sustainable development" remain in the subtitle. Since it would have been impossibly awkward for both "development" and "sustainable development" to appear in the subtitle, Brazil reverted to its earlier insistence on including "development" in the main title. In the face of an emerging consensus behind the original Brazilian formulation, Joan Spero made one last appeal for "elegance in this historic document." The plenary erupted in a chorus of "boos," and Spero had to relent. The summit document would bear the main title "Partnership for Prosperity and Development."

As the conclave came to a close, it was agreed that the texts would be referred to capitals for final approval, but except for a Canadian quibble

16. Personal interview with Alexander Watson, Washington, 3 June 1996; personal interviews with Latin American and Caribbean participants, spring 1996.

in the telecommunications initiative, governments proposed no further changes. Delegates told their ministers and heads of state that Airlie House had produced a truly consensus document. Moreover, delegations could point out their own contributions. Abdenur cabled back to Itamaraty that he was very happy with the outcome: Most Rio Group points were reflected in the final texts and the language had been raised to the presidential level. Abdenur found the Declaration of Principles "high-level, dense, strong, harmonious, and integrated as a set of ideas, principles, and values, to inspire future progress in working on democracy and development in the hemisphere."[17] Jorge Pinto was pleased with his additions on civil society and energy, as well as the recognition given to the rights of migrant workers in the human rights initiative.[18] Senior US officials were relieved that a good document was completed a full two weeks before the summit, and US experts were generally content that perhaps 75 percent of the meat of the initiatives remained intact.

The final document established a new agenda for the Western Hemisphere. It overcame the North-South divide by including the United States and Canada in its definition of the hemispheric community of nations. It dramatically expanded the scope for collective action in the hemisphere. It provided for action across an unprecedented range of issues, including political, economic, social, and environmental matters. It gave unusual attention to implementation mechanisms.

Certainly, the plan of action had its weaknesses. With 23 initiatives and more than 150 action items, it was too broad and ambitious. Many initiatives lacked clear priorities and timetables. Some diplomats may have felt reassured that they were not committing their governments to binding obligations backed by credible enforcement mechanisms. And outside of the existing resources of the multilateral development banks, no significant new financial resources were provided. Notwithstanding these shortcomings and omissions, most delegates were proud of their accomplishments and in the following days began to refer with evident satisfaction to the "spirit of Airlie House."

The Success of Airlie House

Airlie House succeeded for several reasons. The ascendancy of hemispherism and intellectual convergence around important political and economic values, accompanied by the end of the Cold War, had created the right preconditions. The near completion of the trade initiative had provided the immediate goodwill: "Countries were willing to make concessions to

---

17. Personal interview with Brazilian diplomat, Washington, spring 1996.

18. Personal interview with Jorge Pinto, New York, 9 April 1996.

the United States on such sensitive issues as drugs and the environment because they were looking at access to the US market—the big prize. It was a motivational, not a negotiated, linkage," according to a senior Brazilian diplomat.[19]

Certainly, the way the texts had been negotiated contributed to the smoothness of the Airlie House discussions. Bilateral, plurilateral, and issue-specific coalitions had yielded a cascade of agreements. Diplomats and experts throughout the hemisphere developed a stake in their initiatives and were prepared to defend them against those who would delete or diminish them. Throughout the months of discussions and draft exchanges, negotiators became familiar with concepts that at the outset were sometimes innovative and alarming. At Airlie House, there were a minimal number of surprises.

Some Latin American and Caribbean diplomats credited US flexibility. Jorge Pinto felt that "discussions moved fluidly because of the flexible, open US approach, which avoided polarizations. No one could complain of an absence of discussion. There was no imposition of anything on anyone."[20] A senior Caribbean diplomat noted, "The Rio Group was pushing against an open door."[21] In particular, delegates praised Tony Gillespie for skillfully chairing the plenary sessions, allowing open discussions, and sensing when to bring debate to closure. Mack McLarty was appreciated "for intuitively knowing what could be obtained and what could not."[22]

The summit itself was a final explanation for the success of the presummit preparatory process. As December approached, hemispheric leaders and diplomats came to realize that they had big political and economic stakes in the summit's outcome. The Airlie House diplomats understood that their leaders expected them to cable back "consensus achieved."

---

19. President Clinton noted this positive link in an interview reviewing his first term. "And the third issue is building a new structure of opportunity and peace through trade, investment and commerce. And that's NAFTA, GATT, 200 trade agreements, Ron Brown's 10 emerging nations initiatives, what I did with APEC leaders and what we did with the Summit of the Americas. See, I think that the commerce thing, I think it's been wrongly positioned as are you choosing money over values. It seems to me that if America is in the center of these emerging networks, it dramatically increases our leverage to work with people for peace, for human rights and for stability in the world." Interview with Alison Mitchell, "Despite His Reversals, Clinton Stays Centered," *New York Times*, 28 July 1996, 1.

20. Personal interview with Jorge Pinto, New York, 9 April 1996.

21. Personal interview with Caribbean participant, Washington, 22 April 1996.

22. Personal interview with the head of the Chilean delegation, Juan Martabit, Santiago, Chile, 13 September 1996.

9

Miami

I think you will see a good deal of concrete action that will leave the most determined cynic convinced that this was a historic meeting. . . .—Vice President Al Gore[1]

Latin Americans were not happy with the choice of Miami as the site for the summit. Latin Americans view Washington as a city of power and prestige, and Miami as a city for shopping and money laundering. South Florida is also the stronghold of the fiercely anti-Castro Cuban exile community. Latin Americans feared that the exiles might force Clinton to press for a strong anti-Castro declaration, which would be unacceptable to Latin American opinion, or might even, physically threaten summit participants. Some saw the Miami choice as another sign that the Clinton administration did not take Latin America seriously.

Most of the foreign policy experts in the administration agreed with the Latin Americans. Not only was Washington the seat of power, it was also the home of two major hemispheric institutions: the Organization of American States (OAS) and the Inter-American Development Bank (IDB). Washington was accustomed to hosting large international gatherings and could readily handle the complicated logistical and security arrangements. But several cities—including Phoenix, Chicago, and Miami—lobbied the White House hard to be selected as host for the summit. The president selected Miami. One motive was political: the president was traveling frequently to Florida in hopes of winning in November 1996 a state that

1. Al Gore, press briefing on upcoming Summit of the Americas, Old Executive Office Building, Washington, 8 December 1994.

he had lost by less than two percentage points in 1992. A summit would bolster his image and that of the local Democratic Party leadership. But there were deeper motives, which were foreshadowed in the selection of a Pacific Rim city (Seattle) to host the November 1993 Asia Pacific Economic Cooperation (APEC) summit. The choice of Miami spoke to Clinton's post-Cold War vision of hemispheric relations, a vision of common problems and convergent interests, a community of nations with dissolving borders and interdependent economies. Clinton put it in these words on 11 March 1994 when he announced his choice of Miami as the site of the summit:

> The diversity, the dynamism all make Miami an ideal site for this meeting. Miami's economy is fully integrated with the economies of Latin America and the Caribbean. In so many ways, it represents the promise of hemispheric integration. . . .

If Washington was the seat of the traditionally defined national security agenda, Miami, in the words of the president, was "a genuine multicultural, multiracial society that would be at the crossroads" of this emerging hemispheric community of nations. For Miami the summit was an opportunity to shine as the hub of the Americas. The Miami leadership mobilized its human and financial resources and the vibrancy of its ethnic and cultural melange.[2] Miami embedded the summit in a political and cultural reality that Washington could not hope to emulate.

Setting the Scene

At midday on Friday, 9 December, just hours before the formal opening of the summit, Clinton delivered a speech—his first major address on hemispheric affairs as president and the only one he would deliver during his first term—intended to lay out the main themes of the upcoming weekend's events.[3] They were the same three themes outlined in the memorandum to the president that had sparked the summit just one year earlier: to expand trade, strengthen democracy, and work collectively on a broad agenda of issues requiring collective action.

In this inaugural address, Clinton sought to place the summit in historical context:

> In our own century, President Roosevelt's good neighbor policy, as Vice President Gore said, sought to unite the hemisphere by urging mutual respect among all

---

2. A summit host committee was co-chaired by Governor Lawton Chiles, Lieutenant Governor Buddy MacKay, Metro-Dade County Manager Joaquin Avino, attorney Marilyn Holifield, *Miami Herald* publisher David Lawrence, and businessman Jorge Perez. Luis Lauredo served as executive director.

3. The speech was drafted entirely within the NSC and did not undergo interagency clearance, although agencies had the opportunity to propose language. Robert Boorstin was the lead speechwriter.

and recognizing even then, long ago, the importance of our interdependence. Three decades later, President Kennedy's Alliance for Progress inspired the peoples of the Americas with its vision of social justice and economic growth. Today, we can build on those foundations and do what could not be done in former times.

Speaking before a largely domestic audience, Clinton also rooted the summit themes in domestic interests and drew parallels between the problems facing the United States and those confronting the rest of the hemisphere. He emphasized the links between trade and jobs, drawing a Keynesian open-market vision of a hemisphere in 2005 with more than 850 million consumers with $13 trillion in buying power. US exports to Latin America could double by 2005, Clinton prophesied, exceeding those to Western Europe or Japan and creating more than 1 million new jobs. Already Florida was exporting $9 billion a year to its hemispheric trading partners. In a slap at the AFL-CIO, whose anti-North American Free Trade Agreement (NAFTA) leadership refused to attend the summit, Clinton ad-libbed, "Every American worker in every part of the United States should be glad we are all here today at the Summit of the Americas." But Clinton stopped short of announcing the Free Trade Area of the Americas (FTAA) or its completion date of 2005—saving that announcement for the summit itself.

Clinton also underscored the democracy theme. He noted that at the last hemispheric summit in 1967, 10 countries "suffered under authoritarian rule" and referred to the liberation of Haiti just two months earlier. In addressing the need to strengthen democracy, Clinton referred to his own vice president's reinventing government team.

Clinton stressed that environmental threats respect no border and that the countries of the hemisphere had to work together to fight polio, ban lead from gasoline, and conserve biodiversity.[4]

After the speech, Clinton attended several receptions—for the bipartisan congressional delegation of some 27 members, for the Miami Host Committee, and for the US nongovernmental sector that had provided funding or ideas for the summit. These corporate and nongovernmental organization (NGO) representatives were important constituencies for hemispheric integration whose energies would have to remain engaged for post-Miami implementation of the Plan of Action. On Saturday they would be hosted at meals and briefings by Clinton's entourage of cabinet and other senior officials. The White House provided these officials with a pocket-sized card summarizing the summit themes and US interests in the hemisphere (appendix F).

4. Bill Clinton, remarks at the Jackie Gleason Theater for the Performing Arts, Miami, 9 December 1994.

The Rhythm of the Summit[5]

The summit was choreographed to have three highlights, one per day, each building on the other. Friday was the presidential scene-setter speech. Saturday was the private meetings of the leaders that led to the announcement of the FTAA 2005. Sunday was the signing of the summit texts and the first step toward realization of the free trade area—the announcement that the three NAFTA members would negotiate accession with Chile.

Friday evening Clinton greeted the heads of state and government at the Biltmore Hotel (appendix G). The conversations were brief and light, just long enough for each visitor to be photographed one-on-one with the US president. The leaders proceeded to an adjacent room where, before an enthusiastic crowd of summit constituents, Clinton publicly welcomed his colleagues:

> [The] end of the Cold War has given all of us a great opportunity to build bridges where, for 50 years, only barriers stood. . . . Our goals for the summit are clear. We want to extend free trade from Alaska to Argentina, we want to strengthen our democracies, and we want to improve the quality of life for our people.[6]

The leaders then moved into the Granada Ballroom for dinner. There was no organized, group discussion. Clinton and Menem delivered brief toasts, and the social dinner actually broke early.[7]

Leaders' Meeting

On Saturday, Miami fulfilled its promise, and the day was warm and sunny. Saturday was the heart of the Miami gathering—the day-long, private meeting of the leaders in which they discussed the texts they would sign at the closing ceremony on Sunday. Clinton had enjoyed his roundtable discussion with Asia Pacific Economic Cooperation (APEC) leaders in Seattle in 1993, and this session was modeled on that earlier regional success. Leaders could be accompanied by one aide during two of the three scheduled sessions but would be alone during the third. For the United States, US Trade Representative (USTR) Mickey Kantor sat

5. For an illustrated review of the main events at the summit, see White House Report on the Summit of the Americas, *Building a Partnership for Prosperity* (Washington: White House, 1995).

6. Bill Clinton, remarks to leaders at the Biltmore Hotel, Coral Gables, FL, 9 December 1994.

7. Mrs. Clinton hosted a parallel dinner for her counterparts, and Secretary of State Christopher hosted the foreign ministers. The following day, Mrs. Clinton hosted a Symposium on Children of the Americas, where the first ladies discussed the Plan of Action initiatives as they related to children. See White House Report on the Summit of the Americas, *Building a Partnership for Prosperity*, 36-37.

behind the president during the first session on trade, and Secretary of State Warren Christopher was there for the session on democracy. These aides were armed with a white telephone connected to another aide (Samuel Berger for the United States) waiting in a side room.

This Saturday conclave was held in the Vizcaya Museum and Gardens, an Italian-Renaissance-style villa. A massive square table constructed for the event and decorated at the center with the large summit logo (the hemisphere in green against a blue background) filled the courtyard.

The private meeting was subdivided into two three-hour sessions, dedicated to discussing the Plan of Action's initiatives on economic integration and trade in the morning, sustainable development over a working lunch, and strengthening democratic institutions in the afternoon. The United States had polled governments about which session their leaders preferred to address and then proposed subthemes and specific initiatives for each leader based on preferences revealed during presummit negotiations; only two or three governments requested a change in assignment. The leaders stayed mostly within the bounds established by this choreography. A system of green, yellow, and red lights helped keep interventions brief.

Consensus on FTAA 2005

From the outset, it was apparent that the leaders shared a desire to establish an atmosphere of goodwill and consensus. Leader after leader endorsed the concept of the Free Trade Area of the Americas and the presidents of the two most populous Latin American nations, Zedillo of Mexico and Franco of Brazil, brushing aside their own governments' earlier reservations, blessed the target date of 2005. Leaders spoke about the links between free trade, growth, jobs, social progress, and democratic stability. Several speakers pushed the integrationist theme beyond the summit texts to include immigration but proposed no amendments to the Airlie House texts. It was clear that no leader intended to reopen the Airlie House consensus.

As chair, President Clinton acted to defuse potential dissonance on several occasions. When other leaders raised the immigration issue, Clinton distanced himself from California's antimigrant Proposition 187. He avoided citing NAFTA accession as the only path to hemispheric integration, instead calling upon the Mercosur countries to inform the assembly of their promising enterprise. When the Caribbean Common Market (Caricom) leaders raised their separate problems, Clinton reiterated his commitment to the Interim Trade Program and recognized their continuing problems with external debt.

To cap off the opening session, the leaders agreed to establish the Free Trade Area of the Americas by 2005. Clinton led the leaders out to the Vizcaya's formal garden, where he announced to the international press corps: "We are off to an excellent start. The 34 democratically elected leaders of our hemisphere have agreed to establish a Free Trade Area of the Americas. This historic step will produce real opportunities for more jobs and solid lasting prosperity for our peoples."[8] He called the agreement specific and concrete, with the deadline for negotiating the free trade area set for 2005. Posing for the cameras, the leaders first waved and then clasped and raised their hands in unison. It was a high-water mark in hemispheric convergence.

Sustainable Development and Democracy

After this announcement of FTAA 2005, Vice President Gore chaired the session on sustainable development. Gore focused at first on the Plan of Action's social initiatives, giving the floor to those leaders whose countries had championed initiatives during summit preparations. Violeta Chamorro broached women's rights, Patrick Manning discussed microenterprises, and Carlos Menem promoted his White Helmets. When the conversation moved to environment, the Central Americans spoke about their new Alliance for Sustainable Development, noting what a positive change it signaled compared to the conflict-ridden 1980s. (Later in the day, Clinton and the Central Americans signed CONCAUSA, whereby the United States pledged to assist the subregional sustainable development plan.) Several leaders offered examples of environmental problems that required international cooperation: Jean Chrétien spoke of poaching by fishing vessels flying flags of convenience, Caribbean leaders raised problems created by tourism, and Gonzalo Sánchez de Lozada cited mud slides that flowed from Bolivia into Paraguay. The Latin Americans and Caribbeans noted repeatedly that the industrialized nations ought to provide more financial and technical assistance. As one Caribbean leader put it, if the North could claim rights over hemispheric resources, it also incurred responsibilities to help. Gore replied that the Clinton administration had sharply increased US contributions to international environmental programs.

In the concluding session on democracy, the leaders in effect endorsed the Plan of Action's initiatives on good governance and anticorruption, increasing citizen participation and invigorating civil society, and collectively defending democracy. One after another, leaders denounced bribery, commissions, and money laundering and called for hemispheric cooperation to fight these transborder transgressions. Leaders concurred that their own executive branches, as well as the legislatures and judiciaries, must become more open, efficient, accountable, and honest. One speaker

8. *Building a Partnership for Prosperity*, 33.

went so far as to assert that in Latin America people consider any official who doesn't leave office enriched to be a fool. Again, the Latin Americans and Caribbeans called for more international assistance, this time to help with judicial reform and to fight the poverty that lay at the root of many of these social ills. The president turned the discussion toward narcotics, and the leaders reaffirmed the balanced approach of the summit texts in addressing demand as well as supply and trafficking.

Newly reinstated Jean-Bertrand Aristide led off the discussion on the collective defense of democracy by expressing his gratification to all of those nations that had helped restore democracy to Haiti. Central American presidents spoke about their experiences in overcoming fratricidal conflicts and improving human rights performance and of their current efforts to build more just and participatory democracies. Several leaders linked democracy promotion to the fortification of civil society, and a Caricom representative drew attention to their new Charter of Civil Society.

Brazilian President-elect Fernando Henrique Cardoso delivered an eloquent concluding statement. He admitted that before arriving in Miami he had not appreciated the momentous historical importance of the summit but that it was proving to be a true renaissance, a rebirth of the hemisphere. Cardoso added that the hemisphere was moving beyond zero-sum games and there was a clear will to address transborder problems collectively. President Clinton brought the private sessions to an end by noting that "Vizcaya" means "elevated place" in Basque, and that the villa had indeed been an appropriate location for the summit sessions.

The summit texts received the benediction of the heads of state and government, setting the stage for the formal signing the following day.

Dangers Averted

Many things that might have caused the summit to go awry would not materialize.

The administration and local Cuban-American leaders devised plans to keep the demonstrations peaceful and distant from the main summit events. An anti-Castro silent march had as its destination the Orange Bowl. In his scene-setter speech, Clinton drew applause from the large Miami contingent when he said he hoped that at the next summit "a democratic Cuba will take its place at the table of nations." But both the United States and most of the Latin Americans had no desire to insert an evidently divisive issue into the carefully negotiated consensus. When one leader raised Cuba during the Vizcaya discussion on democracy, others shelved it.

Alberto Fujimori had embarrassed George Bush at the 1992 mini-summit in San Antonio, and the president of Ecuador, dissatisfied with Johnson's foreign assistance package, refused to sign the communiqué at Punta del Este. But in Miami, all the leaders seemed to comprehend that it was in their own interests for the summit to succeed.

Some had feared the newly elected leaders of Mexico and Brazil would not be ready. Zedillo took office less than 10 days before Miami, and Fernando Henrique Cardoso was still president-elect, but both men performed well. Zedillo and Cardoso benefited from the considerable continuity in their governments and foreign ministries. Both leaders saw it in their interests to establish good relations with the president of the United States. Generally, Clinton was impressed by his counterparts and at one point during the Vizcaya deliberations leaned over to Gore and praised them as intelligent and impressive.

Initial media skepticism gave way to positive coverage as it became clear that the Plan of Action included important initiatives. FTAA 2005 fit into concepts the media could grasp as being part of a broader administration policy to open markets and create jobs. Passage of the General Agreement on Tariffs and Trade (GATT) in early December increased US credibility on its trade commitments. The enthusiasm of the Latin Americans infected the 3,000 journalists covering the summit. Coverage was more extensive, however, in Latin America than in the US media. The very absence of divisiveness in Miami discouraged coverage.[9] But the Clinton administration was also to blame for the modest coverage in the United States. Distracted by competing events, including a sudden presidential trip to Europe just days before the summit, the administration public affairs team failed to focus sufficiently on Miami and adequately explain its significance.

Signing of the Summit Texts

The Sunday morning closing plenary was witnessed by over 1,000 invited guests. The leaders were seated on stage at a horseshoe table, with their national flags and the summit logo as backdrops. Representatives of the major subregional groups spoke briefly.[10] Speaking on behalf of the Caribbean, Owen Arthur of Barbados proclaimed that such a summit would have been impossible 10 years earlier and improbable five years earlier and affirmed: "There is now a consensus that the chief vehicles for development are integration and trade." Representing North America, Ernesto Zedillo also lauded free trade and expressed the hope that future economic

9. For a survey of US media coverage of international issues as strongly predisposed toward reporting crises and conflicts, see Stephen Hess, *International News and Foreign Correspondents* (Washington: Brookings Institution, 1996).

10. The quotations that follow are from *Building a Partnership for Prosperity*, 43-45.

development would "reduce regional disparities and dissipate the current fears over migration." Speaking on behalf of Central America, José María Figueres of Costa Rica underscored the summit's pledge to bolster democracy: "We have learned from our own crisis that for democracy to grow it is necessary to dethrone corruption, increase the role of civil society in decision making. . . ." Representing South America, Itamar Franco drew attention to the new level of cooperation in the hemisphere, saying, "We are beginning a lasting process that will need to be constantly reactivated."

The heads of the main regional organizations also spoke. IDB President Enrique Iglesias, who had attended the 1967 summit at Punta del Este, noted that this time countries did not reiterate old demands but sought shared prosperity, with a new pragmatism and maturity, with democracy and a real economic capacity to address poverty. He pledged the IDB's newly replenished resources to advance the summit agenda. OAS Secretary General Cesar Gaviria declared that the summit signaled the end of distrust and fear and the creation of a new unity founded on common values. He lauded the leaders for completing the dismantling of the "wall which has so separated the North from the rest of the hemisphere." The Plan of Action presented a "pragmatic vision of the possible," he said, and sent a loud warning to would-be *golpistas* that the people they would crush will not stand alone.

Clinton delivered the plenary's closing remarks.[11] He emphasized the substance of the Plan of Action, referring to its "23 separate and specific initiatives and more than 100 action steps. . . ." Returning to the next chapter of summit implementation, Clinton said, "Our goal is to create a whole new architecture for the relationship of the nations and the peoples of the Americas to ensure that *dichos* become *hechos*, that words are turned into deeds." He ended with a rhetorical flourish: in the four languages of the hemisphere, he called on future leaders to remember the "spirit of Miami."

After the speeches, leaders came to sign the text from each side of the horseshoe table where they were waiting, arrayed by alphabetical order by country. This random pairing at the signing table produced some odd couples, such as the slight, left-wing Aristide and the heavy, right-wing Calderon Sol of El Salvador, but caught up in the emotions of the moment the two leaders embraced. When Ernesto Zedillo found himself with Eugenia Charles of Dominica, he took her hand and kissed it. Spontaneously, the other paired leaders shook hands as they signed the Declaration of Principles. It was a fitting finale.

---

11. Bill Clinton, closing remarks to the plenary session, James L. Knight Center, Miami, 11 December 1994, in USIA Wireless File, "Special Edition: Summit of the Americas in Miami," (11 December 1994), 10-11.

First Step toward Implementation

Immediately after the closing plenary, the leaders from the three NAFTA countries joined with President Eduardo Frei to announce their decision to negotiate Chile's accession. Chrétien stole the show with the comment, "For one year now, we have been the three amigos. Starting today, we will become the four amigos." This coda was meant to be the first step toward implementation of the summit vision.

10

From *Dichos* to *Hechos*

The transformation of *dichos* into *hechos*, words into deeds, in President Clinton's phrase, had been uppermost in the minds of the US summit planners. They did not want the Miami summit to suffer the same fate of the other two 20th-century hemispheric summits: festival followed by fizzle. During the pre-Miami negotiations, the United States built implementation mechanisms into most of the initiatives. At Airlie House, the Latin Americans suggested it would be clearer and more elegant to separate them, so the Plan of Action compiled the list of implementation mechanisms in an appendix. This in effect laid the foundations for a new inter-American system consisting of three pillars: the international organizations, ministerial meetings, and public-private sector partnerships (figure 10.1). The traditional inter-American system centered around the Organization of American States (OAS) (and the foreign ministries that control it) and Cold War security concerns. The new tripodal architecture expanded the inter-American system beyond the foreign ministries and their OAS instrument to encompass the many other government and private-sector players now active in inter-American affairs. The summit process thus redefined the system governing hemispheric relations.

The first pillar comprised the principal multilateral agencies that had received mandates from the summit: OAS, the Inter-American Development Bank (IDB), and the UN Economic Commission on Latin America and the Caribbean (ECLAC), headquartered in Santiago, Chile. By drawing the IDB into a wider range of issues, including some formerly considered political, the summit pulled the regional development bank toward the center of hemispheric affairs. The leadership of all three institutions

Figure 10.1 The postsummit inter-American system

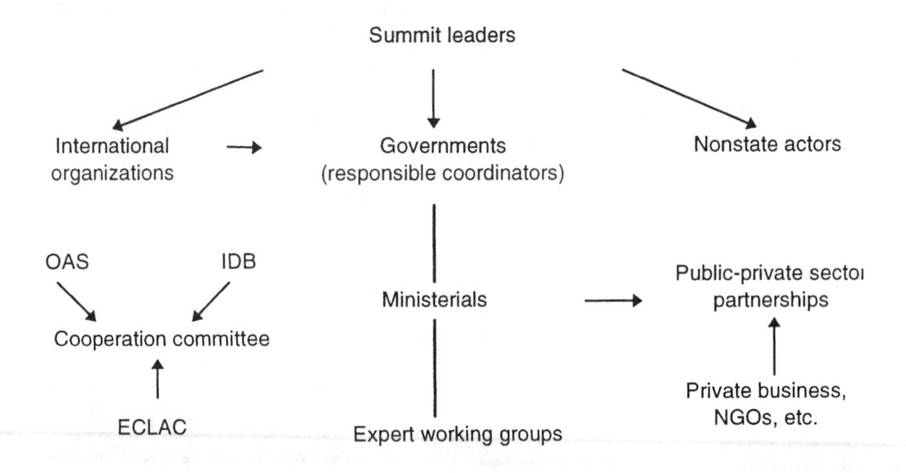

had been consulted frequently during summit preparations and considered the summit initiatives generally consistent with their ongoing programs. Some summit initiatives touched on the activities of more than one international organization. The Plan of Action called on both the OAS and IDB to help implement numerous initiatives, including those on trade, human rights, corruption, narcotics trafficking, cultural values, science and technology cooperation, and pollution prevention. Partly in response to these overlapping summit mandates, the IDB, OAS, and ECLAC decided to activate a tripartite cooperation committee to coordinate their activities.[1]

The second pillar of this newly emerging inter-American system was the series of ministerial and expert-level meetings that expanded participation beyond the foreign ministries to engage the functional agencies. The Plan of Action proposed meetings to advance initiatives dealing with money laundering, narcotics, terrorism, trade, finance, science and technology, health, energy, and sustainable development. These were the agencies with the expertise and resources to carry out the leaders' directives.

The third pillar consisted of the public-private sector partnerships. The nongovernmental actors (NGAs) had fought, with remarkable success, to gain an endorsement of their participation in summit follow-up. Fourteen

1. The growing overlapping of jurisdictions between the OAS and IDB reflected the gradual breaking down of the old categories of "politics" and "economics." Increasingly, it was recognized in academic and policy circles that issues formerly considered politics, such as judicial systems, affected economic development, while economic issues such as health, education, and poverty alleviation had important political dimensions. The push toward greater collaboration between the OAS, controlled by the more political foreign ministries, and the IDB, controlled by economics ministries, reflected at the institutional level this theoretical grasp of political economy.

initiatives were singled out as appropriate for input by the nonstate sector through public-private partnerships. The Plan of Action called for such partnerships for several initiatives in which the NGAs had been especially involved during summit preparations, including microenterprises and sustainable development, as well as in other areas in which they had not played a particularly significant presummit role, such as in infrastructure and cultural values.

This new architecture flowed directly from the way the summit texts had been negotiated. As described in chapters 5 and 6, decentralized functionalism had involved the experts in many US government agencies, who through modular multilateralism had interacted with their counterparts in other countries. These discussions strengthened existing networks and built new ones. For example, individuals interested in combating corruption, part of the informal anticorruption coalition that wrote the summit corruption initiative, were now aware of their common concerns. Moreover, they had built into their initiative a series of steps that required their continued participation and joint action.

These three pillars could and did work together in carrying out some initiatives. As will be explained below, in the trade initiative, the multilateral agencies prepared reports for ministerials, and private sector representatives and government officials devised regular channels for exchanging information and policy advice.

Two New Engines: The Summit Implementation Review Group and Responsible Coordinators

During 1995-96, summit implementers devised two additional mechanisms to monitor and energize postsummit activities. The summit had created mechanisms for carrying out specific initiatives but had not mandated a mechanism to oversee the whole process. At first, the United States suggested forming an executive committee with representatives from the foreign ministries of the major subregional groups to monitor implementation, but countries wanted direct representation, so an all-parties Summit Implementation Review Group (SIRG) was formed. With representation at the vice ministerial level and below, and with officials from the OAS, IDB, ECLAC, and Pan American Health Organization (PAHO) also present, the review group met seven times during 1995-96 to monitor and guide implementation.[2] In its capacity as summit host, the United States chaired the sessions.

2. The review group met during 1995 on 6 March in Washington; 5 May in San Salvador, El Salvador; 26 May in Washington; and 19 September in Washington. In 1996 it met on 22 January in Santiago, Chile; 17 May in Kingston, Jamaica; and 1 October, in Washington. Sessions were also held to discuss summit implementation at the OAS General Assem-

In turn, the group created a system of responsible coordinators intended to decentralize and energize implementation and to disperse leadership throughout the region. The system—clearly an offspring of cascading modular multilateralism—suggested that countries volunteer to coordinate initiatives of special interest to them. Not surprisingly, countries that volunteered to serve as responsible coordinators were the same countries that had been leaders in composing the relevant initiatives during the presummit negotiations. Thus, Venezuela became the responsible coordinator for corruption (with Honduras and the OAS as co-coordinators), Argentina took the lead on terrorism and White Helmets (a rapid-reaction international assistance corps), and Nicaragua volunteered to coordinate the women's rights initiative (for a full list of responsible coordinators, see appendix H). The review group defined the tasks of coordinators to include convening meetings, communicating information, developing work plans, mobilizing resources and attention, and reporting activities to the review group. Coordinators could ask the international organizations for assistance as needed.

Putting the Plan in Action

The summit did not mandate a systematic effort, public or private, to monitor implementation of the Plan of Action. To begin to fill this void, the North-South Center of the University of Miami and the Institute for International Economics commissioned papers to assess progress on 12 of the initiatives—those on democracy, human rights, civil society, corruption, narcotics, education, women's rights, energy, pollution prevention, biodiversity, capital market liberalization, and trade integration.[3]

What follows is an initiative-by-initiative review of progress toward implementation of the summit's Plan of Action that draws heavily on

blies, in Haiti in June 1995 and Panama in June 1996. At the October meeting, four additional sessions were scheduled for 1997.

3. These papers were presented in draft at a workshop in Washington on 29 May 1996 and published as working papers by the North-South Center, University of Miami, in October-December 1996. They include: Richard L. Bernal, "Developing and Liberalizing Capital Markets"; Kimberly Ann Elliott, "Combating Corruption"; Eduardo A. Gamarra, "Combating Illegal Drugs and Related Crimes"; International Center for Research on Women and the Inter-American Dialogue, "Strengthening the Role of Women in Society"; Jeffrey M. Puryear, "Reforming Education Systems"; Robin I. Rosenberg, "Invigorating Civil Society Participation"; José M. Salazar-Xirinachs, "Promoting Free Trade in the Americas"; Michael Shifter and Sean Neill, "Guaranteeing Democracy and Human Rights"; Justin Ward, Arturo García-Costas, S. Jacob Scherr, and Robert Watson, "Building Sustainable Development Partnerships."

Table 10.1 Implementation of the Plan of Action

Initiative	Progress	Architecture	International organization involvement	Public-private partnership
Democracy/human rights	**	**	***	*
Civil society	****	***	****	****
Corruption	***	**	*****	**
Narcotics and money laundering	**	**	***	–
Education	**	**	**	**
Women's rights	**	–	**	*
Energy	***	****	***	****
Pollution prevention	***	**	***	***
Biodiversity	–	–	–	–
Capital market liberalization	**	***	***	**
Trade	**	****	***	***

Ratings: ***** = strong, ****= very good, *** = good, ** = modest, * = minor,
– = very little movement (see footnote 4, below)

Progress: Rating of progress toward implementation of initiative's action items in summit's plan of action.

Architecture: Efficacy and depth of implementation mechanisms composed of one or more elements in the tripodal architecture together with the initiative's responsible coordinator.

IO Involvement: Involvement in terms of leadership, ideas, and resources, of the IDB, OAS, PAHO, and ECLAC.

Public-private partnership: Engagement and access to decision making of NGAs, including NGOs and the private corporate sector.

those papers.[4] Table 10.1 summarizes progress on these 12 initiatives. The papers and table necessarily emphasize international activities because little systematic information was available on implementation at the national level.

Democracy and Human Rights

When Brazil and Canada volunteered to be responsible coordinators, they proposed combining the democracy and human rights initiatives, and at

4. The ratings in table 10.1 and the following descriptions are solely the responsibility of the author. In some cases, they include information drawn from sources other than the workshop papers, including unpublished official sources, and interviews by the author with participants, as well as the author's own participation in summit implementation.

their request the OAS's Special Committee on Inter-American Summit Management established a working group on democracy and human rights. Interestingly, the working group's co-chairs were drawn not from foreign ministries but from Brazil's Ministry of Justice and Canadian human rights commissions.[5] To date, the working group had listed ideas for pilot projects but had not begun implementation of any. The OAS relied primarily on its Unit for the Promotion of Democracy to carry out these summit initiatives. As called for in the Plan of Action, the OAS increased the unit's budget and broadened its mandate. Consistent with the summit text, the unit focused on reforming electoral laws and supervising electoral observation teams and broadened its range of activities to include programs on local conflict resolution, postconflict peace-building programs in Central America and Haiti, and the strengthening of legislatures. But with a budget still less than $4 million, the unit lacked the necessary resources to catalyze the member states to fully act on summit initiatives. Nevertheless, six more countries ratified the Washington Protocol, which provides for the expulsion of a state from the OAS if democratic rule is interrupted.

Without a system to track what individual countries are doing to carry out the Plan of Action, it is impossible to evaluate their national-level implementation of the democracy and human rights initiatives. Anecdotal examples of progress include six countries that established human rights ombudsmen. In the spirit of the summit, Brazil launched its national human rights plan in May 1996. Certainly many countries in the region undertook some of the prodemocracy reforms endorsed by the summit, as the democracy wave that surged in the 1980s continued to swell. There were no cases of forced interruptions of democratic rule.

In their contributions to the workshop convened by the Institute for International Economics and the North-South Center, Michael Shifter and Sean Neill concluded that "The Plan of Action may have accelerated somewhat" the gains on democracy and human rights, however, "progress to date has been slow and diffuse."[6] Perhaps more important than any individual action item, the symbolism of 34 democratically elected leaders declaring democracy the sole legitimate form of government undoubtedly affected political attitudes and the willingness of governments to act collectively to defend democracy. When General Lino Oviedo threatened Paraguay's constitutional order in April 1996, a unified hemisphere forced the strongman to retreat and helped to restore civilian authority. Most significantly, the foreign ministers of Brazil and Argen

5. José Gregori, chief of cabinet of Brazil's minister of justice, and Mary MacLennon, chair of the Nova Scotia Human Rights Commission and a member of the Canadian Human Rights Commission.

6. Shifter and Neill, "Guaranteeing Democracy and Human Rights," 5.

tina descended on Asunción and threatened to expel a nondemocratic Paraguay from Mercosur. It is difficult to overstate the historical significance of this willingness of South America's largest economies to intervene—boldly and openly—in the domestic affairs of another Latin American state. The United States joined in the hemispheric chorus denouncing Oviedo and backed Mercosur's tough diplomacy with its own threat of economic sanctions. OAS Secretary General Cesar Gaviria flew to Asunción to place his moral weight behind constitutional continuity and to help stabilize the rule of President Juan Carlos Wasmosy.

A few days after returning from Asunción, Gaviria said, "The summit cemented the understanding that any military coup would be isolated. The summit strengthened the legitimacy of collective actions to defend democracy and made it clear that democracy is the sine qua non for hemispheric economic integration and the standing of all of the Latin American countries."[7]

Civil Society

The drafters of the summit texts proposed to invigorate civil society by calling for involvement of civil society in political decision making and for the formation of 14 public-private sector partnerships to help carry out specific summit initiatives.

There has been real progress on all the action items enumerated in initiative number three. During Airlie House, the Latin Americans had weakened the verb from "endorse" to "consider" directing the IDB to develop a civil society program. Mexico and Brazil vetoed such a fund in the IDB executive board in 1995, but IDB management and staff have nonetheless sought to embody the spirit of the initiative by attempting gradually to make NGA participation an important part of many bank projects.[8] Furthermore, the IDB's new Unit of State Reform and Civil Society, with the US Agency for International Development (USAID), undertook the summit-mandated review of national regulatory frameworks for civil society participation.

Table 10.1 displays the degree of nongovernmental participation in other summit initiatives. Where public-private sector partnerships have failed to form, the fault may lie with government inactivity or inaccessibility or with the NGAs themselves for failing to seize opportunities. In some areas, participation has been highly visible. More than 1,000 corporate executives attended the private-sector sessions held in conjunction with the trade ministerials in Denver in June 1995 and Cartagena, Colombia, in March 1996. The Council of the Americas, the Consejo Empresario de

---

7. Personal interview with Cesar Gaviria, Washington, 13 May 1996.

8. Personal interview with IDB senior official Steven Quick, Washington, 11 June 1996.

América Latina (CEAL), and the Consejo Interamericano Para el Comercio y la Producción (CICYP) organized a private-sector meeting at the May 1996 meeting of finance ministers in New Orleans. The agenda for the December 1996 meeting in Santa Cruz, Bolivia, on sustainable development was prepared with assistance from the World Resources Institute and an elaborate system was established to facilitate consultations with scores of NGAs from around the hemisphere. In the North-South Center paper on civil society, Robin Rosenberg concluded that, "As perhaps its greatest contribution, the Miami process will continue to unleash an unprecedented series of opportunities for direct civil society participation in the policy process . . . where the private sector and other NGAs not only will continue to pursue meaningful involvement in hemispheric policy formulation but will also press for a strengthening of government commitments to such involvement."[9]

Corruption

Combating corruption was one of the summit's early success stories. The same coalition responsible for the summit initiative drove implementation: the United States, with its interest in making multilateral the ban on bribery by international business, worked with Venezuela and other Latin Americans interested in pursuing and punishing bribe takers and other corrupt officials.

Venezuela volunteered to be the responsible coordinator for this initiative with Honduras and the OAS as co-coordinators. The summit initiative called on the OAS to develop a hemispheric approach to acts of corruption "through negotiation of a new hemispheric agreement or new arrangements." President Caldera's government promptly submitted draft language for an inter-American convention, and the OAS's Working Group on Probity and Public Ethics, chaired by Edmundo Vargas Carreno (who had played an important role in drafting the summit initiative), negotiated the text with member governments. On 29 March 1996 a special conference of the OAS produced the Inter-American Convention Against Corruption, which 21 countries immediately signed. Article VIII in effect internationalizes the Foreign Corrupt Practices Act of the United States by obliging signatories to criminalize transnational bribery. As Venezuela wanted, the convention provides for extradition, mutual legal assistance, seizure of assets, and technical assistance in the battle against corrupt acts. The convention ". . . is the only treaty instrument addressing the problem of corruption, and it is the first cooperative agreement on this issue negotiated by both developed and developing countries."[10]

---

9. Rosenberg, "Invigorating Civil Society Participation," 11-12.

10. Elliott, "Combating Corruption," 7. Two countries must ratify the convention for it to enter into force. In the United States, Senate approval will be required.

The convention incorporates domestic reforms emphasized in the Plan of Action, including establishing conflict-of-interest standards and facilitating public access to information. The convention even went beyond the language of the initiative to incorporate the broader spirit of the summit by encouraging "participation by civil society and nongovernmental organizations in efforts to prevent corruption."

However, the treaty is weak in important respects. Article 10 requires a member state to notify the OAS when it has adopted the legislation making transnational bribery and illicit enrichment crimes, but the treaty does not explicitly provide for monitoring or review by the OAS or any other body. Second, signatories only "agree to consider" the applicability of important measures within their own institutional systems. Nor are there any follow-up steps specified in the convention for encouraging or monitoring implementation of these measures. As Elliott noted, the ultimate effect of the convention will depend on whether "the troops—the NGOs, business firms, and the media"—keep the pressure on.[11]

Politically, the convention responded to the original US motivation in placing corruption on the hemispheric agenda: to deprive authoritarians of the anticorruption banner and to begin to identify democracy with honesty in government. In a very short time, in the Western Hemisphere corruption had journeyed from being a forbidden theme to becoming an issue in which the United States and Latin America together had assumed leadership on an issue suddenly of importance worldwide.

Education

In contrast to anticorruption activity, the education initiative has moved forward slowly on several fronts. Mexico agreed to be the responsible coordinator (President Zedillo had been Minister of Education), but the preliminary background document it presented to the SIRG at its January 1996 meeting was not ready for implementation and the somewhat more elaborated Action Plan presented to the March 1997 SIRG was still well short of an actionable policy proposal. USAID had spearheaded the initiative as a vehicle for promoting its partnerships for educational reform. Hillary Clinton announced launchings of these partnerships at the annual conferences of Hemispheric First Ladies in Asunción, Paraguay, in October 1995 and in La Paz, Bolivia, in December 1996. USAID finally approved a grant of $1.1 million a year over five years in September 1996. This funding will allow the Inter-American Dialogue (which had worked with USAID to design the summit initiative) to launch a consortium of public and private groups aimed at promoting policy reform through a

11. Elliott, "Combating Corruption," 7.

series of workshops, policy publications, and monitoring.[12] These USAID-funded partnerships are very similar in purpose to the ongoing IDB-funded Program to Promote Education Reform in Latin America and the Caribbean (PREAL), and the two may eventually be joined.

In preparing for Miami, the United States had asked the IDB to help design the social initiatives, but the bank had been too involved in grappling with the fallout from its own eighth replenishment and an internal reorganization.[13] In its emphasis on social programs, that replenishment was generally consistent with the summit texts, but the IDB ignored many of the specific action items in the summit's social initiatives. It did not, for example, seek to monitor national attainment of the education initiative's targets of a primary completion rate of 100 percent and a secondary enrollment rate of 75 percent, nor did it seek to increase lending to lagging countries. While consistent with the summit initiative, its education project remained a small, low-key effort.

The education initiative had not been controversial. There was widespread agreement in the hemisphere that educational systems were a weak link in the region's development and were badly in need of greater attention and reform. Why, then, was there not more energy behind the education initiative? The low-intensity presummit consultations led by USAID had not generated much enthusiasm. The summit did not place any institution in charge, and the proposed implementing mechanism—the consultative partnerships—was inchoate. No new resources were provided, despite the fact that the presummit negotiations had expanded the list of goals. Furthermore, neither Mexico as responsible coordinator nor any of the international institutions sought to provide strong leadership. But a few dedicated individuals, mainly in USAID and a US-based think tank, did keep the education initiative alive.

Women's Rights

Because issues having to do with women's rights permeate so many aspects of societal decision making, progress toward carrying out that summit initiative is particularly difficult to assess. Many of the initiative's action items require decisions by national governments, and the summit did not specify a way to monitor them. Nicaragua, which took on the mantle of responsible coordinator, lacked the resources to follow up. The Nicaraguan Institute for Women (INM), which had also participated in preparing for Miami, had applied to the IDB for a budget to coordinate

12. For a fuller description of these programs, see Puryear, "Reforming Education Systems," 3-5.

13. Personal interview with IDB senior official Steven Quick, Washington, 11 June 1996.

the women's rights initiatives but as of this writing had not cleared all the bank's bureaucratic hurdles.

Two of the nongovernmental organizations (NGOs) that had promoted the initiative—the International Center for Research on Women (ICRW) and Inter-American Dialogue—surveyed international actions.[14] They found that:

- the IDB was establishing a Women's Leadership and Representation Fund to promote female participation in public and civic life and had commissioned ICRW and the Dialogue to help identify factors impeding women's integration and to provide policy recommendations;
- the only visible initiative to promote women's economic potential was the IDB's microenterprise lending, which benefits women disproportionately; also, the OAS's Inter-American Commission on Women and PAHO had signed a cooperative agreement to work on the problem of violence against women;
- PAHO was helping national public health services to reduce maternal mortality to one-half of 1990 levels by the year 2000, as specified in the summit initiative on health;
- women's rights issues were rescheduled to be addressed at several upcoming international meetings.

The ICRW Dialogue paper concluded that "much of what has been accomplished at and post-Miami is at the level of statements— *dichos*— rather than action. In the case of initiative 18, *dichos* may be a sign of progress, if governments take these issues seriously. . . ."[15]

The women's rights initiative of the Miami summit suffered from inadequate follow-up, tracking, and budgetary resources and the failure to establish clear priorities among its many ambitious goals. Moreover, although interested NGOs could keep the initiative alive, they did not have the leverage or resources to coerce the United States or other major governments into action. But, along with other major international conferences such as the United Nations Conference on Women held in Beijing in 1995, the summit of the Americas elevated women's rights on the international agenda. As a result, several international organizations, including the OAS, IDB, and PAHO, were probably emphasizing women's rights more than they might otherwise have done.

---

14. International Center for Research on Women and the Inter-American Dialogue, "Strengthening the Role of Women in Society," 3-9.

15. International Center for Research on Women and the Inter-American Dialogue, "Strengthening the Role of Women in Society," 9.

Counternarcotics

In the 1980s, counternarcotics became a very divisive issue in inter-American relations. Latin American and Caribbean nations argued that US demand was the chief factor fueling the drug trade, but US officials accused other countries of not doing enough to stem production and trafficking. By the early 1990s, it was recognized in official circles that both supply and demand were driving the drug trade, and the Clinton administration sought to fashion a balanced approach to tackling production, transshipment, and consumption. But politicians and the media throughout the hemisphere continued to blame other countries for not doing enough to combat the narcotics industry. Latin Americans were particularly upset with the certification process required by US law whereby the US president each year unilaterally judges whether countries have cooperated fully with the United States in combating narcotics.[16]

Several countries had told Vice President Gore that narcotics should be on the summit agenda, and he had concurred. Yet State Department efforts to negotiate a presummit consensus on a counternarcotics strategy for the 21st century foundered against the objections of major coca-producing countries and concerted efforts by Brazil to prevent the narcotics issue from being high profile at Miami. Discussions spearheaded by the US government eventually yielded agreement on an initiative that, in broad terms and with few concrete follow-up steps, called for an integrated, balanced approach to combating all aspects of drug trafficking and that ratified the basic components of previous international agreements.[17] More innovative was the antimoney-laundering proposal Colombia pushed, which began as a separate initiative but which was eventually folded under the counternarcotics umbrella. It called for legislation to permit the proceeds of money laundering to be frozen and forfeited, forfeited assets to be shared among governments, and effective procedures to allow the collection of relevant information from financial institutions to be developed. The initiative approved at Airlie House called for a ministerial meeting to consider an inter-American convention to combat money laundering.

In assessing implementation of the counternarcotics initiative, Eduardo Gamarra concluded, "Overall there has been progress toward satisfying [its] basic outline."[18] Some progress was made on developing programs

16. For a summary of the 1996 certification process, see State Department, Bureau for International Narcotics and Law Enforcement Matters, *International Narcotics Strategy Report,* (Washington: US Department of State, March 1996), xii.

17. These included the 1988 UN Convention Against the Illicit Traffic of Narcotics and Psychotropic Substances (the Vienna Convention), the Cartagena Agreement of 1989, and the San Antonio Declaration of 1992.

18. Gamarra, "Combating Illegal Drugs," 2.

to reduce the demand for illicit drugs; the IDB, OAS, and the UN Drug Control Program have been working with NGOs to mount demand-reduction programs in several countries. In the United States, demand trends in the 1990s have been mixed, with the total number of illegal users having declined sharply since the mid-1980s. But the number of hard-core users remains high, and teenage drug use seems to have jumped since 1992.[19] Summit pledges to cut the cultivation of crops used for illicit drugs achieved few short-term gains, and overall coca production in Latin America actually increased.[20] Many countries have taken steps to adopt laws to control precursor chemicals. Spurred by Mexico, the summit called for a global counternarcotics conference, and the United States dropped its earlier opposition and agreed to a 1998 Special Session of the UN General Assembly for that purpose. The OAS, through its Inter-American Drug Abuse Control Commission (CICAD), ultimately reached agreement on a comprehensive 42-point "Anti-Drug Strategy in the Hemisphere" in December 1996; but governments had yet to determine priorities or assign resources. Most significantly, a ministerial conference in Buenos Aires in December 1995 approved a strong declaration criminalizing money laundering and laying foundations for cooperation among financial regulatory agencies (agreements underscored at the meeting of finance ministers in New Orleans in May 1996).

If there was some progress toward implementing components of the summit initiative, by 1996 drugs had again become a highly contentious issue in inter-American relations. The US campaign against Colombian President Ernesto Samper—which included decertification of Colombia, the lifting of Samper's visa, and a series of hostile public statements by the US ambassador and the State Department's senior antinarcotics official—touched raw nerves even among those Latin Americans who felt little sympathy for Samper himself. US pressures to unseat an elected Latin American head of state, and US threats to raise tariff barriers against some Colombian imports, were widely seen as being inconsistent with the spirit of Miami.

Sustainable Development: Energy, Pollution Prevention, Biodiversity

Having been leaders in the preparations for Miami, the government of Venezuela (through its Ministry of Energy and Petroleos de Venezuela) and the US government (through its Department of Energy) became joint responsible coordinators for the two energy initiatives. They co-hosted a hemispheric energy symposium in October 1995. At the symposium, countries agreed to create a steering committee, which in turn grouped

19. Gamarra, "Combating Illegal Drugs," 3.

20. Gamarra, "Combating Illegal Drugs," 3.

the summit commitments into eight outcomes, each of which was the responsibility of one country.[21] Each outcome leader was to develop work plans with action items. The IDB, World Bank, and United Nations Development Program (UNDP) pledged to work closely with the region's energy ministries.[22] Private-sector representatives also attended the symposium, and each outcome leader was charged with involving private-sector firms.

Whether this elaborate committee structure yields tangible results remains to be seen. So far, the steering committee has focused on conducting additional studies, compiling data, and exchanging information. The vigorous working group on clean energy is designing regulatory frameworks and has identified some 10 projects worthy of finance. Natural Resources Defense Council (NRDC) analysts judged that "Notwithstanding progress in some areas, the sustainable energy implementation process has tended to concentrate more on formulating new blueprints for action rather than following through concretely with existing commitments."[23] Nonetheless, the energy partnership has managed to catalyze a hemispheric process that promises to eventually yield some concrete results.

In November 1995 the US Environmental Protection Agency, the OAS, and PAHO co-sponsored a technical meeting on pollution prevention. Of the various topics addressed at the Puerto Rico meeting, the phase-out of leaded gasoline has developed the most momentum. The World Bank coordinated a comprehensive survey to collect information on the technical, economic, and political barriers to the phase-out in various countries. The survey found that five countries (Bermuda, Bolivia, Brazil, Colombia, and Guatemala) were using lead-free gasoline by 1995, with another five countries (Argentina, Costa Rica, El Salvador, Honduras, and Nicaragua) planning to be lead-free by the end of 1996. Four other countries plan to be lead-free by the year 2000 (Barbados, Ecuador, Mexico, and Trinidad and Tobago).[24]

NRDC analysts concluded that "since the Summit of the Americas, there has been no intergovernmental activity focused on implementation of the biodiversity partnership."[25] They attributed this vacuum to the withdrawal of the US Department of the Interior, which had been important in pre-Miami planning but which had been diverted to defending

21. The eight working areas were financing, clean energy options, regulatory cooperation, petroleum, natural gas, energy efficiency, rural electrification, and joint implementation.

22. Enrique Iglesias, James Gustave Speth, and Shahid Javed Burki, "Joint Statement to the Hemispheric Energy Symposium" (Washington, 31 October 1995).

23. Ward et al., "Building Sustainable Development Partnerships," 4.

24. Alconsult, "Study Concerning the Elimination of Lead Gasoline in Latin America and the Caribbean," August 1996.

25. Ward et al., "Building Sustainable Development Partnerships," 5.

its core domestic programs against severe attacks by the Republican majority in Congress.

Capital Market Liberalization

Although disappointed that the Plan of Action failed to endorse a capital-market liberalization code, the US Treasury remained sufficiently interested in the initiative to take on the task of responsible coordinator. It convened the Committee on Hemispheric Financial Issues as mandated by the summit, which culminated in a meeting of hemispheric ministers of finance in New Orleans in May 1996. The ministerial meeting praised the IDB for fulfilling one of the initiative's action items—preparation of a list of national capital-market regulations—and created a technical working group on national financial market regulations to use the IDB survey to identify policies that "encourage the development, liberalization, and integration of the region's financial markets."[26] The working group will report to the Committee on Hemispheric Financial Issues, which will, in turn, prepare a second ministerial gathering within two years. The finance ministers also called on the IDB to host three meetings among policymakers, regulators, and market participants to identify the main problems in developing deep, liquid financial markets and to recommend solutions.

Meetings of ministers of finance could parallel the periodic meetings of ministers of trade and commerce.[27] The financial agenda remains primarily one of "transparency" (e.g., information exchange) and voluntary unilateral market liberalization because there is as yet no firm consensus on the pace and depth of market integration. The financial agenda is notably modest as compared with the much more ambitious targets and dense architecture of the trade ministers. Nevertheless, these early stirs of institutional ties among finance ministers could grow into an important component of hemispheric economic integration.

The Free Trade Area of the Americas

The Miami accord on the hemispheric free trade area was the product of a happy confluence of forces. The dynamics of the global marketplace and the structural reforms of the 1980s in Latin America provided the

---

26. Joint communiqué, Summit of the Americas Meeting of Western Hemisphere Finance Ministers, New Orleans, 18 May 1996.

27. The possibility of institutionalizing the finance ministerials is noted in Bernal, "Developing and Liberalizing Capital Markets." APEC finance ministers have been meeting annually since 1994.

requisite backdrop, and a favorable alignment of political forces provided the final push. The hemisphere signed on to the Free Trade Area of the Americas (FTAA) 2005 as a result of the momentum of North American Free Trade Agreement (NAFTA) approval, the Asia Pacific Economic Cooperation (APEC) forum free trade initiative, the successful conclusion of the Uruguay Round, and the energy and political imperatives generated by summit planning itself. But this political alignment proved to be not sustainable. The boldness of the summit's trade initiative exceeded the leaders' grasp, as the underlying political forces in the critical countries were not willing to support the Plan of Action. Even before Miami, there were signs in the United States and Brazil that not everyone was behind hemispheric free trade. Under pressure from blue-collar constituencies and the impending presidential elections, the Clinton administration had temporarily abandoned fast track and NAFTA parity—two building blocks in the prospective free trade edifice—and the November 1994 congressional elections had brought in a new breed of representatives seemingly skeptical of free trade. Brazil had balked at hemispheric free trade from the outset, and only after significant progress had been made toward its strategic Mercosur goals in mid-1994 did it feel more comfortable signing on. Immediately after Miami, both the United States and Brazil began to talk of trade fatigue, implying it was time to consolidate gains and pause before undertaking new challenges.

The Collapse of the Mexican Peso

Within two weeks of the summit the Mexican peso collapsed. Mexico's financial crisis was the result of imprudent fiscal policies, excessive government borrowing at short-term maturities, and mismanagement of exchange rate policies.[28] These had little to do with trade policy, but Mexico's financial distress and free trade were linked in the public mind, and NAFTA's critics were quick to blame the widening US trade deficit with Mexico—clearly the result of Mexico's recession and reduced demand for imports—on Clinton's trade agreement. The Mexican financial crisis was probably not decisive in determining the next steps for US trade policy in the hemisphere, but the peso collapse did deflate FTAA enthusiasts, especially on Capitol Hill.

As a result of NAFTA, the administration had a big political stake in Mexico, and the summit had further educated senior officials about the US stake in Latin America. NAFTA and the summit, therefore, were factors behind the Clinton administration's decision to amass a $50 billion

28. The various causes of the peso crisis are lucidly analyzed in Nora Lustig, *The Mexican Peso Crisis: The Foreseeable and the Surprise,* Discussion Paper in International Economics No. 114 (Washington: Brookings Institution, 1995).

rescue package to stabilize the peso. In fact, the rescue package shortened the Mexican recession and protected markets for US goods and services, but it gave the anti-NAFTA camp another weapon—linking free trade with financial bailout.

Retreat from NAFTA Expansion

As it had in 1994, in 1995 the administration again abandoned efforts to gain fast-track approval and NAFTA-parity legislation. Fast track continued to founder over the inability of Congress and the White House to find common ground on labor rights and environmental protection. The Republicans on the House Ways and Means Committee wanted a clean bill that, while not explicitly excluding labor and the environment from trade agreements, would not require their inclusion, but US Trade Representative (USTR) Mickey Kantor insisted on explicit inclusion. Republicans such as Representative Jim Kolbe accused Kantor of walking away from a deal, and some USTR staff agreed that Kantor had not made a serious effort to find a compromise. Politically, it appeared that Kantor preferred not to highlight new trade initiatives that would be unpopular with the AFL-CIO as the 1996 elections approached, just as Republicans increasingly sought to deny Clinton legislation that he might be able to tout during his reelection campaign.

The Chilean government was furious with the Clinton administration when it abandoned efforts to secure fast-track authority. President Eduardo Frei complained bitterly to visiting Americans, making it clear that having been jilted first by Bush and then by Clinton, the Chileans considered the United States an unreliable ally. Please, no more promises about fast track, the Chileans told visiting US diplomats, just let us know when you have congressional authority in hand. Then we can talk.[29] The Chileans did not want to negotiate without fast track, fearing that in its absence the US Congress would reopen any deals that Chile struck with the executive branch.

The Caribbean and Central American countries were also once again disappointed when the administration failed to find a legislative vehicle for NAFTA-parity legislation. White House Counselor Mack McLarty made a major effort to bolster administration interest in legislation that had, after all, been publicly endorsed by both the president and the vice president. But USTR had other priorities, and senior officials at the State Department, National Security Council (NSC), and National Economic Council (NEC) were inattentive. Important administration officials (notably Mickey Kantor and White House Chief of Staff Leon Panetta) saw

29. This was the message, for example, delivered to the US delegation that accompanied Hillary Rodham Clinton during her stopover in Santiago in October 1995.

too many political obstacles: opposition from influential textile firms, some southern Democrats, and some labor unions, compounded by the budget costs of tariff-reducing legislation. Although this opposition was by no means overwhelming, it was sufficient to sink legislation that had no powerful and determined backing.

Indeed, by the end of 1995 USTR turned its attention to slowing NAFTA implementation in the face of labor opposition. Specifically, Kantor persuaded Secretary of Transportation Federico Peña to postpone carrying out the trucking agreement because the teamsters' union was fiercely opposed to allowing Mexican truckers into the US market. Kantor also seemed concerned that NAFTA opponents—and the Republicans—might seize on any accidents or safety violations by Mexican truckers and make them an issue in the 1996 presidential campaign.[30]

The United States was not alone in being unprepared to sprint toward the FTAA goal. Brazil urged caution: "We want to avoid generating or feeding unrealistic expectations," warned Foreign Minister Luiz Felipe Lampreia.[31] Brazil repeatedly emphasized that it gave priority to consolidating Mercosur to allow its entrepreneurs to adjust gradually to market openings and more intensified international competition and, it was understood, to expand Mercosur's relations with other South American nations. An enlarged and unified SAFTA (South American Free Trade Area) would allegedly be in a better position to bargain with the United States and NAFTA.

Nor was Mexico particularly anxious to reach the FTAA goal any time soon. Why share its preferential access to the US market with Brazilian competitors? The inevitable rivalry between Mexico and Brazil for leadership among Latin American countries intensified in 1995-96, as NAFTA and Mercosur jockeyed for position. Many Brazilians gloated when the Mexican ego collapsed along with the peso.

Thus, the three major economies in the hemisphere—the United States, Brazil, and Mexico—preferred a pause in trade liberalization, each for its own reasons. (Two other major economies—Canada and Argentina—were more eager to reach the FTAA goals, but they were secondary players in their own subregional agreements and could not by themselves force the pace of events.) This lack of enthusiasm for trade liberalization did not preclude engaging in preparations for future negotiations, however. It was still possible to fulfill the mandates of the Plan of Action and embark on its calendar of preparatory meetings.

---

30. David Sanger, "Standing by His Man in Role after Role," *New York Times*, 2 November 1996, 21.

31. Address to the Second Summit of the Americas Trade Ministerial, Cartagena, 21 March 1996, as quoted in OAS, *Trade Bulletin* 1, no. 4 (May-June 1996), 5. For the views of a senior Brazilian trade negotiator, see José Botafogo Goncalvez, "The Challenges of Hemispheric Integration: A Brazilian View," *Brazil File* 5, no. 1 (2 February 1996), 7-8.

The Emerging Architecture of Trade Negotiations

The ministers of trade met in June 1995 in Denver, and in March 1996 in Cartagena. The ministers created 11 working groups to consider work plans for the main functional issues listed in the summit initiative (and which mirrored the NAFTA agenda): market access, customs procedures and rules of origin, investment, standards and technical barriers to trade, sanitary and phytosanitary measures, subsidies, antidumping and countervailing duties, government procurement, intellectual property rights, services, competition policy, and, at the insistence of Jamaica and other Caribbean Basin economies, issues related to smaller economies. Also, it was agreed in Cartagena that a 12th working group on dispute settlement procedures should be established after the third trade ministerial in 1997. To allow wide participation and dispersion of leadership, a different country chaired each working group.

At Cartagena, seven working groups submitted their initial accomplishments, which were largely limited to data and information collection.[32] The United States at first had hoped for agreement on a series of "early harvest" steps to reduce trade barriers, but Brazil and other countries balked. Ministers agreed on information dissemination: the data bases on market access would be made public, and a customs procedures manual and guidebook on investment regimes would be published. No accord was possible, however, on business facilitation (customs, standards, sanitary and phytosanitary measures, and investment) or limited scope agreements (market access, subsidies, antidumping, and countervailing duties). Opposition to these proposals stemmed from several concerns. First, just as the Latin Americans had lost interest in the trade and investment councils of the Bush administration's Enterprise for the Americas Initiative (EAI), they again balked at making concessions without reciprocity from the United States (whose credibility was impaired without fast-track authority). Second, some countries wanted all topics to be on the table at once, to permit trade-offs and cross-issue bargaining. Third, some felt uneasy about making commitments in unfamiliar terrain on complex issues without thorough discussions. Finally, Brazil preferred to focus on subregional trade accords and to defer major progress on hemispheric trade liberalization. Nevertheless, the Cartagena ministerial meeting directed all the working groups "to make concrete proposals on areas for immediate attention" before the 1997 ministerial.[33]

---

32. This discussion of the Cartagena trade ministerial follows Salazar-Xirinachs, "Promoting Free Trade in the Americas."

33. Joint Declaration, Summit of the Americas Second Trade Meeting, Cartagena, 21 March 1996.

The summit had stopped short of defining how the FTAA would actually be negotiated.[34] The United States had NAFTA accession in mind, but Brazil increasingly imagined a grand bargain between NAFTA and Mercosur (that is, the United States and Brazil).[35] A third possibility would be all-parties GATT- or WTO-like negotiation. This critical issue was only lightly touched upon at the Denver and Cartagena ministerials, but the Cartagena declaration instructed the vice ministers to make specific recommendations before the 1997 ministerial and assess when and how to launch the FTAA negotiations.

At the instigation of Secretary of Commerce Ron Brown, the United States hosted a forum for more than 1,000 corporate executives immediately after the first trade ministerial in Denver. In Cartagena, some 1,500 executives met just before the trade ministers convened and presented them with the results of their deliberations. This emerging public-private sector partnership is becoming institutionalized as the Americas Business Forum and will meet again at the scheduled trade ministerials in Belo Horizonte, Brazil, in 1997 and in San José, Costa Rica, in 1998. Private-sector efforts are under way to strengthen ties among the major business associations to improve forum effectiveness and augment the influence of the private sector on the trade integration process, for example by gaining access to the working group sessions.[36]

The Plan of Action directed the OAS to work with the IDB and ECLAC to assist integration through data systematization and economic studies. Through their tripartite cooperation committee, these three institutions have coordinated their efforts to provide technical backup to the working groups and to prepare several major studies on the current state of the subregional integration pacts. Initially uncomfortable with an OAS role in trade, the United States has gradually accepted this multilateral intrusion into hemispheric trade discussions, so long as it serves to promote convergence through transparency and eschews overt advocacy on controversial policies.

These new mechanisms apply the pillars of the tripodal inter-American system to trade integration. In only two years, these steps taken together amount to considerable progress in laying the foundations for negotiations

---

34. For an insightful discussion of possible pathways to an FTAA, see Stephan Haggard, *The Political Economy of Regionalism in the Western Hemisphere*, Research Paper 96-01, Graduate School of International Relations and Pacific Studies (San Diego: University of California, 1996).

35. The United States recognized Brazil's economic importance at the time of the April 1995 state visit of President Fernando Henrique Cardoso when it agreed to undertake a bilateral study of trade flows. See Joint Ministerial Report, *Brazil-United States Bilateral Trade Review*, 25 October 1995.

36. For a description of the Business Network for Hemispheric Integration, see Salazar-Xirinachs, "Promoting Free Trade in the Americas."

should the political environment become more propitious. The regular meetings of vice ministers and ministers create useful deadlines and pressure to demonstrate progress. The working groups are gathering necessary data and creating a hemispheric community of trade negotiators. The private sector is becoming a potentially powerful constituency for hemispheric free trade that could influence crucial countries as well as multilateral organizations. The OAS trade unit and the tripartite cooperation committee amount to an incipient secretariat for the FTAA.

As measured in real flows of trade and capital, hemispheric economic integration proceeded apace in 1995-96. Barriers continued to fall within the subregional trading areas, and trade flows increased. United States direct and portfolio investment in Latin America continued to expand. Despite the peso crisis, economic reform also progressed: country readiness indicators improved markedly for all of the major subregional trading pacts.[37] The logic of economic integration remained persuasive even if its timing was uncertain.

The Interim Scorecard

The Plan of Action encompasses so many issues and invites the participation of so many actors that the results to date are inevitably mixed. For each of the 12 initiatives, Table 10.1 rates:

- overall progress toward implementation of the action items, with an emphasis on activities at the international level since little systematic information is available on implementation at the national level;
- the efficacy and depth of implementation mechanisms, whether of the multilateral institutions, ministerial meetings, or public-private sector partnerships, as well as the effectiveness of the responsible coordinator;
- the degree of involvement of the international organizations; and
- the engagement of nonstate actors, their access to public officials, and the vitality of the public-private sector partnerships.

Ratings are from five to zero: five (strong), four (very good-very active), three (good-active), two (modest), one (minor), and zero (little to no movement). While these ratings are in each case based on an empirical body of information, they inevitably involve subjective judgments.[38]

---

37. Gary C. Hufbauer, "Update on Readiness Indicators" (Washington: Institute for International Economics, forthcoming).

38. For another effort at scoring implementation of international agreements, see George M. Von Furstenberg and Joseph P. Daniels, *Economic Summit Declarations, 1975-1989: Examining the Written Record of International Cooperation*, Princeton Studies in International Finance No. 72 (Princeton, NJ: Princeton University, 1992).

The ratings indicate very good or good progress in implementation on four initiatives (civil society, corruption, energy, and pollution prevention) and modest progress on seven more (democracy, human rights, narcotics and money laundering, education, women's rights, capital markets, and trade). Little movement was registered on biodiversity. Within two years of the summit, this is not a bad report card.

The tripodal architecture was supporting most of the initiatives, four very strongly or strongly and five modestly. The international organizations were very active or active in eight initiatives. Public-private sector partnerships had emerged very strongly or strongly in four cases. In many although not all of the initiatives, the new inter-American system was indeed taking shape as the drafters of the summit texts had hoped.

As this survey suggests, the Summit of the Americas affected agendas and attitudes in ways that were sometimes as important as the more readily measurable outcomes. By taking some issues from political silence to international salience—such as corruption and women's rights—the Miami summit altered international norms and affected future international conferences and perhaps the allocation of resources by multilateral agencies. Some national governments may have felt more accountable as well. On other issues that already were on the international agenda, such as democracy and money laundering, the summit helped to consolidate attitudes and facilitate future cooperation as unanticipated threats arose.

Problems Requiring Mid-Course Correction

The summit and its offspring, the SIRG and responsible coordinators, spurred an impressive amount of activity during 1995-96. Indeed, some Latin Americans complained that their governments lacked the human resources to attend the many meetings being held around the hemisphere. Yet it soon became evident that there were significant impediments to full implementation.

There were too many initiatives and action items. Despite efforts by the summit negotiators to limit the agenda, it expanded to 23 initiatives and more than 150 action items. The hemisphere lacked the organizational capacity, and the political will, to implement this large number of items, many of which were overarching and ambitious.

The summit had failed to allocate new financial resources, even though some of the initiatives, particularly in the social and environmental areas, would require major investments. Some of the initiatives lacked the essential elements of good policy formulation—measurable goals, priorities, and timetables. The Brazilians, through the Rio Group, had succeeded in deleting these critical details from many initiatives before and during the Airlie House negotiations.

Many governments lacked the requisite administrative capacity and resources to carry out some of the actions, and the summit did not provide compensatory assistance. The international organizations took their summit mandates seriously, but bureaucratic routine often overwhelmed them. The OAS and IDB sought to implement some initiatives assigned to them but allowed other mandates to slip.

Monitoring mechanisms were weak to nonexistent. Latin American governments had resisted reporting requirements to prevent international oversight from impinging on national sovereignty and, perhaps, to allow them to not adopt those summit commitments that they found politically inconvenient or financially too costly.

There was no great action-forcing event. Ministerial meetings could sometimes force decisions, but during 1995-96 there was no second summit on the schedule that would stimulate international agencies and national governments to work hard to fulfill the commitments made in Miami. At Miami, there was a general sentiment favoring a second summit, but the foreign ministers postponed the decision to consider such an event until the OAS General Assembly in June 1996.

There was no central coordinating mechanism responsible for overseeing and monitoring implementation. The review group and responsible coordinators tried to fill this void with some success, but the review group lacked a permanent staff (other than the shrinking Summit Coordinating Office in the US Department of State) and the effectiveness of the coordinators varied widely among the national governments.

In sum, the weaknesses lie in some of the very same factors that contributed to the spirit of Airlie House. Compromises on clarity of objectives, dilution of monitoring mechanisms, and the addition of new language to keep all parties satisfied took their toll as countries turned toward implementation. The refusal of the United States to consider even a small commitment of new financial resources deprived the process of seed money that could have catalyzed actions in many areas. The sweep and vagueness of the mandates ascribed to the IDB and OAS made it easier to win their backing but also made it easier for them to stand by as some summit objectives remained unfulfilled.

US Government Implementation

Within the US government, the deputies turned their attention to other problems and other presidential priorities and after one postsummit meeting ceased to concern themselves with summit follow-up. There was no presidential event on the calendar demanding that summit implementation be a success. In the immediate afterglow of Miami, the White House pondered a presidential trip to Latin America, but by the spring of 1995 Clinton's calendar was filled instead with foreign travel that was judged to offer greater domestic political payoffs. In 1995-96, Clinton traveled repeatedly to Europe and the Middle East but became the first US president since World War II not to set foot in Latin America or the Caribbean (outside of a few hours in Haiti) during his first term. The NSC acceded to a State Department appeal to give it the lead in coordinating summit follow-up, accepting the argument that this was more an issue of operations (the prerogative of the State Department) than decision making (which could justify NSC leadership). In practice, State's Summit Coordinating Office served to coordinate information flow and to backstop the review group but could not provide the leadership that the White House had generated in the run-up to the summit. The Summit Coordinating Office quickly dwindled, and it lacked the leverage to mobilize bureaucratic resources from within the State Department or the scattered executive branch. The now State-chaired comprehensive interagency working group met occasionally but performed more as an information exchange than a decision-making body. Presidential counselor Mack McLarty, whom Clinton tasked with leadership over summit follow-up, fought hard to draw public attention to summit implementation and to keep trade initiatives on track, but he lacked line authority and adequate bureaucratic and staff underpinning.

Within the executive branch, many agencies and individuals that had become engaged in a particular summit initiative during the pre-Miami process took implementation seriously. Until her elevation to acting USTR when Mickey Kantor moved to the Department of Commerce, Charlene Barshefsky attended the scheduled vice ministerials, and the staff pressed hard to make the ministerial agendas significant. The Department of Energy worked with interested NGAs and with its counterparts in its energy coalition to mount a carefully structured implementation process. Law enforcement officials at Treasury, Justice, and State helped negotiate comprehensive accords on money laundering and combating corruption. These departments and their experts, often in partnership with NGAs, became the true heroes of summit implementation.

The outcome from Miami compares very favorably with the results of the 1956 and 1967 summits. The summit texts and associated inter-American architecture have provided powerful momentum for progress on important issues. Yet, as some of the energy generated by a presidential summit gradually dissipated, forward motion was often stalled. There are important lessons to be learned—from both these successes and mistakes—that can improve future efforts to realize the vision of Miami and to augment the yield of future summits.

11

Making Hemispheric Summits Work

The Miami Summit of the Americas worked because hemispherism was ascendant in the United States and Latin America while contrary forces were at their nadir.[1] Individuals in the US government, allied with nongovernmental actors (NGAs) in the private sector and nongovernmental organizations (NGOs), were able to overcome many of the vested interests and bureaucratic obstacles that stood in the way of hemispheric summitry. After months of discussions about the values and regimes governing inter-American relations, the region's representatives approved the most far-reaching documents in the history of hemispheric diplomacy. The summit texts codified the principles governing hemispheric relations and ratified a detailed action plan for transforming them into realities. It elevated new issues onto the hemispheric agenda and expanded the scope for collective action. Summit leaders pledged not only to align their trade regimes but also to seek convergence on a wide array of political and social issues.[2]

The road to Miami was paved by crews from throughout the hemisphere. It was noted by Jamaican Ambassador Richard Bernal and others that whereas President George Bush's Enterprise for the Americas Initia-

---

1. As defined in chapter 1, "hemispherism" is the active attempt by the nations of the hemisphere to seek closer ties with one another with the goals of bolstering republican institutions and promoting mutual prosperity.

2. In the most thorough assessment of the summit published to date, Hays concludes that Miami achieved a "maximally substantive agenda," *Building the Hemisphere Community: Lessons from the Summit of the Americas Process*, Occasional Papers in Hemispheric Governance No. 3 (Washington: Inter-American Dialogue, July 1996), 11.

tive (EAI) was *for* the Americas (in that it was unilaterally proclaimed without direct consultations with the region), the Miami summit was *of* the Americas. In fact, Latin Americans and Caribbeans have often helped mold US policies in the region, as occurred with EAI, the North American Free Trade Agreement (NAFTA), and the Free Trade Area of the Americas (FTAA) 2005. Summit preparations assured Latin America unsurpassed opportunities for influence through participation in issue-oriented coalitions, plurilateral groupings, and bilateral conversations; through their representation in the regional institutions; and through common cause with NGAs. Despite its imperfections, the Miami process was so open that even those Latin Americans who had reacted with skepticism to Vice President Al Gore's Mexico City announcement recognized that the texts approved at Airlie House in Warrenton, Virginia, expressed the many voices of the hemisphere.[3]

Like a sculptor working with a block of marble, the makers of Miami carved out of the post-Cold War hemisphere a new multidimensional system that revealed the rich texture of inter-American relations. No longer confined to the one-dimensional security system of the post-World War II OAS and the Rio Pact, the architecture of hemispheric relations now encompassed the cabinets and ministries of governments and the *fuerzas vivas* (living forces) of organized society. One of the greatest contributions of the Miami summit was their recognition and legitimization.

In 1995-96, this new inter-American system made significant progress toward implementing portions of the summit Plan of Action (chapter 10). But ideas that militated against hemispherism suddenly regained ground. Within weeks of Miami, the collapse of the Mexican peso reignited the US belief that the United States derives no benefit from close associations with its Latin American neighbors (chapter 1), just as the outbreak of hostilities between Peru and Ecuador rekindled the deep-seated distrusts that still divide Latin America. As the 1996 US presidential elections approached, the politics of the frustrating antinarcotics campaign created opportunities for aggressive voices within the Clinton administration to attack Latin American governments for laxity in combating drugs. Candidate Robert Dole proposed mobilizing the National Guard to interdict the flow of narcotics at the border, rekindling the fears and distrust inherent in the great power asymmetries between the United States and Latin America. Especially damaging to the Miami agenda, both presidential candidates stayed clear of free trade themes, and both were content to allow free trade legislation to lie dormant in the US Congress.

The Miami summit had failed to arm the hemisphere against a cyclical resurgence of antihemispherism. Without an institutionalized summit structure

---

3. Hays concluded that "most countries now concede that the United States acted in good faith and was able to be an honest broker in preparing the summit agenda." In Hays, *Building the Hemisphere Community*, 11.

to keep hemispheric leaders focused on their common interests, prohemispheric advocates lost a potentially potent instrument. Within the senior spheres of the US government, attention quickly drifted away from the hemisphere toward more crisis-ridden regions. Nor did the summit give birth to a strong secretariat or other bureaucracy with interests in keeping alive the spirit of Miami.

The planning and aftermath of Miami suggest important lessons for managing inter-American relations in the years ahead. At Miami, Secretary of State Warren Christopher readily gained agreement among his fellow foreign ministers that they would consider a second summit at the margins of the OAS General Assembly in Panama in June 1996. There ministers unanimously accepted Chile's offer to host a second summit in early 1998. This second summit of the Americas in Santiago offers another major opportunity to advance the hemispheric idea.

US Interests and Strategy

There should be no doubt in the minds of US leaders that the Miami summit served US interests. It provided the vehicle—absent before—through which the United States gained explicit hemispheric support for many of its major objectives in Latin America. Miami multilateralized the agenda established in the Presidential Decision Directive 28 on US policy toward Latin America and the Caribbean. Future hemispheric summits could build on this promising foundation.

Nor should there be any doubt that the United States has important interests in Latin America and the Caribbean. US exports to the region now total $100 billion or over 15 percent of total US exports, and if current trends continue, exports to the region will surpass those to Western Europe. FTAA promises to maintain and enhance US access to that growing market, just as NAFTA increased US market share in Mexico. Moreover, forward momentum on FTAA will accelerate the opening of Latin American economies and should stimulate more rapid GDP growth. Progress on the trade and capital markets initiatives will also make the region's capital markets more efficient and more open to US equity and portfolio investors. The debt crisis of the 1980s and the Mexican peso crisis of 1994-95 made evident the potential negative impact that Latin American financial instability can have on financial markets in other emerging markets as well as the United States.

If momentum is maintained, FTAA will advance other US interests as well. It serves as a building block for more open global markets and nudges forward liberalization in other forums—regional and global. Of economic and geopolitical interest, a dynamic FTAA will lessen the Latin American tendency to look elsewhere—to Europe and Asia—for leadership in the international political economy. The Miami summit fortified the trend toward democratic stability. Recurrent US interventions throughout the Caribbean Basin have typically been stimulated by political instability perceived to threaten US interests. Many of these interventions have occasioned extremely divisive political debates in the United States, most recently as a result of the civil wars in Central America. If summitry can continue to codify democratic practices and promote collective actions to strengthen Latin American democracies, it can help free US foreign policy from this destructive whirlpool.

The Miami summit reinforced those political factions in Latin America that favor hemispheric and global markets and seek democratic stability. Rarely, if ever, has the United States had the opportunity to work with so many potential allies that share its core values throughout the Americas. If the United States can build on the Miami vision of a hemispheric community of democracies, it will find many countries in the region willing to participate in global activities of interest to the United States. Already, many Latin American and Caribbean countries adhere to nonproliferation objectives, join in international peacekeeping efforts, and support the promotion of human rights.

Miami also demonstrated that the Western Hemisphere provides fertile ground for the United States to undertake innovations in foreign policy that may be replicable elsewhere. Since Miami, which yielded the world's first anticorruption convention, fighting corruption—with its links to drug traffickers and other international criminals—has become a concern for US foreign policy worldwide. But much work remains for future summiteers, who must battle against corrupt individuals that use modern technology to pursue their ends.

The degree of involvement of nongovernmental actors in the Miami process also harbors positive implications for an assertive US foreign policy. In the post-Cold War world, US leaders must broaden citizen interest in foreign affairs if they are to pursue policies of international engagement. The Miami process opened avenues for the engagement of corporate and financial communities and NGOs in partnering with the government to design and advance US foreign policy objectives. The Miami summit failed to attract much interest in Hispanic communities outside of Florida, but the Hispanic population, which is fast becoming the largest minority group in the United States, may voice louder interests in its motherlands as it becomes more established and better organized. The process of summitry in the Americas provides one multifaceted mechanism for Hispanic involvement.

Finally, geographic proximity gives the United States an interest in avoiding negative spillover effects from potentially harmful developments in Latin America and the Caribbean. The Miami summit did not make much progress on counternarcotics, nor did it address illegal migration. In the future, summitry may facilitate better working relations on such conflictive issues. Miami did, however, make important progress on issues of environmental protection; the elimination of lead from gasoline will improve air quality in cities throughout the hemisphere.

Today, Latin America is a region at peace and, by and large, is interested in good relations with the United States. Rather than complacently ignore the region, the United States should build a structure of inter-American relations capable of making progress on current problems and prepared to manage the frictions and downturns that the future will inevitably bring. This is an opportunity for farsighted statesmanship.

The attention summits confer to Latin America need not require assertions that the region is more or even as important as other regions of the world. Senior-level attention and official financial resources required to pursue the Miami agenda are not overwhelming and are relatively modest compared to the potential gains for future generations. It would, however, imply marginal reallocation of traditional decision-making energies, away from global crisis management and toward strategic planning for longer-term gains in the Western Hemisphere.

The United States commands more than 75 percent of the hemisphere's GDP, offers by far the richest markets for trade and capital, generates a flood of pop culture and mass entertainment, is home to a vibrant civil society, and houses in Washington a collection of ministries and diplomatic corps whose capacities are without equal in the region. Other countries can be leaders and propose ideas that help to mold the hemispheric agenda, but without active US engagement summitry cannot succeed. The failure of the Bolivian hosts to develop a constructive working relationship with the United States in preparing their conference on sustainable development led to the frustrations surrounding that December 1996 meeting in Santa Cruz. But for summits to have a palpable effect on hemispheric relations, the United States must do more than attend: the hemisphere's predominant power must be actively engaged in summit preparations, be prepared to place detailed proposals on the table and to work actively for their acceptance by crucial countries and NGAs, and put its muscle behind implementation.[4] The United States did not so engage in the 1956 Panama summit, worked harder to prepare the 1967 Punta del Este summit but did not follow-up, and, having learned from history, performed far better in the Summit of the Americas.

But lack of sustained attention to Latin America is a chronic problem in the US government. Europe, the Middle East, and portions of Asia command constituencies throughout the federal bureaucracy and the US Congress—not to mention the media—that Latin America cannot match.

---

4. In a study of Group of Seven summits, Robert D. Putnam and Nicholas Bayne also concluded that progress was most likely when the United States asserted strong leadership in alignment with at least one other major power. In *Hanging Together: Cooperation and Conflict in the Seven-Power Summits* (London: Sage Publications, 1987), 271-73.

Figure 11.1 Proposed US government organization for the 1998 Santiago summit

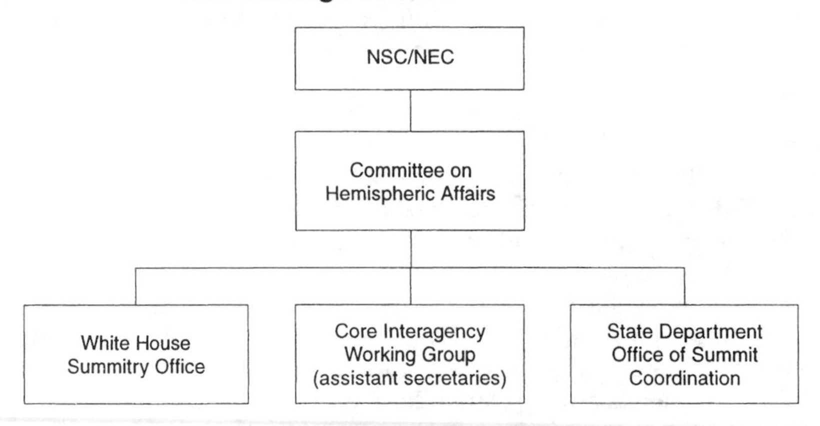

It is true that the evolution of cabinet diplomacy has linked executive branch departments with their counterparts throughout the hemisphere, creating an emergent inter-American system with great promise. But this new system can prosper only if it receives periodic attention and some resources from the leadership of the United States.

Summits offer an alternative to crises as a way of focusing attention on Latin America. Indeed, in the post-Cold War world, they may be the only way. When summits are held in the United States, senior-level attention is assured because the prestige of the president is at stake. But summits held overseas may seem less vital: although presidential aides will not want the president to be seen as participating in an international event that fails, the president's prestige will be less engaged in Santiago than it was in Miami, and there will be no Miami community to cultivate for domestic political advantage.

How can we assure strong US engagement in the Santiago and subsequent summits? How can we keep US policy on track and consistent with the spirit of summitry between summits? It is conceivable that senior foreign policy advisers will take sufficient interest, but the realities of crisis management and bureaucratic interests diminish those prospects. Therefore, I propose four organizational initiatives (see figure 11.1).

First, establish a deputies-level committee on hemispheric affairs co-chaired by presidential envoy Mack McLarty. In announcing his second-term cabinet, President Clinton gave McLarty the additional title of special envoy for the Americas, and included among his major tasks US preparation for the Santiago summit. McLarty has gained the respect of the hemisphere's leaders and is a good judge of their reactions to US initiatives, but he needs more operational authority to fulfill his mandate successfully. Under McLarty's stewardship, a senior Committee on Hemispheric

Affairs (CHA) would serve two purposes: to set US policy on hemispheric summits and to assess possible US policies on a range of issues in terms of their effect on overall hemispheric relations.

The CHA would be the senior body for coordinating summit planning and implementation. Under the president, it would be the ultimate authority for summitry in the Western Hemisphere. It would establish a mechanism for agencies to report on their progress in implementing the Miami initiatives, as well as guide preparation for Santiago. The committee would seek to keep crucial summit initiatives on track. And it would seek better consistency across the range of US policies toward Latin America and the Caribbean. It would not, however, attempt to control policymaking on many functional issues. Existing or specialized channels, with their superior expertise and authority, will and should continue to be the primary foci for policymaking on most issues.

Summit momentum cannot be maintained if between meetings US policy is driven by antihemispherism. The CHA could seek to hold in check the pressures that inevitably arise from domestic politics and certain government agencies that oppose the letter or spirit of summit accords. This does not mean that the United States will not from time to time take actions, including sanctions, which anger Latin Americans, but the CHA would weigh whether such actions are sufficiently important to US interests and how best to minimize the collateral danger to summitry.

Second, create a permanent working group for Western Hemisphere summits at the assistant secretary level. Officials at the cabinet and vice cabinet levels can be useful in policy coordination, articulation, and resource allocation and in establishing guidelines on major issues, but (chapter 5) often lack the time and expertise to manage the many details involved in hemispheric summitry. As Miami summit preparations showed, assistant secretaries of the critical agencies would be a more efficient locus for decision making on most substantive matters.[5] A core of 5 to 10 such officials would gather sufficient expertise and representation to make most important policy decisions. In the event of deadlocks or issues requiring presidential involvement, the core interagency working group (IWG) would prepare recommendations for the CHA or other appropriate body.

Third, give Vice President Gore and UN Ambassador Bill Richardson major roles in hemispheric summitry. Gore was the originator of the Summit of the Americas and supported some of its most innovative initiatives. He has earned widespread respect throughout the hemisphere and, although not a regional expert, he is knowledgeable about many of the major issues,

---

5. I. M. Destler makes a similar recommendation for economic policy in general: "The NEC [National Economic Council] should constitute and empower assistant-secretary working groups in ongoing issue areas, with authority to resolve issues at their level or refer disagreements to the Deputies." In *The National Economic Council: A Work in Progress* (Washington: Institute for International Economics, 1996), 65.

including democratic governance, environmental protection, international crime, and trade. President Clinton should again engage his vice president in hemispheric summitry by giving him the US lead in one of these important areas.

Bill Richardson speaks fluent Spanish and has a long history of involvement in Latin America. A senior team of Gore, McLarty, and Richardson would bring international prestige and bureaucratic clout to US summitry.

Fourth, set up an office in the White House to coordinate US policy toward multilateral summits, including summits of the Americas, the Asia Pacific Economic Cooperation (APEC) forum, and the industrial-country Group of Seven (G-7). This summitry office would help provide consistency in US policy toward the major regional and multilateral groups. It would work to overcome the regional-global tension by making regional initiatives consistent with global regimes. The summitry office would also facilitate cross-fertilization among the three summits, for example enabling the Western Hemisphere to learn from APEC's experience in such areas as organizational secretariats, trade negotiations, and financial market liberalization.

These four proposals seek to capture the strengths of decentralized functionalism as expressed in the core IWG while drawing on the authority vested in more senior officials. The IWG would mobilize the working-level expertise of the functional agencies. With McLarty and the official from the summitry office, the committee on hemispheric affairs could set priorities, support the innovative individuals in the functional agencies, and seek budgetary resources and occasional presidential involvement.

Hemispheric Diplomacy

At the 1 October 1996 Summit Implementation Review Group (SIRG) meeting in Washington, it was agreed that the review group itself should become the primary intergovernmental forum for negotiating the agenda for the Santiago summit.[6] This represented a partial counterrevolution by the foreign ministries, an attempt to wrest control over the summit process and the inter-American system away from the functional ministries and organized civil society. But the landscape of inter-American relations had changed too much to permit the diplomats to ignore the new components. Both the US and Chilean delegations referred to the importance of civil society's participation in preparing summit agendas.[7]

6. Personal interviews with participants, October 1996, and written presentations by the US and Chilean delegations. The United States will retain the chair of the review group on matters related to the Miami plan of action, but Chile will lead, with US support, during discussions related to the Santiago agenda.

7. The US delegation argued that "in the spirit of continuing the advances made following the Miami summit regarding invigorating civil society, private sector interest groups and nongovernmental organizations should be consulted by governments in the formulation of

Bowing to decentralized functionalism, the US delegation allowed that separate expert meetings may need to be convened to help draft action items, and trade will continue to be negotiated on a separate but parallel track. Both the Chilean and US delegations also urged that the third leg of the tripodal inter-American system, the international organizations—namely, the four official observers of the Miami summit: the Organization of American States (OAS), the Inter-American Development Bank (IDB), UN Economic Commission on Latin America and the Caribbean (ECLAC), and Pan American Health Organization (PAHO)—be consulted. Ideally, this review-group-led process will bring more order to summit preparation while still capturing the benefits of participation by the full inter-American system.

For any initiative, one predictor of success in implementation is the intensity of negotiation. Agreements reached quickly by a few parties (as with the Miami education initiative, for example) are unlikely to engage the bureaucratic and NGA attention and commitment required for compliance. Prolonged negotiations and democratic diplomacy are a good investment that will yield payoffs after the summit leaders have adjourned.

Fortunately, the long lead time before the March 1998 Santiago summit offers a superb opportunity for NGAs to engage their respective governments and to form cross-border alliances to feed their recommendations directly into the SIRG process. These proposals should be based on a critical assessment of progress on implementation of the Miami Plan of Action. Santiago preparations should take stock of Miami progress and undertake necessary mid-course corrections. Evaluations would benefit from official as well as nongovernmental assessments.

Chapter 10 drew on private expert surveys of implementation of the Miami plan of action to assess summit weaknesses. *Santiago can improve on Miami by tackling a more limited set of initiatives and many fewer action items.*[8] *Each initiative should embody measurable goals and phased timetables. Sufficient human and financial resources are needed to catalyze other official and private flows. Mandates should be made clear to international organizations, and financial targets should be set when appropriate. Reporting requirements for governments and international agencies and monitoring mechanisms to oversee implementation would also be useful.*

It is time to create a secretariat for hemispheric summitry.[9] APEC benefits from a small, low-budget secretariat in Singapore that preserves records,

---

positions on agenda items. Such groups should be encouraged to meet months in advance of the Santiago summit to produce position papers on issues they believe important."

8. The agreement by Chile and the United States to circumscribe the agenda early on may be a step in the right direction so long as it does not shut out innovative initiatives.

9. Miles Kahler suggests that regional integration may proceed in a curvilinear fashion. When economic integration is shallow, information gathering is required before stronger and more centralized institutions can emerge. Later, when transparency has increased but

coordinates paper flow, keeps the calendar of events, and helps to staff meetings. The incipient tripartite cooperation committee (OAS, IDB, and ECLAC) should be given a staff that could perform such functions, manage surveys of summit implementation, and collate information from other monitors.[10] With perhaps two dozen professionals drawn from member institutions and expert hiring, the cooperation committee could adequately staff the summit implementation review group. A more robust cooperation committee would provide continuity and multilateralism. The tripartite committee could also assist responsible coordinators, which remain a useful instrument for spreading leadership among the countries of the hemisphere.[11]

Most important, Santiago should declare that summits will be a permanent feature of the inter-American system. APEC has benefited mightily from the regular leaders' summits begun in Seattle in 1993. These annual events have driven APEC integration by pressuring countries to agree each year to action items in line with the ultimate goals of free trade by 2020. (In contrast, the G-7 summits suffer from the absence of such end-state goals, leaving leaders each year to search afresh for some presidential-level initiative.) APEC began in 1989, so direct comparisons with FTAA results to date would be unfair, but certainly its annual summits are one explanation for APEC's superior ability to agree on actions such as the alignment of national standards, the harmonization of tariff nomenclature and customs clearance, and other business facilitation measures. Summits also allow for the sort of presidential involvement that was critical in gaining prompt consensus on innovative initiatives, such as the Information Technology Agreement at the November 1996 APEC summit in Subic Bay, the Philippines. The annual APEC summits also build personal relations among major regional leaders that not only help close summit deals but also make it easier to manage unforeseen crises that may arise between summits.

---

uncertainty remains about the preferences of governments, more centralized institutions with greater monitoring and enforcement capabilities can arise. Finally, when information about preferences and reputations is plentiful and cheap, decentralized reputation-based systems may suffice. In Miles Kahler, *International Institutions and the Political Economy of Integration* (Washington: Brookings Institution, 1995), 16.

10. A precedent for such a multilateral committee was the Inter-American Committee of the Alliance for Progress (CIAP), whose primary function was to undertake reviews of countries' national economic plans. Through CIAP, the Latin American countries examined their own performances and plans and pinpointed issues of national and regional importance.

11. This proposal would add a line between the cooperation committee and government responsible coordinators (figure 10.1). It would be beneficial for review group leaders to meet periodically with the committee, as well as directly with the multilateral agencies to cement their focus on summit initiatives.

After Santiago, the leaders should copy the APEC model of annual summits for the next two to three years. After that, summits every two years should be enough to maintain momentum for compliance on accords and for agreement on new initiatives consistent with common goals.

There is always the risk, of course, that summits in the Western Hemisphere will become routine exercises in empty rhetoric and unkept promises.[12] Full engagement of the tripodal inter-American system, fortified by the reforms advocated here, would be the region's best protection against summit entropy. In the end, leadership (or its absence) by the United States and by Latin American nations will also be crucial in determining the fate of hemispheric summits.

Gaining Brazilian and Mexican Cooperation

The heart of the drama of Miami was Brazil's struggle to establish itself as the interlocutor for South America and the Rio Group. For the Santiago summit, securing Brazilian cooperation is complicated by the natural leadership position that Chile will occupy. Chilean diplomatic skills will be tested as they struggle to balance the aspirations of Brazil and the United States. Chile can help build a coalition of states that want the Santiago summit to succeed, just as the United States did before Miami, thereby compelling Brazil to adopt a more affirmative posture if it wants to remain a leader. The traditionalists at Itamaraty often will bend on substance to remain ahead on their diplomatic scoreboard. Moreover, Itamaraty has already accomplished its main strategic objective of consolidating Mercosur and pulling other South American countries into the Mercosur orbit through a series of bilateral and subregional trade agreements, thereby establishing Brazil as the logical lead South American representative in any negotiations with the United States and its NAFTA partners on the terms of hemispheric trade integration.

Presidents Bill Clinton and Fernando Henrique Cardoso are remarkably similar in personality and world outlook. The chemistry between the two leaders was excellent in Miami and at a spring 1995 state visit in Washington. The summit process would benefit tremendously if the two men began to converse regularly in order to foster more constructive win-win attitudes on the part of their representatives.[13] Exploring their common interests could promote cooperation.

---

12. For a critical assessment of the G-7 summits tempered with hope for reform, see C. Fred Bergsten and C. Randall Henning, *Global Economic Leadership and the Group of Seven* (Washington: Institute for International Economics, 1996).

13. As the Santiago summit approaches, President Clinton should speak directly with his counterparts in key countries, as he routinely does with European and Asian leaders.

Itamaraty prefers centralized, foreign ministry-driven summit planning because that maximizes its ability to influence events. Decentralized functionalism and spreading preparation throughout the tripodal inter-American system dilute the influence of Itamaraty, generally to the benefit of hemispherism and effective collective action.

Mexico was not a major player in the Miami process. But a friendship between Presidents Clinton and Zedillo has been forged in the crucible of the peso crisis. For their part, Brazilian diplomats have struggled to identify Mexico with NAFTA and marginalize Mexico from South American diplomacy. The United States has an interest in encouraging deeper Mexican involvement in hemispheric diplomacy, while allowing Mexico sufficient political space to retain Latin American credentials. The Mexican foreign ministry remains distrustful of multilateral interventions on behalf of democratic governance within nations, but Mexico can play constructive roles in fostering regional cooperation on economic and social issues. A more engaged Mexico could assist Chile in the run-up to the Santiago summit in building a winning coalition of prosummitry states.

Summitry and Hemispherism

Trade integration was the centerpiece in Miami and remains the yardstick whereby Santiago will be judged. If significant progress on trade integration is anticipated, the Latin Americans are more likely to cooperate on issues that infringe on traditional notions of sovereignty and that entail domestic political costs. In this indirect but very real way, progress on trade is positively correlated with cooperation on environment, narcotics, and other contentious issues.

The Miami summit pledged to make significant progress by the end of the century toward concluding negotiations on FTAA. That means that the Santiago summit will have to find a way to attain that goal promptly. The building blocks are already in place: the ministerial meetings and their 11 working groups, the OAS trade unit, the tripartite cooperation committee, the private-sector constituencies, and the dynamic subregional trading blocks, especially NAFTA and Mercosur. What is needed are political decisions in Washington and Brasilia. Leaders in both countries must build the political coalitions necessary to sustain progress toward hemispheric free trade. President Clinton must do what he did not do in 1995-96: he must make it a clear priority to gain congressional renewal of fast-track authority, and this authority should be broad enough to permit Chilean accession to NAFTA and to negotiate an FTAA. The legislation must be passed before the Santiago summit if US diplomats are to have sufficient credibility for serious negotiations with the Latin Americans. The administration must work hard to find a formula on trade and environment issues that is satisfactory to a broad bipartisan coalition and be prepared to expend the political capital necessary to either satisfy or defeat organized labor's congressional allies. President Clinton cannot allow this faction to jeopardize the host of US interests in the hemisphere that are tied to progress on trade liberalization.

Selection of 2005 as the completion date for FTAA negotiations was rather arbitrary. The Clinton administration felt that the 2000 target proposed by some Latin American countries was too stringent but that a date was needed that was at least as ambitious as APEC'S free trade targets (2010 for the industrialized countries, 2020 for the entire region).[14]

Why not set a more ambitious time line but one that allows sufficient time for countries to undertake the necessary domestic economic and political adjustments? Before Santiago, the hemisphere should agree on some minor business facilitation steps (such as customs clearance and tariff nomenclature harmonization) and one more significant measure such as a code on direct foreign investment. This progress would demonstrate countries' goodwill and capacity to negotiate integration and catch up to APEC. With these achievements under their belts, *at Santiago the leaders should announce this bold decision: to launch negotiations with the goal of reaching agreement on FTAA during 2000.* This timetable would still allow for more time than it took to negotiate the groundbreaking NAFTA text and would enable President Clinton to add FTAA to his foreign policy legacy. Actual implementation, of course, would come only gradually, perhaps over 15 years as allowed for by NAFTA and over an even longer time frame for the smaller and poorer economies, just as the APEC process allows a more gradual pace for its developing country members. This would provide plenty of time for countries to carry out the economic reforms that help prepare their economies for open trade.

Such accelerated negotiations would probably have to be an all-parties' GATT/WTO-style process; whatever the modalities, the United States and Brazil will inevitably be meeting in an anteroom to cut the major deals. The existing 11 working groups could continue to function as useful venues for data collection and analysis and the negotiation of specific agreements. The OAS Trade Unit and the tripartite cooperation committee could evolve into a hemispheric trade secretariat.

The Santiago summit should undertake one additional and highly innovative step: announce that only democracies will be welcome to participate in hemispheric trade integration. The exclusion of Cuba from Miami implied that only democracies would be invited to participate in regional trade accords; however, the linkage was not explicit and was not tested by the emergence of a noncommunist authoritarian state. The 1996 Paraguay

14. Personal interview with Mack McLarty, Washington, 16 January 1997. In fact, the APEC timetable was similar to that set for FTAA. The 2010 and 2020 APEC deadlines were for the implementation of agreements, whereas the 2005 FTAA deadline was only for the completion of negotiations.

crisis demonstrated in stark relief the positive links between trade integration and democratic solidarity when the Mercosur countries threatened to expel Paraguay from their economic club if it abandoned fundamental democratic norms. The hemisphere should seek to deter any future authoritarian threats by threatening similar expulsion from the broader regional trading arrangement. In addition, the trade-democracy link might be fortified by amending the 1991 Santiago Declaration requiring the OAS to take emergency action in the event of a challenge to democratic rule, by calling for the suspension of IDB and even possibly of bilateral loans if constitutional rule is violated. In fact, the IDB has already begun to display such politically aware behavior.

Santiago will also want to address social issues, even if follow-up to Miami has been relatively weak in this area. Problems of poverty and gross inequality are simply too central to future economic development and democratic stability to be ignored. Although the lack of consensus in the United States and throughout the hemisphere on how best to resolve social problems inhibits workable accords, it should be feasible to identify a few achievable goals. This time, hemispheric leaders should seek to mobilize the resources of the international institutions in pursuit of the chosen objectives more forcefully. The Miami summit's educational reform proposals, if given the necessary political backing and financial resources, are worthy of a second endorsement. Summit action could make a positive difference in educational attainment throughout the Americas. The Santiago summit could help energize a series of national policy dialogues on educational reform involving governments and relevant stakeholders, the sharing of best practices, establishment and implementation of regional standards (including those established at Miami regarding school completion rates), and technical assistance and resource transfers from international agencies.

The Miami summit revealed that there are many issues of valid concern on which agreement on collective action is possible. But antihemispherism remains very much alive in both the United States and in Latin America. And politicians may weary of summits that pressure them to reach international accords that entail domestic costs.

The challenge to the Clinton administration is to build on the foundations laid in the first term in Miami, to advance and possibly even complete the most dramatic initiative ever conceived of in the Western Hemisphere—agreement on FTAA. Such an accord would create the diplomatic conditions for progress on a wide range of other issues, from capital market liberalization to educational reform, from the collective defense of democracy to the criminalization of official corruption, from energy cooperation to environmental protection. It could open the gates to meaningful accords on such highly contentious matters as immigration and narcotics. Such a new hemispheric alliance would be a major strategic achievement and an important boost to US prosperity and global economic competitiveness and would also be a major building block in an eventual global free trade regime.

For Latin America, to embrace FTAA and to negotiate and carry out detailed summit agreements would be equally historic. It would imply the victory of the hemispheric ideal and the defeat of those who fear, distrust, or disdain the United States. It would recognize that the future of Latin America lies in a comprehensive, working alliance with its powerful northern neighbor. It would not separate Latin America from the rest of the world any more than it would impede the United States from pursuing trade liberalization and other objectives in other regional and multilateral forums.

As the Miami Summit of the Americas demonstrated, summits are now the most effective way to propel the Western Hemisphere forward. The "summitization" of hemispheric affairs implies that countries can look beyond crisis management to strategic vision, that bureaucracies can learn from past errors at hemispheric summitry and are willing to translate words into deeds, that the broader and deeper inter-American system—the international organizations, cabinet ministries, and civil society—can be mobilized, and, most important, that leaders will seize this moment to attain the hemispheric ideal. In 200 years, we have never been closer to realizing that promise.

APPENDICES

Appendix A
Summit of the Americas: Chronology of Events

1 December 1993	Vice President Al Gore announces summit at an address to the Mexican, American, and Latin American Chambers of Commerce in Mexico City.
20 December	Interagency working group (IWG) is proposed by US Secretary of State Warren Christopher.
5 January 1994	First US summit IWG meeting. Eleven initiatives presented. Themes: democracy and governance, growth and prosperity, and social agenda.
7 February	First meeting of US Deputies Committee.
11 March	President Bill Clinton announces location and month of summit and invites leaders of the hemisphere.
20-21 March	Vice President Gore visits Bolivia, Argentina, and Brazil, discusses summit with Presidents Sánchez de Lozada, Menem, and Franco.
21 March	Rio Group meets, discusses summit.
8 April	US IWG meets to discuss 39 proposed initiatives.
21-23 April	US Under Secretary of State Joan Spero visits Mexico City.
23 May	A US team led by Under Secretary of the Treasury Lawrence Summers and Assistant Secretary of State for Inter-American Affairs Alexander Watson consults with Rio Group in Brasilia, Brazil.
24 May	Vice President Gore meets with Central American Presidents in Tegucigalpa, Honduras.
27 May	Vice President Gore briefs hemispheric ambassadors in Washington.
31 May-2 June	Spero visits Barbados, meets with Prime Minister Erskine Sandiford, Caricom Bureau, and meets with Prime Minister Patrick Manning in Trinidad and Tobago.
3 June	Deputy Secretary of State Strobe Talbott visits with President Rafael Caldera in Caracas, Venezuela.
5-6 June	US delegation to OAS General Assembly in Belem, Brazil discusses summit with delegations from Argentina, Brazil, Chile, Colombia, Mexico.

9 June	OAS General Assembly creates Summit of the Americas Working Group.
15 June	End of first phase of consultations.
28 June	President Eduardo Frei of Chile visits President Clinton at the White House.
15 July	OAS summit working group reviews initiative that calls for OAS participation.
19 July	Vice President Gore meets with Prime Minister Jean Chrétien in Ottawa, Canada.
20 July	First House Western Hemisphere Subcommittee hearings on the summit.
15 August	First meeting of the OAS working group on public ethics.
21 August	Presidential elections in Mexico. Ernesto Zedillo Ponce de Léon, of the ruling PRI party, wins with 50.18 percent of the vote.
22 August	Phase Two consultations begin. US circulates menu of 14 initiatives.
22-26 August	US consultation team visits Santiago, Chile; Buenos Aires, Argentina; and Brasilia.
1-3 September	US consultation team visits Colombia.
6-7 September	Rio Group coordinators meet in Brazil, discuss summit documents.
9-10 September	Summit of Rio Group presidents in Brazil.
12-14 September	US consultation team meets with Caricom countries in Trinidad and Tobago.
12-14 September	IDB hosts conference on strengthening civil society.
15 September	César Gaviria inaugurated as OAS secretary general.
16 September	IDB hosts conference on governance and the modernization of the democratic state. Vice President Gore speaks at event.
20 September	Special Rio Group meeting in Washington to prepare presentation on summit to US government.
21 September	Rio Group representatives present preliminary reaction to documents at US State Department.

29 September	US consultation team meets with Canadian representatives at US State Department.
3 October	Presidential elections in Brazil. Fernando Henrique Cardoso is elected president with 53 percent of the vote.
10-11 October	US consultation team meets with Central American foreign ministers in Managua, Nicaragua.
12 October	Vice President Gore in Managua to witness signing of Alliance for Sustainable Development by Central American leaders.
13-14 October	San Antonio Seven plus Brazil and Chile meet on narcotics in Mexico City.
13-14 October	Summit consultation team in Mexico, meets with President-elect Zedillo.
15 October	Second phase of summit consultations ends.
15 October	President Jean-Bertrand Aristide, ousted in a coup in September 1991, returns to power in Haiti.
18 October	Rio Group coordinators meet to prepare draft declaration in Rio de Janeiro.
18-21 October	OAS's CICAD semi-annual meeting in Santiago.
21-28 October	US hosts trade consultations with Canada, Chile, Caricom, Central America, Andean Pact, and Mercosur.
24 October	Rio Group transmits draft declaration to US government.
26-27 October	Hemispheric consultations on environmental initiatives in Quito.
26-29 October	Hemispheric seminar on ethics in Quito.
27 October	US holds consultations with OAS in Washington.
1-2 November	Microenterprise workshop in Trinidad and Tobago.
7-8 November	US summit team meets with Caricom heads in Kingston.
7-8 November	US consultation team in Lima.
10-11 November	Rio Group coordinators meet to prepare draft plan of action in Brasilia.

11-13 November	New Moment in the Americas meeting in Annapolis, Maryland.
21 November	Rio Group draft plan of action is transmitted to the US government.
21-23 November	Mack McLarty visits Brasilia and Caracas.
21-23 November	Trade consultations with all subregional trade groups in Washington, with concluding plenary session.
25 November	Preparatory meeting of the Rio Group participants at Airlie House negotiations, in Washington.
28-29 November	Airlie House meeting, Warrenton, Virginia.
1 December	Ernesto Zedillo Ponce de Léon inaugurated as Mexico's president.
2 December	Final, all-parties trade consultation hosted by USTR in Washington.
9-11 December	Summit of the Americas, Miami. All 34 leaders sign declaration of principles and plan of action.

Sources: Department of State; interviews with hemispheric diplomats.

Appendix B

NATIONAL SECURITY COUNCIL
WASHINGTON D C 20506

November 29, 1993

ACTION

MEMORANDUM FOR THE VICE PRESIDENT
ANTHONY LAKE

FROM: WILLIAM WISE
RICHARD E. FEINBERG

SUBJECT: Proposed Hemispheric Summit

The proposed Memorandum to the President at Tab I asks him to approve a summit meeting of heads of state of the Western Hemisphere in Washington in May 1994 and to authorize the Vice President to announce this initiative in Mexico City on Wednesday.

RECOMMENDATION

That you sign the Memorandum to the President at Tab I.

Attachment
Tab I Memorandum to the President

Declassified/Released on 3/8/96
under provisions of E.O. 12953
by D. Van Tassel, National Security Council

~~CONFIDENTIAL~~
Declassify on: OADR

UNCLASSIFIED
~~CONFIDENTIAL~~

THE WHITE HOUSE
WASHINGTON

ACTION

MEMORANDUM FOR THE PRESIDENT

FROM: THE VICE PRESIDENT
ANTHONY LAKE

SUJBECT: Proposed Hemispheric Summit

Purpose

To seek your approval for a summit meeting of Western Hemisphere heads of state in Washington in May 1994 to build on the NAFTA victory to generate a broad hemispheric consensus behind our key policy objectives. The Vice President would announce your intention to convene such a summit in his address in Mexico City on Wednesday.

Background

The moment is ripe for an historic initiative -- of the weight of the Good Neighbor policy and the Alliance for Progress -- to establish the themes for inter-American relations for the rest of the decade and beyond:

-- The NAFTA is the foundation for the gradual expansion of hemispheric free trade. Prior to the summit we still would need to decide the modalities, timetable and eligibility criteria -- you have already defined the vision.

-- The region is solidly democratic (except Haiti and Cuba), and old restraints of "non-intervention" are giving way to the collective defense of democracy. We can strengthen the OAS and other mechanisms to prevent or react to coups. To enhance democratic legitimacy, we can launch a "good governance initiative" to strengthen the institutions of government.

-- Our new global agenda -- environmental protection, immigration and refugees, family planning and sustainable development -- can take concrete form in this hemisphere. The region has made considerable progress on traditional security issues (nonproliferation, conventional arms control) and could be encouraged to do more.

-- Hemispheric institutions, including the OAS and Inter-American Development Bank and now the NAFTA institutions, can be forged into the vital mechanisms of hemispheric governance.

The organizing concept could be a hemispheric "Community of Democracies" increasingly integrated by economic exchange and shared political values. Whatever the slogan, your vision of an integrated Western Hemisphere could be a model for international relations in general and for North-South relations more specifically.

We have nearly completed a draft Presidential Decision Directive on Latin America which can provide the basic guidelines for our own deliberations. We would of course hold intensive consultations with Latin America and the Caribbean prior to the May summit. One outcome of the summit could be a "Charter of Hemispheric Solidarity" which would codify a set of shared principles.

RECOMMENDATION

That you approve a summit meeting of heads of state of the Western Hemisphere for May in Washington, and that the Vice President announce your intention to convene such a summit in his address in Mexico City.

Approve _____ Disapprove _____

~~CONFIDENTIAL~~
Declassify on: OADR

cc: Vice President
Chief of Staff

Appendix C

SUMMIT DOCUMENTS

Fourteen Summit Agenda Initiatives Presented by the United States to Governments of the Hemisphere

The United States believes the Summit of the Americas will accelerate the development of a hemispheric community based on democratic rule, increased economic integration, and shared values and interests. It represents an unprecedented opportunity for the leaders of this hemisphere to affirm a joint vision of the future and to lay a foundation for hemispheric cooperation into the next century. Taken together, initiatives developed in preparation for the Summit will unite the governments and people of the hemisphere in an historic partnership. The following proposed initiatives are being discussed throughout the hemisphere.

THEME ONE — MAKING DEMOCRACY WORK: REINVENTING GOVERNMENT

Initiative 1

No to Corruption: A hemispheric call on governments and international businesses to recognize the need for transparency and accountability, to refrain from offering or seeking bribes, and to take specific actions necessary for compliance. Discussions might include 1) how to participate in implementation of the May 1994 recommendation of the Council of the OECD on bribery in international business transactions; 2) development of national action plans to strengthen formal and operational mechanisms for combatting corruption, e.g., review of law and practice relating to management of public funds, procurement, conflict of interest of public officials, donations to political parties, and auditing structures; 3) adoption of strong criminal, civil, and administrative prohibitions against bribery of foreign officials in international business transactions; and 4) greater cooperation to improve public procurement, civil service, and business regulation.

Initiative 2

Battle Plan against the Cartels: A hemisphere-wide commitment to law enforcement measures against the major drug traffickers and to demand/production targets.

The initiative would focus on moving our long-established efforts on the continent to a new plateau of cooperation and sophistication. The theme would be a call for a modernized, forward-looking drug agenda grounded on the understanding that the narcotics trade is a fundamental

3

threat to democracy and sustainable development throughout the hemisphere.

We will pursue discussions, commitments, and initiatives focused on two separate but reinforcing objectives. The first will be an enforcement challenge to the cartels that calls for regional and institution-building programs that deprive traffickers and their operations the opportunity to elude law enforcement. This will be broad enough to encompass the particular interests of each participating government: chemical controls for some; money laundering, interdiction, and kingpin investigations for others. Several Latin American governments have expressed particular interest in strengthening regional efforts against money laundering.

The second objective will be a call to reject the legalization of drugs and commit to a substantial reduction in drug cultivation and consumption by the year 2000. The goal will be to eliminate opium poppy production and significantly reduce illicit coca cultivation by the year 2000 and to resume, at a faster rate, the downward trend in drug abuse in the United States. For its part, the United States will be willing to step up technical, operational, and financial support for eradication and to lead an international effort to raise billions of dollars in sustainable development assistance over the remainder of the decade to create economic alternatives for drug producers.

Initiative 3

Regulatory Reform: Financial market integrity and investor protection are necessary to maximize capital inflows. Leaders could endorse the activities of existing regional regulatory bodies such as the Council of Security Regulators of the Americas (COSRA) and the Center for Monetary Studies of Latin America (CEMLA), lending them greater legitimacy. In addition, the U.S. is prepared to expand IRS and customs programs that provide training to national authorities in the collection of taxes and tariffs.

Initiative 4

Making Civil Society Work: An integrated program would include a model legal/tax framework for the operation of NGOs, start-up financing through an IDB civil society fund, better support through organized hemispheric networking, and an OAS prize to recognize outstanding individual contributions. The Summit would react to existing analyses and proposals for improving the climate for creation and operation of civic-minded NGOs and private voluntary associations. It would endorse the creation of a fund within the IDB which would stimulate private philanthropy by providing matching funds for the endowment of "Mentor Foundations" in the civic development area. The mentors would advocate needed tax and regulatory policy reform in individual countries and help other organizations get started. The Summit would also endorse networking among NGOs to share experience.

Initiative 5

Enhance OAS Capacity to Strengthen Democracy: Commitment for OAS 1) to assist member states to strengthen their legislative branches though technical assistance and increased interaction with their democratic counterparts and 2) to enhance the capacity of the organization to preempt or manage situations in member states that threaten the democratic order. A proposed mediation and reconciliation service would be able to call on outside notables to facilitate peaceful constitutional solutions before the democratic order is broken. Creation of a crisis management center would enable the OAS to respond more effectively when and if a breakdown occurs.

THEME TWO — MAKING DEMOCRACY PROSPEROUS: HEMISPHERIC ECONOMIC INTEGRATION

Advancing Trade and Investment
Strengthening Financial Linkages

Initiative 6

Hemispheric Free Trade: The Summit offers the opportunity to affirm the vision of free trade in the Western Hemisphere based on the principles of "open regionalism." Senior U.S. government trade officials will consult with governments of the hemisphere on ways and means to make this powerful vision a reality.

Initiative 7

Hemispheric Capital Movements Liberalization: Barriers to the free movement of capital hamper investment and economic growth. Leaders could commit to progressive liberalization of capital flows. Those leaders prepared to move ahead now could give momentum to this process by agreeing to launch negotiations for a Hemispheric Capital Movements Code that would provide for a standstill and the progressive liberalization of capital restrictions. This code would facilitate the free flow of capital, promote comparable financial standards, bolster transparency, and reduce opportunities for corruption. Development and advancement of the code may require establishment of a committee on hemispheric capital markets comprised of senior financial officials meeting periodically to examine issues related to cross-border capital flows in the region.

In addition, the leaders might consider other agreements that could provide private investors assurances about the future openness of their investment regimes.

Initiative 8

Hemispheric Infrastructure:

Part A — Hemispheric Infrastructural Protocol: The goal of this initiative is to reduce the cost of financing the tremendous infrastructure requirements of the hemisphere, including those in the telecommunications, transportation, energy, and public utility grids. Leaders could agree to develop a protocol to facilitate international financing for private infrastructure projects that could 1) enunciate the policies and principles that governments should follow to support private financing of infrastructure; 2) establish procedures for consultations before enacting policy changes affecting an infrastructure project; and 3) agree to compensate investors in private sector infrastructure projects for damages caused by government failure to respect the commercial integrity of such projects.

In addition, this initiative would benefit from harmonization of inconsistent standards and regulations across borders. It would complement initiatives in the environmental domain to ensure that infrastructure development is consistent with sound environmental policies.

Part B — Information for the Americas: Sharing information is essential to making markets work and to promoting democratic institutions and sustainable development. Today, the primary means of sharing information is electronic. The leaders could endorse private investment, competition, open access to networks, universal service, and flexible regulatory frameworks as the basic principles of a hemispheric information infrastructure linked to the global information infrastructure. These could be achieved through an energized Inter-American Telecommunications Commission (CITEL) that would serve as the regional forum and focal point for telecommunications development activities. Working individually and through CITEL, countries could set a goal to put the Americas online by ensuring hemisphere-wide access points connecting major hospitals, universities, libraries, and research institutions to the Internet within one year.

THEME THREE — MAKING DEMOCRACY ENDURE: SUSTAINABLE DEVELOPMENT

Major challenges are investing in people, the hemisphere's most valuable resource, and creating an alliance with nature to ensure that our natural resources are available to sustain future generations.

A. Investing in People

The Summit offers the opportunity to call for policies that would allow all members of the hemisphere's societies to partake of the benefits of development. The proposed initiatives in this area focus on population segments — the poor, women, and indigenous populations — likely to remain excluded from full benefits of development unless specific policy measures are taken.

Initiative 9

Universal Access to Quality Primary Education: Obtain a commitment from the hemisphere's governments to refocus existing resources more effectively toward quality primary education. A hemispheric partnership proposes to achieve 100 percent primary school completion rates and 75 percent secondary school enrollment by the year 2000. Aim at education sector reforms in financing, decentralization, and a reordering of budget priorities, so that an increased proportion of government budgets would be invested in primary education. The hemisphere initiative would approve the design of a plan of action involving all nations. The action plan would be monitored by a region-wide consultative partnership involving governments, NGOs, the business community, and international organizations. Achievement of the goal would enable all citizens to participate productively and democratically in a maturing economic and political environment.

Initiative 10

Equitable Access to Basic Health Care: Summit leaders would call for each country's commitment to ensure equitable, universal access to basic health services so as to reduce child mortality rates in the region by one-third and maternal mortality rates by one-half by the year 2000. Health reform commissions would be designated in each country and include public and private participants and donors to help plan, monitor, and mobilize resources for reforming the health sector and ensuring equitable access to services. Under the country plans, reforms will include decentralizing services, reorienting budgetary allocations to favor essential services for the poor, developing new financial mechanisms, and encouraging privatization of some services and greater use of NGOs. As a result, countries should be able to ensure access to a basic, cost-effective WHO and World Bank-endorsed package of clinical and public health services. The Pan American Health Organization (PAHO) and other existing regional mechanisms will monitor implementation of the country plans, consistent with the Nariño Accord, and provide a forum for sharing information and expertise.

Initiative 11

Nurturing Microenterprises: The IDB group could take the lead in crafting a pilot project to integrate the poor into the formal economy through reducing legal obstacles to enterprise growth and through development of financial services targeted specifically at small businesses and microenterprises. Specifically, it could 1) provide assistance to improve the marketing, management, and financial capabilities of NGOs that sponsor successful savings associations and financial companies for microenterprises so that they can operate on market terms and conditions; 2) provide financial and technical assistance to commercial banks and saving institutions to help lower transaction costs associated with originating and monitoring small loans to entrepreneurs; 3) develop and provide seed capital and technical support for a network of locally owned business advisory services affiliates; and 4) assist in efforts to reduce legal obstacles to microenterprises, e.g., simplification of business registration and tax codes and improved land titling.

B. Alliance with Nature

The alliance with nature's overall objectives are 1) to ensure that resource use today does not reduce the quality of life of future generations, 2) to halt and reverse resource waste and environmental degradation in the hemisphere, and 3) to strengthen natural resource stewardship by facilitating increased participation of indigenous people, local communities, and non-governmental organizations.

The initiatives described below build on the agreements reached at UNCED 1992, including the Climate Change and Biodiversity Conventions and Agenda 21. Follow-up would be focused on at a ministerial-level meeting on sustainable development, proposed to be held in Bolivia in 1995.

Initiative 12

Energy: Summit leaders would agree to begin implementation by 1998 of programs to promote sustainable energy use based on the principles of integrated resource planning and consideration of the full range of energy and capacity resources. Leaders would call for the identification and financing of non-conventional renewable energy and energy efficiency, especially by the multilateral development banks, which would be asked to increase financing for sustainable energy projects. As a first step, energy ministers will develop national work programs to promote energy efficiency, renewable energy, and natural gas use for discussion at the November 1995 meeting of the Latin American Energy Organization (OLADE). Technical cooperation could be coordinated by OLADE and Renewable Energy in the Americas (REIA).

Initiative 13

Hemispheric Partnership for Nature: The leaders would reaffirm their commitment, utilizing existing international agreements and the newly replenished Global Environmental Fund (GEF) to build cooperative action on the management and conservation of living resources. The partnership would focus on enhancing scientific and management capacity in forest management, management of coral reef and marine resources, and parks, reserves, and migratory species. Special emphasis would be placed on support for natural resource management efforts of indigenous communities. The leaders would call on the OAS to establish a Western Hemisphere convention office to report on progress of the initiative.

Initiative 14

Environmental Protection and Compliance Regimes: Leaders would agree to pursue an agreement to develop and strengthen compatible environmental laws, standards, and enforcement regimes to reduce environmental problems and negative impacts, promote a level playing field for industries operating in the hemisphere, increase demand for environmental technologies and services, and offer opportunities for public participation in the environmental policy-making process. This "upward" harmonization of environmental standards in the Americas would strengthen legal frameworks, enhance environmental compliance and enforcement capacity, and build institutions through technical cooperation, training, and education. A first step would be to focus on a sector or sectors of critical importance to human health, such as pesticides, lead, mercury, or industrial pollution, as well as on developing mechanisms to promote public involvement in the decision-making process. Leaders should also call on appropriate regional institutions to provide technical coordination linking government agencies, NGOs, the private sector, and professional groups. Leaders could announce an initial set of principles and commitments, e.g., pollution prevention, cost internalization, ecosystem protection, and the right of nations to adopt levels of protection more stringent than international levels.

Appendix D

Summit of the Americas Declaration of Principles

Partnership for Development and Prosperity: Democracy, Free Trade and Sustainable Development in the Americas

The elected Heads of State and Government of the Americas are committed to advance the prosperity, democratic values and institutions, and security of our Hemisphere. For the first time in history, the Americas are a community of democratic societies. Although faced with differing development challenges, the Americas are united in pursuing prosperity through open markets, hemispheric integration, and sustainable development. We are determined to consolidate and advance closer bonds of cooperation and to transform our aspirations into concrete realities.

We reiterate our firm adherence to the principles of international law and the purposes and principles enshrined in the United Nations Charter and in the Charter of the Organization of American States (OAS), including the principles of the sovereign equality of states, non-intervention, self-determination, and the peaceful resolution of disputes. We recognize the heterogeneity and diversity of our resources and cultures, just as we are convinced that we can advance our shared interests and values by building strong partnerships.

To Preserve and Strengthen the Community of Democracies of the Americas

The Charter of the OAS establishes that representative democracy is indispensable for the stability, peace and development of the region. It is the sole political system which guarantees respect for human rights and the rule of law; it safeguards cultural diversity, pluralism, respect for the rights of minorities, and peace within and among nations. Democracy is based, among other fundamentals, on free and transparent elections and includes the right of all citizens to participate in government. Democracy and development reinforce one another.

We reaffirm our commitment to preserve and strengthen our democratic systems for the benefit of all people of the Hemisphere. We will work through the appropriate bodies of the OAS to strengthen democratic institutions and promote and defend constitutional democratic rule, in accordance with the OAS Charter. We endorse OAS efforts to enhance peace and the democratic, social, and economic stability of the region.

We recognize that our people earnestly seek greater responsiveness and efficiency from our respective governments. Democracy is strengthened by the modernization of the state, including reforms that streamline operations, reduce and simplify government rules and procedures, and make democratic institutions more transparent and accountable. Deeming it essential that justice should be accessible in an efficient and expeditious way to all sectors of society, we affirm that an independent judiciary is a critical element of an effective legal system and lasting democracy. Our ultimate goal is to better meet the needs of the population, especially the needs of women and the most vulnerable groups, including indigenous people, the disabled, children, the aged, and minorities.

Effective democracy requires a comprehensive attack on corruption as a factor of social disintegration and distortion of the economic system that undermines the legitimacy of political institutions.

Recognizing the pernicious effects of organized crime and illegal narcotics on our economies, ethical values, public health, and the social fabric, we will join the battle against the consumption, production, trafficking and distribution of illegal drugs, as well as against money laundering and the illicit trafficking in arms and chemical precursors. We will also cooperate to create viable alternative development strategies in those countries in which illicit crops are grown. Cooperation should be extended to international and national programs aimed at curbing the production, use and trafficking of illicit drugs and the rehabilitation of addicts.

We condemn terrorism in all its forms, and we will, using all legal means, combat terrorist acts anywhere in the Americas with unity and vigor.

Recognizing the important contribution of individuals and associations in effective democratic government and in the enhancement of cooperation among the people of the Hemisphere, we will facilitate fuller participation of our people in political, economic and social activity, in accordance with national legislation.

To Promote Prosperity Through Economic Integration and Free Trade

Our continued economic progress depends on sound economic policies, sustainable development, and dynamic private sectors. A key to prosperity is trade without barriers, without subsidies, without unfair practices, and with an increasing stream of productive investments. Eliminating impediments to market access for goods and services among our countries will foster our economic growth. A growing world economy will also enhance our domestic prosperity. Free trade and increased economic integration are key factors for raising standards of living, improving the working conditions of people in the Americas and better protecting the environment.

We, therefore, resolve to begin immediately to construct the "Free Trade Area of the Americas" (FTAA), in which barriers to trade and investment will be progressively eliminated. We further resolve to conclude the negotiation of the "Free Trade Area of the Americas" no later than 2005, and agree that concrete progress toward the attainment of this objective will be made by the end of this century. We recognize the progress that already has been realized through the unilateral undertakings of each of our nations and the subregional trade arrangements in our

Hemisphere. We will build on existing subregional and bilateral arrangements in order to broaden and deepen hemispheric economic integration and to bring the agreements together.

Aware that investment is the main engine for growth in the Hemisphere, we will encourage such investment by cooperating to build more open, transparent and integrated markets. In this regard, we are committed to create strengthened mechanisms that promote and protect the flow of productive investment in the Hemisphere, and to promote the development and progressive integration of capital markets.

To advance economic integration and free trade, we will work, with cooperation and financing from the private sector and international financial institutions, to create a hemispheric infrastructure. This process requires a cooperative effort in fields such as telecommunications, energy and transportation, which will permit the efficient movement of the goods, services, capital, information and technology that are the foundations of prosperity.

We recognize that despite the substantial progress in dealing with debt problems in the Hemisphere, high foreign debt burdens still hinder the development of some of our countries.

We recognize that economic integration and the creation of a free trade area will be complex endeavors, particularly in view of the wide differences in the levels of development and size of economies existing in our Hemisphere. We will remain cognizant of these differences as we work toward economic integration in the Hemisphere. We look to our own resources, ingenuity, and individual capacities as well as to the international community to help us achieve our goals.

To Eradicate Poverty And Discrimination In Our Hemisphere

It is politically intolerable and morally unacceptable that some segments of our populations are marginalized and do not share fully in the benefits of growth. With an aim of attaining greater social justice for all our people, we pledge to work individually and collectively to improve access to quality education and primary health care and to eradicate extreme poverty and illiteracy. The fruits of democratic stability and economic growth must be accessible to all, without discrimination by race, gender, national origin or religious affiliation.

In observance of the International Decade of the World's Indigenous People, we will focus our energies on improving the exercise of democratic rights and the access to social services by indigenous people and their communities.

Aware that widely shared prosperity contributes to hemispheric stability, lasting peace and democracy, we acknowledge our common interest in creating employment opportunities that improve the incomes, wages and working conditions of all our people. We will invest in people so that individuals throughout the Hemisphere have the opportunity to realize their full potential.

Strengthening the role of women in all aspects of political, social and economic life in our countries is essential to reduce poverty and social inequalities and to enhance democracy and sustainable development.

To Guarantee Sustainable Development and Conserve Our Natural Environment for Future Generations

Social progress and economic prosperity can be sustained only if our people live in a healthy environment and our ecosystems and natural resources are managed carefully and responsibly. To advance and implement the commitments made at the 1992 United Nations Conference on Environment and Development, held in Rio de Janeiro, and the 1994 Global Conference on the Sustainable Development of Small Island Developing States, held in Barbados, we will create cooperative partnerships to strengthen our capacity to prevent and control pollution, to protect ecosystems and use our biological resources on a sustainable basis, and to encourage clean, efficient and sustainable energy production and use. To benefit future generations through environmental conservation, including the rational use of our ecosystems, natural resources and biological heritage, we will continue to pursue technological, financial and other forms of cooperation.

We will advance our social well-being and economic prosperity in ways that are fully cognizant of our impact on the environment. We agree to support the Central American Alliance for Sustainable Development, which seeks to strengthen those democracies by promoting regional economic and social prosperity and sound environmental management. In this context, we support the convening of other regional meetings on sustainable development.

*****

Our Declaration constitutes a comprehensive and mutually reinforcing set of commitments for concrete results. In accord with the appended Plan of Action, and recognizing our different national capabilities and our different legal systems, we pledge to implement them without delay.

We call upon the OAS and the Inter-American Development Bank to assist countries in implementing our pledges, drawing significantly upon the Pan American Health Organization and the United Nations Economic Commission for Latin America and the Caribbean as well as sub-regional organizations for integration.

To give continuity to efforts fostering national political involvement, we will convene specific high-level meetings to address, among others, topics such as trade and commerce, capital markets, labor, energy, education, transportation, telecommunications, counter-narcotics and other anti-crime initiatives, sustainable development, health, and science and technology.

To assure public engagement and commitment, we invite the cooperation and participation of the private sector, labor, political parties, academic institutions and other non-governmental actors and organizations in both our national and regional efforts, thus strengthening the partnership between governments and society.

*****

Our thirty-four nations share a fervent commitment to democratic practices, economic integration, and social justice. Our people are better able than ever to express their aspirations and to learn from one another. The conditions for hemispheric cooperation are propitious. Therefore, on behalf of all our people, in whose name we affix our signatures to this Declaration, we seize this historic opportunity to create a Partnership for Development and Prosperity in the Americas.

Appendix E

Plan of Action
Table of Contents

I. Preserving and Strengthening the Community of Democracies of the Americas

1. Strengthening Democracy
2. Promoting and Protecting Human Rights
3. Invigorating Society/Community Participation
4. Promoting Cultural Values
5. Combating Corruption
6. Combating the Problem of Illegal Drugs and Related Crimes
7. Eliminating the Threat of National and International Terrorism
8. Building Mutual Confidence

II. Promoting Prosperity Through Economic Integration and Free Trade

9. Free Trade in the Americas
10. Capital Markets Development and Liberalization
11. Hemispheric Infrastructure
12. Energy Cooperation
13. Telecommunications and Information Infrastructure
14. Cooperation in Science and Technology
15. Tourism

III. Eradicating Poverty and Discrimination in Our Hemisphere

16. Universal Access to Education
17. Equitable Access to Basic Health Services
18. Strengthening the Role of Women in Society
19. Encouraging Microenterprises and Small Businesses
20. White Helmets—Emergency and Development Corps

IV. Guaranteeing Sustainable Development and Conserving Our Natural Environment for Future Generations

21. Partnership for Sustainable Energy Use
22. Partnership for Biodiversity
23. Partnership for Pollution Prevention

Summit of the Americas
Plan of Action

The heads of state and government participating in the 1994 Summit of the Americas in Miami, Florida, desirous of furthering the broad objectives set forth in their Declaration of Principles and mindful of the need for practical progress on the vital tasks of enhancing democracy, promoting development, achieving economic integration and free trade, improving the lives of their people, and protecting the natural environment for future generations, affirm their commitment to this Plan of Action.

I. PRESERVING AND STRENGTHENING THE COMMUNITY OF DEMOCRACIES OF THE AMERICAS

1. Strengthening Democracy

The strengthening, effective exercise and consolidation of democracy constitute the central political priority of the Americas. The Organization of American States (OAS) is the principal hemispheric body for the defense of democratic values and institutions; among its essential purposes is to promote and consolidate representative democracy, with due respect to the principle of non-intervention. The OAS has adopted multilateral procedures to address the problems created when democratic order has been interrupted unconstitutionally. In order to prevent such crises, the OAS needs to direct more effort toward the promotion of democratic values and practices and to the social and economic strengthening of already-established democratic regimes.

Governments will:

- Give expeditious consideration to ratifying the Cartagena de Indias, Washington and Managua Protocols to the OAS Charter, if they have not already done so.

- Strengthen the dialogue among social groups and foster grass roots participation in problem solving at the local level.

- Support efforts by the OAS to promote democracy by:

  ◊ Encouraging exchanges of election-related technologies and assisting national electoral organizations, at the request of the interested state.

  ◊ Strengthening the Unit for the Promotion of Democracy so that it can provide assistance at the request of the interested state on such matters as legislative and judicial processes, government reforms (including administration of justice, technical modernization of national legislative bodies, simplification of government regulations and promotion of participation by community organizations in local democracy), and other institutional changes.

- ◊ Encouraging opportunities for exchange of experiences among member states' democratic institutions, particularly legislature-to-legislature and judiciary-to-judiciary.

- ◊ Fostering understanding, dialogue and political reconciliation, at the request of the affected state and bearing in mind that national reconciliation comes from within.

- ◊ Requesting the OAS to promote and follow up on these commitments.

2. Promoting and Protecting Human Rights

Great progress has been made in the Hemisphere in the development of human rights concepts and norms, but serious gaps in implementation remain. While courts ultimately have the responsibility for enforcing legal rights and obligations, reforms in other institutions are needed to contribute to the further development of a climate of respect for human rights. There must also be universal access to justice and effective means to enforce basic rights. A democracy is judged by the rights enjoyed by its least influential members.

Governments will:

- Give serious consideration to adherence to international human rights instruments to which they are not already party.

- Cooperate fully with all United Nations and inter-American human rights bodies.

- Develop programs for the promotion and observance of human rights, including educational programs to inform people of their legal rights and their responsibility to respect the rights of others.

- Promote policies to ensure that women enjoy full and equal legal rights within their families and societies, and to ensure the removal of constraints to women's full participation as voters, candidates and elected and appointed officials.

- Review and strengthen laws for the protection of the rights of minority groups and indigenous people and communities to ensure freedom from discrimination, to guarantee full and equal protection under the law, and to facilitate active civic participation. Support a process to review and enhance the protection of indigenous rights in OAS member states and to develop promptly an effective United Nations declaration on indigenous rights.

- Review national legislation affecting people with disabilities, as well as benefits and services for them, and make any changes needed to facilitate the enjoyment by these individuals of the same rights and freedoms as other members of society.

- Undertake all measures necessary to guarantee the rights of children, and, where they have not already done so, give serious consideration to ratifying the United Nations Convention on the Rights of the Child.

- Guarantee the protection of the human rights of all migrant workers and their families.

- Take the necessary steps to remedy inhumane conditions in prisons and to minimize the number of pretrial detainees.

- Review training curricula for law enforcement agents to ensure that they adequately cover proper treatment of suspects and detainees as well as relations with the community.

- Exchange experiences on protection of human rights at the national level and, where possible, cooperate in the development of law enforcement and security force training or other programs to reduce the potential for human rights violations.

- Call on the OAS and the Inter-American Development Bank (IDB) to establish or to reinforce programs, as appropriate, to support national projects for the promotion and observance of human rights in the Western Hemisphere.

- Further strengthen the Inter-American Commission on Human Rights and the Inter-American Court of Human Rights.

3. Invigorating Society/Community Participation

A strong and diverse civil society, organized in various ways and sectors, including individuals, the private sector, labor, political parties, academics, and other non-governmental actors and organizations, gives depth and durability to democracy. Similarly, a vigorous democracy requires broad participation in public issues. Such activities should be carried out with complete transparency and accountability, and to this end a proper legal and regulatory framework should be established to include the possibility of obtaining technical and financial support, including from private sources.

Governments will:

- Review the regulatory framework for non-governmental actors with a view to facilitating their operations and promoting their ability to receive funds. This review will emphasize the management and oversight of resources as well as transparency and the accountability to society of said actors.

- Take steps to improve the participation in social activities and initiatives of groups traditionally marginalized, including women, youth, indigenous people and the extremely poor.

- Exchange progress reports on activities in the civil society area at the 1996 Summit Conference on Sustainable Development in Bolivia.

Consider the development by the IDB of a new Civil Society Program to encourage responsible and accountable philanthropy and civic engagement in public policy issues.

4. Promoting Cultural Values

Cultural development is a fundamental and integral component of development in the Americas and has an inherent capability to enrich our societies and to generate greater understanding among our countries.

In order to promote cultural values, governments will:

- Encourage more dynamic relations among public and private institutions and organizations, including universities, museums, and centers of art and literature, as well as among individual cultural actors. Such exchanges emphasize our cultural diversity, recognize the value of our local cultures and contribute to improving hemispheric understanding.
- Request that the OAS and IDB reinforce their plans and programs to facilitate these cultural exchanges and the flow of cultural and historical information within and among our nations.

5. Combating Corruption

The problem of corruption is now an issue of serious interest not only in this Hemisphere, but in all regions of the world. Corruption in both the public and private sectors weakens democracy and undermines the legitimacy of governments and institutions. The modernization of the state, including deregulation, privatization and the simplification of government procedures, reduces the opportunities for corruption. All aspects of public administration in a democracy must be transparent and open to public scrutiny.

Governments will:

- Promote open discussion of the most significant problems facing government and develop priorities for reforms needed to make government operations transparent and accountable.
- Ensure proper oversight of government functions by strengthening internal mechanisms, including investigative and enforcement capacity with respect to acts of corruption, and facilitating public access to information necessary for meaningful outside review.
- Establish conflict of interest standards for public employees and effective measures against illicit enrichment, including stiff penalties for those who utilize their public position to benefit private interests.
- Call on the governments of the world to adopt and enforce measures against bribery in all financial or commercial transactions with the Hemisphere; toward this end, invite the OAS to establish liaison with the OECD Working Group on Bribery in International Business Transactions.

- Develop mechanisms of cooperation in the judicial and banking areas to make possible rapid and effective response in the international investigation of corruption cases.

- Give priority to strengthening government regulations and procurement, tax collection, the administration of justice and the electoral and legislative processes, utilizing the support of the IDB and other international financial institutions where appropriate.

- Develop within the OAS, with due regard to applicable treaties and national legislation, a hemispheric approach to acts of corruption in both the public and private sectors that would include extradition and prosecution of individuals so charged, through negotiation of a new hemispheric agreement or new arrangements within existing frameworks for international cooperation.

6. Combating the Problem of Illegal Drugs and Related Crimes

The problems of illegal drug and related criminal activities pose grave threats to the societies, free market economies, and democratic institutions of the Hemisphere. Drug use imposes enormous social costs; drug money and income are net drains on economic growth; and drug lords and criminal organizations endanger the security of our people through corruption, intimidation, and violence. While drug trafficking continues to be a significant source of illegal funds, the money laundering industry increasingly deals with the proceeds of all types of criminal activity. An integrated and balanced approach that includes respect for national sovereignty is essential to confront all aspects of these problems. For these reasons, a broad coordinated hemispheric strategy to reduce drug use and production, including new enforcement methods that can disrupt drug trafficking and money laundering networks and prosecute those engaged in such activities, is required. In this context, governments note the work of the 1992 San Antonio Summit, endorse the efforts of the Inter-American Commission on Drug Abuse Control, and agree to work together to formulate a counter-narcotics strategy for the 21st Century.

Governments will:

- Ratify the 1988 United Nations Convention Against the Illicit Traffic of Narcotics and Psychotropic Substances and make it a criminal offense to launder the proceeds of all serious crimes.

- Enact legislation to permit the freezing and forfeiture of the proceeds of money laundering and consider the sharing of forfeited assets among governments.

- As agreed by ministers and representatives of Caribbean and Latin American governments in the Kingston Declaration, November 5-6, 1992, implement the recommendations of the Caribbean Financial Action Task Force on Money Laundering and work to adopt the Model Regulations of the Inter-American Commission on Drug Abuse Control (CICAD).

- Encourage financial institutions to report large and suspicious transactions to appropriate authorities and develop effective procedures that would allow the collection of relevant information from financial institutions.

- Work individually and collectively to identify the region's narcotics trafficking and money laundering networks, prosecute their leaders, and seize assets derived from these criminal activities.

- Adopt programs to prevent and reduce the demand for and the consumption of illicit drugs.

- Adopt effective and environmentally-sound national strategies to prevent or reduce substantially the cultivation and processing of crops used for the illegal drug trade, paying particular attention to national and international support for development programs that create viable economic alternatives to drug production.

- Pay particular attention to the control of precursor chemicals and support comprehensive drug interdiction strategies.

- Strengthen efforts to control firearms, ammunition, and explosives to avoid their diversion to drug traffickers and criminal organizations.

- Hold a working-level conference, to be followed by a ministerial conference, to study and agree on a coordinated hemispheric response, including consideration of an inter-American convention, to combat money laundering.

- Convene a hemispheric-wide conference of donors, including multilateral development banks and UN agencies, to seek resources for alternative development programs aimed at curbing the production, trafficking, and use of illicit drugs, and the rehabilitation of addicts.

- Support the discussion the OAS has initiated with the European Union on measures to control precursor chemicals.

- Support the convening of a global counter-narcotics conference.

7. Eliminating the Threat of National and International Terrorism

National and international terrorism constitute a systematic and deliberate violation of the rights of individuals and an assault on democracy itself. Recent attacks that some of our countries have suffered have demonstrated the serious threat that terrorism poses to security in the Americas. Actions by governments to combat and eliminate this threat are essential elements in guaranteeing law and order and maintaining confidence in government, both nationally and internationally. Within this context, those who sponsor terrorist acts or assist in their planning or execution through the abuse of diplomatic privileges and immunities or other means will be held responsible by the international community.

Governments will:

- Promote bilateral and subregional agreements with the aim of prosecuting terrorists and penalizing terrorist activities within the context of the protection of human rights and fundamental freedoms.
- Convene a special conference of the OAS on the prevention of terrorism.
- Reaffirm the importance of the extradition treaties ratified by the states of the Hemisphere, and note that these treaties will be strictly complied with as an expression of the political will of governments, in accordance with international law and domestic legislation.

8. Building Mutual Confidence

The expansion and consolidation of democracy in the Americas provide an opportunity to build upon the peaceful traditions and the cooperative relationships that have prevailed among the countries of the Western Hemisphere. Our aim is to strengthen the mutual confidence that contributes to the economic and social integration of our peoples.

Governments will:

- Support actions to encourage a regional dialogue to promote the strengthening of mutual confidence, preparing the way for a regional conference on confidence-building measures in 1995, which Chile has offered to host.

II. PROMOTING PROSPERITY THROUGH ECONOMIC INTEGRATION AND FREE TRADE

9. Free Trade in the Americas

1) While pursuing economic integration and free trade in the Hemisphere, we reinforce our strong commitment to multilateral rules and disciplines. We endorse full and rapid implementation of the Uruguay Round, active multilateral negotiations in the World Trade Organization, bilateral and subregional trade agreements, and other trade arrangements that are consistent with the provisions of the GATT/WTO and that do not raise barriers to other nations.

2) Extraordinary achievements have been made by countries of the Hemisphere in trade liberalization and subregional integration. Free trade and increased economic integration are key factors for sustainable development. This will be furthered as we strive to make our trade liberalization and environmental policies mutually supportive, taking into account efforts undertaken by the GATT/WTO and other international organizations. As economic integration in the Hemisphere proceeds, we will further secure the observance and promotion

of worker rights, as defined by appropriate international conventions. We will avoid disguised restrictions on trade, in accordance with the GATT/WTO and other international obligations.

3) We will strive to maximize market openness through high levels of discipline as we build upon existing agreements in the Hemisphere. We also will strive for balanced and comprehensive agreements, including among others: tariffs and non-tariff barriers affecting trade in goods and services; agriculture; subsidies; investment; intellectual property rights; government procurement; technical barriers to trade; safeguards; rules of origin; antidumping and countervailing duties; sanitary and phytosanitary standards and procedures; dispute resolution; and competition policy.

4) We recognize that decisions on trade agreements remain a sovereign right of each nation. In addition, recognizing the importance of effective enforcement of international commitments, each nation will take the necessary action, in accordance with its own legislation and procedures, to implement the agreements in the areas covered by this Plan of Action.

5) As we work to achieve the "Free Trade Area of the Americas," opportunities such as technical assistance will be provided to facilitate the integration of the smaller economies and increase their level of development.

Immediate Action Agenda

We direct our ministers responsible for trade to take the following concrete initial steps to achieve the "Free Trade Area of the Americas."

6) With the objective of ensuring full and complete discussion among the parties to the various trade agreements in the Hemisphere, we direct that meetings be held under existing trade and investment fora. Members of these fora will determine areas of commonality and divergence in the particular agreements under review and should consider the means of improving disciplines among them and bringing them together. We further direct that members of these fora inform ministers of the status of their discussions and make recommendations for achieving the "Free Trade Area of the Americas."

7) Transparency in, and a clear understanding of, the subregional and bilateral agreements achieved to date among the nations in the Hemisphere are critical for advancing trade and investment integration in the Americas. We will direct the OAS Special Committee on Trade, with the support of the IDB, ECLAC, and other specialized regional and subregional organizations, to assist in the systematization of data in the region and to continue its work on studying economic integration arrangements in the Hemisphere, including brief comparative descriptions of the obligations in each of the Hemisphere's existing trade agreements. We will further direct the Special Committee on Trade to prepare a report of its work by June 1995 for the meeting of ministers.

8) We direct our ministers responsible for trade to: (a) review the progress of work undertaken in the fora noted in paragraphs 6 and 7; (b) provide guidance with respect to further work; and (c) consider areas for immediate attention—such as customs facilitation and product testing and certification with a view to mutual recognition agreements—that could be taken up in the appropriate fora.

9) Therefore, today we launch the "Free Trade Area of the Americas" by initiating the following process. We will direct the OAS to assist the host country in arranging the ministerial meetings.

January 1995 o Initiation of work programs and establishment of schedules in the fora in paragraph 6 and in the Special Committee on Trade.

June 1995 o Meeting of Ministers responsible for trade.

— preliminary report on status of work in the fora described in paragraph 6.

— preliminary Special Committee on Trade report.

— areas for immediate consideration.

March 1996 o Meeting of Ministers responsible for trade.

— final report to ministers by the Special Committee on Trade.

— final reports to ministers from the fora described in paragraph 6.

— timetable for further work.

10. Capital Markets Development and Liberalization

The availability of capital at competitive rates is essential to finance private sector investment—a vital ingredient in economic development. Developing, liberalizing and integrating financial markets domestically and internationally, increasing transparency, and establishing sound, comparable supervision and regulation of banking and securities markets will help to reduce the cost of capital by enhancing investor and depositor confidence.

Governments will:

- Form a Committee on Hemispheric Financial Issues to examine steps to promote the liberalization of capital movements and the progressive integration of capital markets, including, if deemed appropriate, the negotiation of common guidelines on capital movements that would provide for their progressive liberalization.

- Prepare, in cooperation with the Inter-American Development Bank, a comprehensive list of national capital regulations in order to promote transparency and support the discussions in the Committee on Hemispheric Financial Issues.

- Support the cooperative endeavors of the Association of Latin American and Caribbean Bank Supervisors and the Council of Securities Regulators of the Americas to provide sound supervision and regulation that support the development and progressive integration of markets.

The Committee on Hemispheric Financial Issues should also review problems of debt in the Hemisphere, taking account of ongoing work and drawing, as appropriate, on a broad range of expertise.

11. Hemispheric Infrastructure

Development in this Hemisphere depends on urgent infrastructure measures, including the priority allocation of financial resources, in accordance with national legislation and with the participation of both the public and private sectors. Strengthening the flow of private productive capital to economically and environmentally sound projects has become increasingly vital to countries throughout the Hemisphere as the growth of official sources of capital has failed to keep pace with the area's needs.

Governments will:

- Charge multilateral development banks to work with governments and, as appropriate, private concerns, to develop mechanisms to deal with lending and investment issues.

- Draw on other regional and sub-regional experiences within the Hemisphere to support infrastructure development.

- Governments that so wish will develop suitable mechanisms, including multilateral and bilateral commitments on regulatory and legal rules and practices, to encourage private investment, both domestic and foreign, in national and transboundary infrastructure projects.

12. Energy Cooperation*

The nations of the Hemisphere have begun a new era of economic growth. This new era is based on greater economic cooperation, freer trade, and open markets. Sustainable economic development requires hemispheric cooperation in the field of energy.

Governments will:

- Convene a follow-up hemispheric officials' meeting in the first semester of 1995 to encourage cooperation to study ways to develop the energy industry within the Hemisphere, consistent with the least cost national energy strategies and the activities described in the "Partnership for Sustainable Energy use" in the following areas:

  ◊ Consideration of ways to use the energy sector to promote sustainable economic growth.

  ◊ Cooperation to study ways to optimize and facilitate the financing mechanisms of international financial institutions to support the development of projects in the energy sector, especially including those pertaining to the enhancement of efficiency in the use of energy and to non-conventional renewable energy.

  ◊ Cooperation to promote capital investment and to foster the use of innovative financial mechanisms to increase investment in the energy sector and the enhancement of efficiency in the use of energy and non-conventional renewable energy, in accordance with each country's legislation and developmental needs.

  ◊ Promotion of the use of efficient and non-polluting energy technologies, both conventional and renewable, leading to a higher degree of knowledge and technical expertise in this area.

  ◊ Consideration of the enhancement of ongoing efforts to establish electric and other energy facilities in accordance with domestic regulatory frameworks and, where appropriate, under sub-regional agreements.

* This initiative is integrally linked with the Partnership for Sustainable Energy Use item.

13. Telecommunications and Information Infrastructure

A country's information infrastructure—telecommunications, information technology, and broadcasting—is an essential component of political, economic, social and cultural development. The information infrastructure development needs in the Americas are immense. The governments of the Americas intend to meet these needs by engaging in multiple actions, where consistent with their respective governing laws, such as: encouraging private sector investment to increase participation in the telecommunications and information infrastructure sectors; promoting competition; implementing flexible regulatory regimes; stimulating diversity of content, including cultural and linguistic diversity; providing access to information networks for service and information providers; and ensuring universal service, so that the benefits of the information infrastructure will be available to all members of our societies.

Governments will:

- Engage in ongoing discussions at the international level of the actions referred to above and endeavor to take those actions in their own countries, taking account of domestic conditions and circumstances.

- Undertake efforts to make government information more publicly available via electronic means.

- Review the availability and interoperability of connections to international networks that facilitate trade, improve education and improve access to health care.

- Encourage major universities, libraries, hospitals and government agencies to have access to these networks, building on the work of the OAS Hemisphere-Wide Inter-University Scientific and Technological Information Network.

- Via the OAS Inter-American Telecommunications Commission (CITEL), and in coordination with the sub-regional telecommunications organizations, develop and carry out a work program to:

  ◊ Evaluate regulatory, technical and legal means to promote liberalization, common standards, interoperability of networks and compatible use of the radio spectrum.

  ◊ Examine ways to promote greater consistency of the certification processes for telecommunications equipment among member countries.

  ◊ Develop regional guidelines for the provision of international value-added network services.

- Support a meeting by 1996, coordinated by CITEL, of senior telecommunications officials to conduct further discussions of the above actions.

14. Cooperation in Science and Technology

There is a need to re-assess the on-going interaction among the region's science and technology (S&T) infrastructure and cooperative mechanisms; to provide impetus for improved cooperation; to reduce barriers to collaboration; to augment the demand for technology; and to disseminate information about technological opportunities using new advances in information technology; and generally to improve communications among the key S&T organizations, researchers in the region, and growing technology-based small and medium-sized enterprises.

The commitment of the countries of the Americas to non-proliferation has gained new momentum with the acceptance of the international safeguard regime by some of our countries.

The outstanding progress achieved in this field is to be commended and should contribute to enhanced opportunities for cooperation in the area of advanced goods and technologies.

Governments will:

- Convene a meeting of ministers responsible for science and technology in the Hemisphere within the next year to assess progress and to promote the Bolivar Programme and the OAS Common Market of Scientific and Technological Knowledge (MERCOCYT) program, to provide the necessary support to improve scientific partnerships and technological ventures in the region, and to explore the possibility of establishing a council on science and technology.

- Use existing multilateral mechanisms in the region to address a wide number of common S&T interests, including enhanced professional technical training, development and implementation of national policies and regional programs, dissemination and standardization of science and technology (including metrology and other technical norms), environmental technology development, and more effective partnerships to promote learning and competitiveness.

- Stimulate greater S&T interaction in the Hemisphere and support efforts already undertaken in other fora, including the Inter-American Institute for Global Change Research, and the International Research Institute for Climate Prediction. Governments will serve to advance and communicate new initiatives such as the Global Learning and Observations to Benefit the Environment (GLOBE) program.

- Confirm their interest in participating in new initiatives driven by a demand from private sector and non-government interests in technological opportunities.

- Confirm their national commitments to share S&T information with others in the Hemisphere, in accord with their respective laws, and to expand cooperation in scientific and environmental research.

15. Tourism

Tourism is important to our economies and valuable in promoting understanding among the people of the Americas.

Governments will:

- Undertake initiatives to stimulate tourism in the Hemisphere.

III. ERADICATING POVERTY AND DISCRIMINATION IN OUR HEMISPHERE

Large segments of society in our Hemisphere, particularly women, minorities, the disabled, indigenous groups, refugees and displaced persons, have not been equipped to participate fully in economic life. Nearly one-half of the Hemisphere's population still lives in poverty. Expanded participation of the poor in the region's economies, access to productive resources, appropriate support for social safety nets and increased human capital investments are important mechanisms to help eradicate poverty. In pursuit of these objectives, we reaffirm our support for the strategies contained within the "Commitment on a Partnership for Development and Struggle to Overcome Extreme Poverty" adopted by the OAS General Assembly.

The World Summit for Social Development to be held in Copenhagen in March 1995, as well as the United Nations World Conference on Women in Beijing in September 1995, will provide unique opportunities to define strategies to promote social integration, productive employment and the eradication of poverty.

16. Universal Access to Education

Universal literacy and access to education at all levels, without distinction by race, national origin or gender, are an indispensable basis for sustainable social and cultural development, economic growth and democratic stability.

Governments will:

- Guarantee universal access to quality primary education, working with public and private sectors and non-governmental actors, and with the support of multinational institutions. In particular, governments will seek to attain by the year 2010 a primary completion rate of 100 per cent and a secondary enrollment rate of at least 75 per cent, and to prepare programs to eradicate illiteracy, prevent truancy and improve human resources training.

- Promote, with the support of international financial institutions and the private sector, worker professional training as well as adult education, incorporating efforts to make such education more relevant to the needs of the market and employers.

- Improve human resources training, and technical, professional and teacher training, which are vital for the enhancement of quality and equity of education within the Hemisphere.

- Increase access to and strengthen the quality of higher education and promote cooperation among such institutions in producing the scientific and technological knowledge that is necessary for sustainable development.

- Support strategies to overcome nutritional deficiencies of primary school children in order to enhance their learning ability.

- Support decentralization including assurance of adequate financing and broad participation by parents, educators, community leaders and government officials in education decision-making.

- Review existing regional and hemispheric training programs and make them more responsive to current needs.
- Create a hemispheric partnership, working through existing organizations, to provide a consultative forum for governments, non-governmental actors, the business community, donors, and international organizations to reform educational policies and focus resources more efficiently.
- Urge the March 1995 World Summit for Social Development and the September 1995 Fourth World Conference on Women to address the issue of universal access to education.

17. Equitable Access to Basic Health Services

Despite impressive gains in the Hemisphere, limitations on health services access and quality have resulted in persistently high child and maternal mortality, particularly among the rural poor and indigenous groups.

Governments will:

- Endorse the maternal and child health objectives of the 1990 World Summit for Children, the 1994 Nariño Accord and the 1994 International Conference on Population and Development, and reaffirm their commitment to reduce child mortality by one-third and maternal mortality by one-half from 1990 levels by the year 2000.
- Endorse a basic package of clinical, preventive and public health services consistent with World Health Organization, Pan American Health Organization (PAHO) and World Bank recommendations and with the Program of Action agreed to at the 1994 International Conference on Population and Development. The package will address child, maternal and reproductive health interventions, including prenatal, delivery and postnatal care, family planning information and services, and HIV/AIDS prevention, as well as immunizations and programs combating the other major causes of infant mortality. The plans and programs will be developed according to a mechanism to be decided upon by each country.
- Develop or update country action plans or programs for reforms to achieve child, maternal and reproductive health goals and ensure universal, non-discriminatory access to basic services, including health education and preventive health care programs. The plans and programs will be developed according to a mechanism to be decided upon by each country. Reforms would encompass essential community-based services for the poor, the disabled, and indigenous groups; stronger public health infrastructure; alternative means of financing, managing and providing services; quality assurance; and greater use of non-governmental actors and organizations.
- Strengthen the existing Inter-American Network on Health Economics and Financing, which serves as an international forum for sharing technical expertise, information and

experience, to focus on health reform efforts. The network gathers government officials, representatives of the private sector, non-governmental institutions and actors, donors and scholars for policy discussions, analysis, training and other activities to advance reform; strengthens national capabilities in this critical area; and fosters Hemisphere-wide cooperation.

- Convene a special meeting of hemispheric governments with interested donors and international technical agencies to be hosted by the IDB, the World Bank and PAHO to establish the framework for health reform mechanisms, to define PAHO's role in monitoring the regional implementation of country plans and programs, and to plan strengthening of the network, including the cosponsors' contributions to it.

- Take the opportunity of the annual PAHO Directing Council Meeting of Western Hemisphere Ministers of Health, with participation of the IDB and donors, to develop a program to combat endemic and communicable diseases as well as a program to prevent the spread of HIV/AIDS, and to identify sources of funding.

- Urge the March 1995 World Summit for Social Development and the September 1995 Fourth World Conference on Women to address the issue of access to health services.

18. Strengthening the Role of Women in Society

The strengthening of the role of women in society is of fundamental importance not only for their own complete fulfillment within a framework of equality and fairness, but to achieve true sustainable development. It is essential to strengthen policies and programs that improve and broaden the participation of women in all spheres of political, social, and economic life and that improve their access to the basic resources needed for the full exercise of their fundamental rights. Attending to the needs of women means, to a great extent, contributing to the reduction of poverty and social inequalities.

Governments will:

- Recognize and give full respect for all rights of women as an essential condition for their development as individuals and for the creation of a more just, united and peaceful society. For that purpose, policies to ensure that women enjoy full legal and civil rights protection will be promoted.

- Include a gender focus in development planning and cooperation projects and promote the fulfillment of women's potential, enhancing their productivity through education, training, skill development and employment.

- Promote the participation of women in the decision-making process in all spheres of political, social and economic life.

- Undertake appropriate measures to address and reduce violence against women.

- Adopt appropriate measures to improve women's ability to earn income beyond traditional occupations, achieve economic self-reliance, and ensure women's equal access to the labor market at all employment levels, the social security systems, the credit system, and the acquisition of goods and land.

- Cooperate fully with the recently-appointed Special Rapporteur on Violence Against Women, its Causes and Consequences, of the United Nations Commission on Human Rights.

- Support and actively work to secure the success of the United Nations World Conference on Women that will take place in Beijing in September 1995.

- Encourage, as appropriate, ratification and compliance with the International Convention on the Elimination of all Forms of Discrimination Against Women and the Inter-American Convention on the Prevention, Punishment and Eradication of Violence Against Women.

- Further strengthen the Inter-American Commission on Women.

- Call upon regional and international financial and technical organizations to intensify their programs in favor of women. Encourage the adoption of follow-up procedures on the national and international measures included in this Plan of Action.

19. Encouraging Microenterprises and Small Businesses

Microenterprises and small businesses account for a large percentage of the employment of the poor, particularly women, and contribute a considerable percentage of the gross domestic product of our countries. Strengthened support for microenterprises and small businesses is a key component of sustainable and equitable development.

Governments will:

- Further pursue or initiate programs of deregulation and administrative simplification.

- Increase efforts to enable enterprises to obtain information on appropriate technologies (especially those that are environmentally sound), markets, processes, raw materials and management systems that will permit them to be more competitive in the global economy.

- Develop programs of financial deregulation to reduce costs in credit transactions and strengthen the institutional capacity of the financial sector servicing microenterprises and small businesses, and encourage the active participation by multilateral and bilateral agencies, development banks, commercial banks and other intermediary credit organizations, consistent with strict performance standards.

- Strengthen the institutions and programs that supply services and facilitate access to training and technical assistance to make possible this sector's participation in the global economy through export of its products and services.

- Encourage cooperation among businesses in this sector to enable them to benefit from the advantages of economies of scale without losing their distinctive characteristics.

- Promote the strengthening of relations among the public, private and mixed (public/private) institutions that support the microenterprise and small business sector through programs of information, training, technical assistance, financing and association-building, enabling this sector to thrive over the long term.

- Recommend to the multilateral development organizations, especially the World Bank and the IDB, the establishment or fortification of funds and other mechanisms to support microenterprises and small businesses.

20. White Helmets—Emergency and Development Corps

The "White Helmets Initiative" is based on the conviction that a concerted international effort of developing and developed countries can facilitate the eradication of poverty and strengthen the humanitarian rapid response capability of the international community to emergency humanitarian, social and developmental needs.

The countries of the Americas could pioneer this initiative through the creation of national corps of volunteers that could respond to calls from other countries in the region. These national corps could eventually be put at the disposal of the United Nations.

Governments will on a voluntary basis:

- Establish, organize and finance a corps of volunteers to work at the national level and, at the same time, be at the disposal of other countries of the Hemisphere and, eventually, the United Nations system, on a stand-by basis, for prevention, relief, rehabilitation, technical, social and development cooperation, with the aim to reduce the effects of natural disasters, social and developmental needs and emergencies.

- Through the creation of a national corps of volunteers, be responsible for the following:

  ◊ Selection and training of its national volunteer corps;

  ◊ Financing of its national corps of volunteers, encouraging the involvement of the private sector;

  ◊ Preparedness to send specialized volunteers, on short notice and at the request of the United Nations, to cope with situations generated by or to prevent the effects of natural disasters and humanitarian emergencies.

- Contribute to the formation of this corps and invite private enterprises, foundations and regional financial institutions to do so.
- Contribute to the development of an international roster of volunteers to be maintained in a master plan in the United Nations to be drawn upon to complement the activities of existing UN mechanisms. The IDB, OAS, and PAHO should be invited to participate and assist in developing this corps.

IV. GUARANTEEING SUSTAINABLE DEVELOPMENT AND CONSERVING OUR NATURAL ENVIRONMENT FOR FUTURE GENERATIONS

21. Partnership for Sustainable Energy Use*

Consistent with Agenda 21 and the Framework Convention on Climate Change, sustainable energy development and use promote economic development and address environmental concerns. Governments and the private sector should promote increased access to reliable, clean, and least cost energy services through activities and projects that meet economic, social, and environmental requirements within the context of national sustainable development goals and national legal frameworks.

Governments will:

- Pursue, in accordance with national legislation, least cost national energy strategies that consider all options, including energy efficiency, non-conventional renewable energy (i.e., solar, wind, geothermal, small hydro, and biomass), and conventional energy resources.
- Emphasize market-oriented pricing, which discourages wasteful energy use.
- Identify for priority financing and development at least one economically viable project in each of the following areas: non-conventional renewable energy, energy efficiency, and clean conventional energy.
- Promote, in cooperation with the private sector and rural and isolated communities, rural electrification programs which take into account where appropriate the utilization of renewable energy sources, in accordance with the domestic regulatory framework.
- Seek to ratify and begin implementation of the provisions of the Framework Convention on Climate Change which entered into force on March 21, 1994.
- Encourage the World Bank and IDB to increase promptly and substantially, as a portion of energy lending, financing of projects in energy efficiency and renewable energy and financing to improve the environmental sustainability of conventional energy sources, in accordance with economic rationality.

- Call on the multilateral financial institutions and other public and private financial institutions to finance regional and national programs in support of this action plan, such as training and exchange programs as well as technology cooperation, in accordance with the needs and conditions of receiving countries.

- Assist with coordination and technical cooperation between countries, using existing regional organizations, including project identification and implementation, training programs, and personnel and information exchanges to increase capacity.

- Promote the identification and implementation of private sector projects that reduce greenhouse gas emissions.

- Convene a Sustainable Energy Symposium in the first half of 1995 to discuss follow-up activities relative to this initiative. In the spirit of cooperation countries will share their experiences and discuss progress on implementing this action plan.

*This initiative is integrally linked with the Energy Cooperation item.

22. Partnership for Biodiversity

Our Hemisphere contains over half the world's biodiversity. To sustain the Hemisphere's social and economic development, we must intensify efforts to understand, assess, and sustainably use this living resource base. We must act now to increase the technical and management capacity and public awareness of national and international efforts in this area. Agenda 21, the Convention on Biological Diversity, and other related international instruments recognize these needs and call for the conservation and sustainable use of biodiversity resources.

Governments will:

- Seek to ensure that strategies for the conservation and sustainable use of biodiversity are integrated into relevant economic development activities including forestry, agriculture, and coastal zone management, taking into account the social dimension and impact of these activities.

- Develop and implement the policies, techniques, and programs to assess, conserve, and sustainably use terrestrial, marine, and coastal biodiversity resources.

- Seek to ratify the Convention on Biological Diversity and pursue opportunities for collaboration under it, and, as appropriate, other international and regional environmental instruments.

- Support democratic governmental mechanisms to engage public participation, particularly including members of indigenous communities and other affected groups, in the development of policy involving conservation and sustainable use of natural environments. The forms of this participation should be defined by each individual country.

- Develop national plans and programs to establish and strengthen the management of parks and reserves, seeking links to economic, social, and ecological benefits for local people.
- Build capacity for the conservation and sustainable use of biodiversity, through programs on management of parks and protected areas, forests and wetlands management, the Small Islands Developing States Action Plan, the Coral Reef Initiative, CITES support projects, and the Caribbean Regional Marine Pollution Action Plan, among others.
- Launch a "Decade of Discovery" to promote hemispheric technical and scientific cooperation and to facilitate the exchange of information relevant to the conservation and sustainable use of biological diversity.
- Increase support of training and education initiatives addressing sustainable use of biodiversity resources and foster activities by universities, non-governmental actors and organizations and the private sector to assist in the training of managers and to empower local communities.
- Call on multilateral financial institutions, including the IDB and the Global Environment Facility, to support eligible regional and national projects.
- Discuss progress on implementation of national and international activities described above at the 1996 Summit Conference on Sustainable Development in Bolivia, and at subsequent annual sustainable development ministerials.

23. Partnership for Pollution Prevention

As recognized in Agenda 21, sound environmental management is an essential element of sustainable development. Cooperative efforts are needed to develop or improve, in accordance with national legislation and relevant international instruments: (1) frameworks for environment protection; and (2) mechanisms for implementing and enforcing environmental regulations. To achieve this goal, a new partnership will promote cooperative activities for developing environmental policies, laws, and institutions; increasing technical capacity; promoting public awareness and public participation; continuing to pursue technological, financial and other forms of cooperation; and facilitating information exchange, including on environmentally sound technologies. The activities of the partnership will build on and advance the implementation of international agreements and principles including those agreed to at the 1992 United Nations Conference on Environment and Development and the 1994 Global Conference on the Sustainable Development of Small Island Developing States, in areas identified as priorities by countries of the Hemisphere.

Governments will:

- Strengthen and build technical and institutional capacity to address environmental priorities such as pesticides, lead contamination, pollution prevention, risk reduction, waste and sanitation issues, improved water and air quality, access to safe drinking water, urban environmental problems, and to promote public participation and awareness.

- Develop and implement national action plans to phase out lead in gasoline.
- Strengthen national environmental protection frameworks and mechanisms for implementation and enforcement, and include sustainability criteria and objectives in national and other development strategies.
- Undertake national consultations to identify priorities for possible international collaboration.
- Support democratic governmental mechanisms to engage public participation, particularly from members of indigenous and other affected communities, in the consideration of policies regarding the environmental impact of development projects and the design and enforcement of environmental laws.
- Convene a meeting of technical experts, designated by each interested country, to develop a framework for cooperative partnership, building on existing institutions and networks to identify priority projects. These projects will initially focus on (1) the health and environmental problems associated with the misuse of pesticides, and (2) the impacts of lead contamination from gasoline and other sources. Subsequent activities could address waste, air, water quality, marine pollution from ships and other sources, and problems associated with urbanization.
- Promote the participation of organizations, such as the IDB, MIF, the World Bank, PAHO, the OAS, and non-governmental actors and organizations, as appropriate, to finance, develop and implement priority projects.
- Develop environmental policies and laws with the goal of ensuring that economic integration of the region occurs in an environmentally sustainable manner.
- Establish mechanisms for cooperation among government agencies, including in the legal and enforcement areas, to facilitate environmental information exchange, technology cooperation and capacity-building.
- Develop compatible environmental laws and regulations, at high levels of environmental protection, and promote the implementation of international environmental agreements.
- Discuss progress on implementation of international and national activities described above at the 1996 Summit Conference on Sustainable Development in Bolivia and at subsequent annual sustainable development ministerials.

Appendix

The primary responsibility for implementing this Plan of Action falls to governments, individually and collectively, with participation of all elements of our civil societies.

Existing organizations or institutions are called upon to implement the package of initiatives that has emerged from this Summit of the Americas. In many instances we have proposed that specific issues be examined by meetings of ministers, senior officials or experts. We are also proposing that some of these initiatives be carried out in partnerships between the public and private sector. Wanting to benefit from existing hemispheric mechanisms, and considering the various proposals included in this Plan of Action, we offer the following recommendations, which shall not impede any government from approaching other institutions not cited herein, as appropriate.

I. Principal Initiatives in Which International Organizations and Institutions Will Be Involved

A) The OAS will have a paramount role in following up on the various decisions of this Summit meeting. Regarding the Plan of Action, the OAS has a particularly important supporting role in connection with the following:

- Strengthening Democracy
- Promoting and Protecting Human Rights
- Combating Corruption
- Eliminating the Threat of National and International Terrorism
- Building Mutual Confidence
- Free Trade in the Americas
- Telecommunications and Information Infrastructure

The Action Plan also envisages roles for the OAS in the following areas:

- Promoting Cultural Values
- Combating the Problem of Illegal Drugs and Related Crimes
- Cooperation in Science and Technology
- Strengthening the Role of Women in Society
- Partnership for Pollution Prevention

B) We call on the Inter-American Development Bank to support the activities specified in this Plan of Action. The policies agreed in the recently completed augmentation of its capital and replenishment of the Fund for Special Operations already move in the directions identified and should receive special emphasis. The IDB has a particularly important role in connection with the following:

- Universal Access to Education
- Equitable Access to Basic Health Services
- Encouraging Microenterprises and Small Businesses
- Partnership for Sustainable Energy Use
- Partnership for Biodiversity
- Partnership for Pollution Prevention

In addition, the Action Plan envisages roles for the IDB and its affiliates in the following areas:

- Promoting and Protecting Human Rights
- Invigorating Society/Community Participation
- Promoting Cultural Values
- Combating Corruption
- Combating the Problem of Illegal Drugs and Related Crimes
- Free Trade in the Americas
- Capital Markets Development and Liberalization
- Hemispheric Infrastructure
- Cooperation in Science and Technology
- White Helmets—Emergency and Development Corps

C) Other international organizations, notably ECLAC and PAHO in the Hemisphere, as well as the World Bank and all agencies of the UN system active in the Hemisphere, are called upon to assist in the implementation of the action items where appropriate.

II. High-Level Meetings

The following high level meetings and conferences are called for to carry out the mandates emanating from the Summit:

- Summit Conference on Sustainable Development (Bolivia, 1996) with follow-on Annual Ministerials
- Ministerial Conference on Combating Money Laundering (preceded by working level meeting)

- Conference of Donors for Alternative Development Programs to Curb Narcotics Trafficking
- Global Counter-Narcotics Conference
- Special OAS Conference on Combating Terrorism
- Regional Conference on Confidence-Building Measures (Chile, 1995)
- Meetings of Ministers Responsible for Trade (June 1995, March 1996)
- Meeting of Committee on Hemispheric Financial Issues
- Hemispheric Meeting on Development of Energy Industries (first semester 1995)
- Meeting of Ministers Responsible for Science and Technology (1995)
- Meeting Between Governments and Donors/Technical Agencies to Establish Health Reform Mechanisms
- Sustainable Energy Symposium (first half of 1995)

III. **Initiatives in Which Public and Private Sector Partnerships Play an Important Role**

- Strengthening Democracy
- Promoting and Protecting Human Rights
- Invigorating Society/Community Participation
- Promoting Cultural Values
- Combating Corruption
- Hemispheric Infrastructure
- Cooperation in Science and Technology
- Universal Access to Education
- Equitable Access to Basic Health Services
- Encouraging Microenterprises and Small Businesses
- White Helmets—Emergency and Development Corps
- Partnership for Sustainable Energy Use
- Partnership for Biodiversity
- Partnership for Pollution Prevention

Appendix F

SUMMIT OF THE AMERICAS
"Partnership for Prosperity:
Democracy & Free Trade in the Americas"
(Miami, December 9 - 11)

President Clinton makes history in the Hemisphere.

- Summit builds upon dramatic move toward free societies and open markets that has swept the Western Hemisphere.
- Last summit held in 1967 in Punta del Este, Uruguay. Ten nations were non-democratic; many economies had not yet begun reform.
- Largest summit ever: all 34 freely elected leaders will attend; Cuba's Castro not invited.

Leaders will address challenges facing the region:

- eliminating barriers to trade and economic integration
- strengthening democratic institutions (e.g. anti-corruption laws)
- assuring sustainable development (promoting environment, health & education)

Focus on Trade

- Goal is *free trade for the Hemisphere.*
- Summit joins NAFTA, APEC, and GATT as elements in Clinton strategy to reduce trade barriers against U.S. exports.
- U.S. is now concluding consultations with hemispheric leaders on Summit trade proposals, as well as political and social initiatives.

The U.S. has critical interests in the Hemisphere:

Economic: Trade = U.S. Jobs

- The Western Hemisphere will be the world's largest market: $13 trillion & 850 million people by 2003.
- With greater trade liberalization, U.S. exports to Latin America could more than triple to $290 billion and support an additional 2-3 million U.S. jobs by 2003.
- The Hemisphere is now the United States' most important export market, and Latin America is the only region with which the U.S. has a substantial trade surplus. U.S. exports to Latin America more than doubled over 1985-93, from $30 billion to $80 billion.
- If trends continue, Latin America will become a larger customer for U.S. exports than Western Europe. Today we sell more to Brazil than to Russia.

Strategic: Democracy = Stability

- Strengthening democracy across the region will preserve peace and assure stability for economic growth of all nations.

Appendix G
Leaders at the Summit of the Americas

Antigua and Barbuda	Prime Minister Lester Bird
Argentina	President Carlos Menem
The Bahamas	Prime Minister Hubert A. Ingraham
Barbados	Prime Minister Owen Arthur
Belize	Prime Minister Manuel Esquivel
Bolivia	President Gonzalo Sánchez de Lozada
Brazil	President Itamar Franco
Canada	Prime Minister Jean Chrétien
Chile	President Eduardo Frei
Colombia	President Ernesto Samper
Costa Rica	President José María Figueres
Dominica	Prime Minister Eugenia Charles
Dominican Republic	President Joaquín Balaguer
Ecuador	President Sixto Durán Bállen
El Salvador	President Armando Calderón Sol
Grenada	Prime Minister Nicholas Brathwaite
Guatemala	President Ramiro de Léon Carpio
Guyana	President Cheddi Jagan
Haiti	President Jean-Bertrand Aristide
Honduras	President Carlos Roberto Reina
Jamaica	Prime Minister P. J. Patterson
Mexico	President Ernesto Zedillo
Nicaragua	President Violeta Chamorro
Panama	President Ernesto Pérez Balladares
Paraguay	President Juan Carlos Wasmosy
Peru	President Alberto Fujimori
St. Kitts and Nevis	Prime Minister Kennedy Simmonds
St. Lucia	Prime Minister John Compton
St. Vincent and the Grenadines	Prime Minister James F. Mitchell
Suriname	President Ronald Venetiaan
Trinidad and Tobago	Prime Minister Patrick Manning
United States	President William Jefferson Clinton
Uruguay	President Luís Alberto Lacalle
Venezuela	President Rafael Caldera

Appendix H

Responsible Coordinators for Summit Implementation

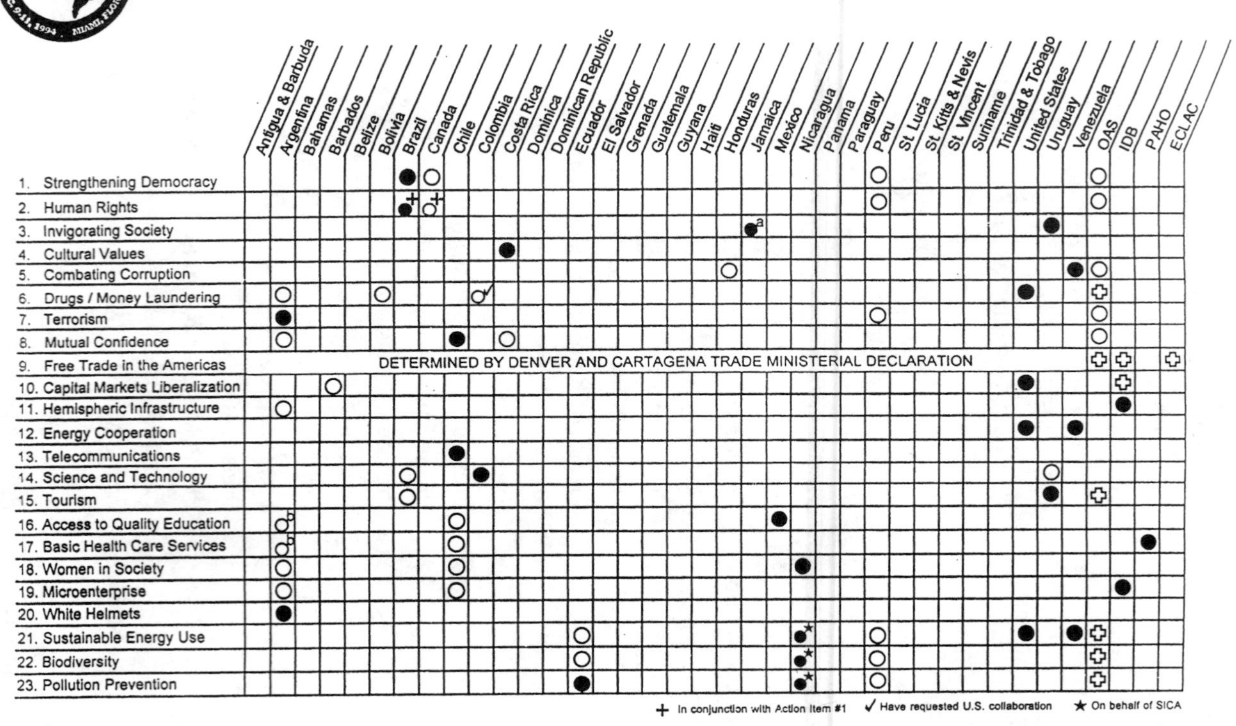

	Antigua & Barbuda	Argentina	Bahamas	Barbados	Belize	Bolivia	Brazil	Canada	Chile	Colombia	Costa Rica	Dominica	Dominican Republic	Ecuador	El Salvador	Grenada	Guatemala	Guyana	Haiti	Honduras	Jamaica	Mexico	Nicaragua	Panama	Paraguay	Peru	St Lucia	St Kitts & Nevis	St Vincent	Suriname	Trinidad & Tobago	United States	Uruguay	Venezuela	OAS	IDB	PAHO	ECLAC
1. Strengthening Democracy							●	○																		○									○			
2. Human Rights							●+	○+																		○									○			
3. Invigorating Society																					●a												●					
4. Cultural Values											●																											
5. Combating Corruption																				○														●	○			
6. Drugs / Money Laundering		○				○				○✓																						●			✚			
7. Terrorism		●																								○									○			
8. Mutual Confidence		○							●		○																								○			
9. Free Trade in the Americas	DETERMINED BY DENVER AND CARTAGENA TRADE MINISTERIAL DECLARATION																																		✚	✚		✚
10. Capital Markets Liberalization				○																												●				✚		
11. Hemispheric Infrastructure		○																																		●		
12. Energy Cooperation																																●		●				
13. Telecommunications									●																													
14. Science and Technology							○			●																							○					
15. Tourism							○																										●		✚			
16. Access to Quality Education		○b							○													●																
17. Basic Health Care Services		○b							○																												●	
18. Women in Society		○							○														●															
19. Microenterprise		○							○																											●		
20. White Helmets		●																																				
21. Sustainable Energy Use														○									●★			○						●		●	✚			
22. Biodiversity														○									●★			○									✚			
23. Pollution Prevention														●									●★			○									✚			

\+ In conjunction with Action Item #1   ✓ Have requested U.S. collaboration   ★ On behalf of SICA

a In coordination with CARICOM   b The comprehensive nutrition, hunger aspects

● Responsible Coordinator
○ Co-Coordinator
✚ Support Role

9/24/96

Appendix I
Glossary

ACDA	Arms Control and Disarmament Agency
APEC	Asian Pacific Economic Cooperation
ARA	Inter-American Affairs Bureau, Department of State
Caricom	Caribbean Common Market
CMM	Cascading modular multilateralism
COSRA	Council of Security Regulators of the Americas
DOD	Department of Defense
DOE	Department of Energy
EB	Bureau of Economic and Business Affairs, Department of State
EPA	Environmental Protection Agency
FTA	Free Trade Area
G-7	Group of Seven
GATT	General Agreement on Tariffs and Trade
HHS	Health and Human Services
ICRW	International Center for Research on Women
IDB	Inter-American Development Bank
ITP	Interim Trade Program
IWG	Interagency working group
JCS	Joint Chiefs of Staff
Mercosur	Southern Cone Common Market
NAFTA/TLC	North American Free Trade Agreement/Tratado de Libre Commercio

NEC	National Economic Council
NED	National Endowment For Democracy
NGA	Nongovernmental actor such as business and labor associations, academic and research institutions, and advocacy and community groups
NRDC	Natural Resources Defense Council
NSA	National Security Advisor
NSC	National Security Council
OAS	Organization of American States
OECD	Organization for Economic Corporation and Development
OMB	Office of Management and Budget
ONDCP	Office of National Drug Control Policy
PAHO	Pan-American Health Organization
PDD	Presidential Decision Directive
PRD	Presidential Review Directive
SIRG	Summit Implementation Review Group
TIC	Trade and Investment Council
UNECLAC	United Nations Economic Commission for Latin America and the Caribbean
USAID	US Agency for International Development
USOAS	US Mission to the Organization of American States
USTR	US Trade Representative
WOLA	Washington Office on Latin America
WTO	World Trade Organization

Index

Abdenur, Roberto, 141-43, 148
Abrams, Eliot, 41
Adams, John Quincy, 16
Agribusiness, 36-37
Aho, Michael, 44*n*
Airlie House meeting, 139-49
  anticorruption initiative, 120
  consensus initiatives, 104
  energy initiative, 123
  microenterprise initiative, 127
  money laundering, 172
  reasons for success, 148-49
  women's rights initiative, 121
Allende, Salvador, 40
Alliance for Progress, 32-33, 100, 194*n*
Alliance for Sustainable Development, 156
Altman, Robert, 94-95, 134
Americas Business Forum, 180
Amorim, Celso, 115
Andean Pact, 40
  trade (1988-94), 50*t*
  trade initiative, 135
Anticommunism, 27, 29, 31-32, 40
Anticorruption initiative, 117-20, 168-69
  authoritarian regime fear, 90
  Caribbean Common Market (Caricom), 145
  coalition, 144
  endorsed at summit, 156-57
  implementation, 164, 168-69
  leadership, 144
  networks, 163
  plan of action (text), 222-23
  significance of Miami summit, 188
  Venezuela, 114, 128
  See also Bribery issue; Corruption issue; Drug war
Antihemispherism, 186-87, 198
Anti-imperialism, 10*t*
Antitotalitarian thinking, 24-25
APEC. *See* Asia Pacific Economic Cooperation forum
Arévalo, Juan José, 27, 27*n*
Argentina
  date certain, 137
  democracy initiative, 114-15
  FTAA goals, 178
  Gore visit, 107-09
  infrastructure initiative, 126
  military tensions, 147
  Paraguay coup attempt, 166-67
  reaction to summit, 105
  terrorism, 164
  ties with Europe, 21
  trade initiative, 135-36
Aristide, Jean-Bertrand, 157
Armacost, Michael, 82*n*

Arthur, Owen, 158
Asia, 37
  hemispheric free trade, 134
Asia Pacific Economic Cooperation (APEC) forum, 193-94
  announces 2020 free-trade date, 137
  Bogor summit, 77
  competitive liberalism, 77
  Seattle meeting, 154
  secretariat, 193-94
  US participation, 45
Atkins, Pope G., 14*n*
Authoritarian regimes
  after 1950s, 26
  anticorruption banner, 90, 169
  Cold War, 40, 42
  disappearance in 1980s, 41
  Kirkpatrick justifies, 40-41
  leaders at summits, 40, 100
  Paraguay coup attempt, 167-68
  sovereignty issue, 28
  US tolerance, 24, 31
Aylwin, Patricio, 49

Baena Soares, Secretary General, 43
Baker, James A., III, 41*n*, 44*n*, 45, 45*n*, 47*n*
Balseiro, José Agustín, 15*n*, 22*n*
Barbados, 113, 158
Barshefsky, Charlene
  Central America, 134-35
  deputies committee, 80
  Gore's Mexico City speech, 56, 72
  knowledge of Latin America, 84
  second round of consultations, 141
  sovereignty issue, 136
  trade expertise, 75
  trade integration initiative, 131-33
  vice ministerial meetings, 184
Bayne, Nicholas, 38*n*, 189*n*
Behr, Peter, 49*n*
Belassa, Bela, 35*n*
Bentsen, Lloyd, 69, 71, 75-76
Berger, Samuel
  at Miami summit, 155
  Chilean accession to NAFTA, 69
  date certain, 78
  deputies committee, 80
  free trade benefits US, 75-76
  summit coordination, 81
  trade expertise, 75
Bergsten, C. Fred, 44*n*, 77*n*, 195*n*
Berle, Adolf, 87*n*
Bernal, Richard L., 134, 164*n*, 175*n*, 185
Betancourt, RXC59,1mulo, 32
Bilateralism strategy, 103-04, 122
Bilbao, Francisco, 15*n*
Biles, Robert E., 27*n*
Biodiversity initiative, 123, 174-75, 238-39
Birdsall, Nancy, 121, 124*n*
Blaine, James G., 18-19
Blanco, Herminio, 111
Blasier, Cole, 29*n*
Bolivarianism, 10*t*, 17, 18*n*, 23
Bolívar, Simón, 15, 15*n*, 17
Bolivia, Gore visit, 107-08
Border disputes, 18-19, 186
Botafogo Goncalvez, José, 178*n*
Boylan, Delia, 103*n*-04*n*
Brady Plan, 34
Brazil
  Cartagena trade meeting, 179-80
  cautions about summit, 115
  date certain, 137
  democracy and human rights initiatives, 165-66
  document title debate, 147
  education initiative, 125
  energy initiative, 122
  Gore visit, 107, 109-10
  human rights, 166
  infrastructure initiative, 126
  Mercosur as priority, 178
  Mexico competition, 178
  Monroe Doctrine, 15
  new ideas resisted, 128
  Paraguay coup attempt, 166-67
  postsummit hesitation over free trade, 176, 178
  pre-Airlie consultations, 140-44
  reaction to summit, 105
  Santiago summit, 195
  target date, 155
  trade initiative, 135-37
  trade with Soviet Union, 28-29
Bribery issue, 119, 168-69
  See also Anticorruption initiative
British-Venezuelan conflict (1902), 21
  Brooke, James, 43*n*
Brown, Ron, 75-76, 180
Bueno, Gerardo M., 35*n*
Bulmer-Thomas, Victor, 19*n*, 23*n*
Bureaucracy
  after Miami summit, 87
  deadlines and end runs, 60-61
  distant deadlines, 102
  fourteen initiatives, 94, 208-12

hemispheric decision making, 79
hemispheric free trade, 67, 72
Burelli, Miguel Angel, 114
Burki, Shahid Javed, 174*n*
Bush, George
Enterprise for the Americas Initiative, 47-49, 48*n*, 105
market reforms, 46
on trade agreements, 65
Butelmann, Andrea, 51*n*, 134

Caldera, Rafael, 114, 118*n*
California, Proposition 187 (antimigrant), 155
Canada
democracy and human rights initiatives, 165-66
free trade agreement, 45
FTAA goals, 178
summit consultations, 115
trade integration initiative, 131-32
Capital markets, Mexican perspective, 111
Capital markets initiative, 146-47, 175
Caribbean Common Market (Caricom), 147
hemispheric code proposed, 92, 146-47
plan of action (text), 227-28
text, 210
US interests, 187
Cárdenas, Victor Hugo, 107-08
Cardoso, Fernando Henrique, 35, 158
accompanies Franco, 109*n*, 141
chemistry with Clinton, 195
civil society, 145*n*
summit address, 157
Caribbean
consultations about summit, 113-14
document title debate, 147
education initiative, 125
English-speaking, 113
USTR draft trade initiative, 136
Caribbean accession to NAFTA, 49, 68
Caribbean Basin, parity with Mexico, 69-71
Caribbean Common Market (Caricom), 40, 113-14
anticorruption initiative, 145
capital markets initiative, 147
civil society, 145
parity with Mexico, 69-70
pre-Airlie consultations, 141
trade (1988-94), 50*t*
trade integration initiative, 131, 134
Carnoy, Martin, 100*n*
Carpio, Ramiro de León, 112*n*
Cartagena meeting, 47, 179-80
Cascading modular multilateralism (CCM), 103-05, 144-46
evaluating, 128-29
implementation, 164
initiatives elongated, 116
Mexican suggestions, 111
middle-level officials, 128
Rio Group, 141
spontaneity, 127
value, 129
See also Cumulative modular multilateralism
Castro, Fidel, 59, 59*n*
See also Cuba
Central America
Congress of Panama, 16
energy initiative, 146
Gore in, 112-13
Interim Trade Program, 112
sustainable development, 156
trade initiative, 134-35
USTR draft trade initiative, 136
wars of 1980s, 33-34
Central American Common Market (CACM), 40
trade (1988-94), 50*t*
trade integration initiative, 131
Central Intelligence Agency (CIA), 81-82
Chamorro, Violeta, 112*n*, 121, 156
Chile
anticorruption issue, 119
energy initiative, 146
Santiago summit, 195
summit role, 115
Chilean accession to NAFTA, 68-69
announced, 154, 160
Bush administration, 48-49
Chilean frustration with US, 177
Chilean motives, 51
Clinton pledge, 68
Chrétien, Jean, 115, 156, 160
Christopher, Warren, 69, 72, 155
Chronology of events for summit, 202-05
Civil society initiative, 167-68
Caricom, 145
democracy working group, 90-91
plan of action (text), 221-22
text, 209
Clavigero, Fr., 14*n*
Clay, Henry, 16

Cline, William R., 34*n*, 42*n*
Clinton administration
NAFTA endorsement, 49, 52, 55, 63*n*, 64*n*
promotion of democracy, 42-44
Clinton, Bill (President)
APEC, 57*n*
chemistry with Cardoso, 195
choice of Miami for summit, 151-52
decision to hold summit, 1
election campaign, 63-64
free trade advantages, 65
free trade commitment, 141
hemispheric focus, 4
Menem meeting, 65
postsummit foreign travel, 183-84
role in summit, 97
speech on hemispheric affairs, 152-53
summit address, 159, 159*n*
summit proposal documents, 206-07
Zedillo relationship, 196
Clinton, Hillary Rodham, 154*n*, 169, 177*n*
Coalition building, issue-specific, 103-04, 117-22, 144-45
Cold War issues, 11*t*
aggressive US policy, 24
effect on hemispherism, 26-31
Cold War hawks, 10*t*
North-Atlanticism, 25
think tanks, 36*n*
Collective security, 24
Colombia
anticommunist parties, 29
Congress of Panama, 16
counternarcotics, 173
Monroe Doctrine, 15
Committee on Hemispheric Affairs (CHA), 190-91
Community of democracies, 52-53, 60
CONCAUSA sustainable development program, 156
Congress of Panama (1826), 15-17
Consejo Empresario de América Latina (CEAL), 167-68
Consejo Interamericano para el Comercio y la Producción (CICYP), 168
Consultations about summit
first round, 107-16
second round, 116-26
Containment strategy, 84-85
Cooper, Richard N., 82*n*
Corrales, Javier, 7*n*
Corruption issue, 90-91, 144-45, 168-69
OAS Inter-American Convention Against Corruption, 168
See also Anticorruption initiative
Costa Rica, 29
Cottam, Martha L., 9*n*, 12*n*
Council of the Americas, 167
Council of Security Regulators of the Americas (COSRA), 92
Counternarcotics
Cartagena meeting, 47
complex established, 91
deputies committee, 83
Peru, 140
See also Drug trafficking; Drug war; Money laundering
Counternarcotics initiative, 172-73
certification process, 172-73
money laundering, 172
plan of action (text), 223-24
text, 208-09
Cristiani, Alfredo, 112*n*
Cuba
Alliance for Progress, 32
democratic trends, 2
excluded from summit, 59
issue in US, 83*n*-84*n*
Miami summit, 197
universalism, 22
Cuban Americans, 111, 151, 157
Cultural values initiative, 147, 222
Cumulative modular multilateralism, 127-29, 164
See also Cascading modular multilateralism
Cutter, Bowman
date certain, 78
deputies committee, 80
free trade benefits US, 75-76
Gore's Mexico City speech, 56
summit coordination, 81
trade expertise, 75
trade mechanisms memo, 133

Dahik, Alberto, 118*n*, 119
Daniels, Joseph P., 181*n*
Davis, Harold Eugene, 17*n*
Deadlines, 61
Debt crisis, 33-34, 46
Decentralized functionalism, 85-88, 90, 104-05, 163, 195-96
Declaration of Lima (1938), 23
Declaration of Principles, Miami summit (text), 213-17
Democracy, 90-91

collective actions recently, 39
Declaration of Principles (text), 213-14
return to, 34-35
stability postsummit, 188
Democracy initiative
Central America, 157
Haiti, 157
implementation, 165-67
Paraguay, 128
plan of action (text), 219-20
at summit, 157, 159
text, 208
Democratic Party (US)
Clinton administration, 42
NAFTA reservations, 63
resentments, 72
trade policy, 67
Denot Medeiros, JosXC41,1 Artur, 136
Dent, David W., 12*n*
Denver trade meeting, 180
Department of Defense (DOD), 83
Department of Energy (DOE), 122-24
Deputies Committee (DC), 80-84
NAFTA accession, 74
trade initiative, 132
Destler, I. M., 75*n*, 88*n*, 191*n*
Developmentalism, 29
Dillon, Douglas, 87*n*
Dilute, John J., Jr., 85*n*
Diplomacy, 99-129
Dispute settlement procedures, 179
Di Tella, Guido, 109
Domínguez, Jorge I., 28*n*, 36*n*, 46*n*
Dominican Republic, US occupation, 24, 28
Donilon, Tom, 95
Dornbusch, Rudiger, 50*n*
Drago Doctrine (1902), 22
Drug trafficking
antihemispheric trends, 37
Caribbean, 114
initiative text, 208-09
Peru, 140
summit discussion, 157
Drug war
1996 US presidential election, 186
democracy initiative, 91
Deputies Committee, 83
Dunham, Constance, 127
Durán Ballén, Sixto, 118

Earth Summit (Rio de Janeiro, 1992), 58, 93
Eaton, Samuel, 99*n*, 100*n*
Economic Commission for Latin America and the Caribbean (ECLAC), 8*n*, 29*n*, 35*n*
economic model, 25
market reforms, 35
state role, 32
Economic liberalism, 25-26
Ecuador, 100, 118-19
Ecuador-Peru conflict, 186
Education initiative, 124-25, 169-70
plan of action (text), 232-33
references to women, 120
Santiago summit, 198
text, 210-11
USAID, 93
Edwards, Sebastian, 35*n*, 49*n*, 50*n*
Egaña, Juan, 15*n*
Eisenhower, Dwight D., 31
Electoral reforms, 41
Elliott, Kimberly Ann, 164, 168*n*, 169, 169*n*
Endara, Guillermo, 112*n*
Energy conservation initiative, 93, 237-38
Energy initiative, 122-24, 128, 146, 173-74, 211, 228-29
Enterprise for the Americas Initiative (EAI),
47-49, 105*n*
compared to Miami summit, 185-86
Mexican proposal, 7
Mexico criticizes, 110
Environmental issues
Clinton speech, 153
Gore in Bolivia, 107
initiative text, 211-12
Mexico, 110
Miami summit gains, 189
Santa Cruz meeting, 168, 189
Environmental protection initiative, 93, 211-12
Esquivel, Manuel, 112*n*
Europe, 13-14
European Commission, 134
Europeanism, 10*t*, 17, 23
Extradition issue, 120

Farer, Tom, 35*n*
Fast-track negotiations
Chilean accession to NAFTA, 69, 134
Clinton endorses, 63-64
postsummit, 177
renewal debate, 74-75
Santiago summit, 196-97
USTR withdraws legislation, 132

Fawcett, Louise, 8*n*
Feinberg, Richard E.
book cited, 85*n*, 133*n*
civil society initiative, 145-46
community of democracies, 60*n*
modular multilateralism, 103*n*-04*n*
Santiago summit proposals, 190-92
trade mechanisms memo, 133-34
Figueres, José, 32, 112*n*, 159
Figueroa, 115
Financial markets initiative, 209
Flecha de Lima, Paulo Tarso, 142
Foreign aid, 29, 41
Foreign Corrupt Practices Act (FCPA), 90, 119, 168
Foreign direct investment, 46
Foreign policy formulation, 82-84
Fourteen original initiatives, text, 208-12
Foxley, Alejandro, 69
Franco, Itamar, 109-10, 140, 159
Frankel, Jeffrey, 45*n*
Free trade
19th century, 19
Latin American counterproposal, 8
reservations in US, 37-38
US postwar adoption, 26
Free Trade Area of the Americas (FTAA), 131-38
acronym choice, 137*n*
date certain, 137, 155-56
Declaration of Principles (text), 214-15
endorsed at summit, 155
Miami summit significance, 4
plan of action (text), 225-27
postsummit, 175-76
US interests, 187-91
See also FTAA 2005; Trade integration initiative
Frei, Eduardo, 32, 118*n*, 160, 177
FTAA 2005, 155-56, 158, 197
Fuerth, Leon, 56-57, 78, 80, 96
Fujimori, Alberto, 43
Functionalism, decentralized, 85-88, 90, 104-05, 163, 195-96

Galtung, Johan, 27
Gamarra, Eduardo, 172-73, 172*n*, 173*n*
Gamble, Andrew, 8*n*
García-Costas, Arturo, 164*n*
Garten, Jeffrey, 56, 71
Garvey, Gerald, 85*n*
GATT. *See* General Agreement on Tariffs and Trade
Gaviria, Cesar, 159, 167
Gelb, Leslie, 80*n*
General Agreement on Tariffs and Trade (GATT)
open regionalism, 8*n*
regional free trade versus, 47, 68-69
shortcomings, 44-45
US credibility, 158
Generalized System of Preferences, 33
Gephardt, Richard, 63, 63*n*
Gergen, David, 75-76, 95
Gil, Federico G., 12*n*, 15*n*
Gillespie, Tony, 140, 142, 149
Golden, Tim, 56*n*
Goldstein, Judith, 25*n*, 28*n*
Good governance initiative, 95-96, 108
Argentina, 109
Central America, 112
Good Neighbor policy, 2-24
Gordon, Lincoln, 33*n*, 87*n*, 100*n*
Gore, Al
books cited, 95*n*
Caribbean accession to NAFTA, 70
Central America trip, 112-13
Chilean accession to NAFTA, 69
consultation with summit partners, 73
cooperation, 9
environmental issues, 95-96
good governance, 95-96
idea for summit, 1
Mexico City address, 2, 57-60, 71, 71*n*
NAFTA, 55-56, 55*n*
new role proposed, 191-92
quote on summit, 151
South America trip, 107-11
summit role, 95-97
sustainable development, 96, 156
Goshko, John, 43*n*
Greenhouse, Steven, 67*n*
Grieco, Joseph M., 12*n*
Group of Seven (G-7), 38*n*
Grunwald, Joseph, 87*n*, 100*n*
Guatemala, 40, 43
Gunboat diplomacy, 21

Haggard, Stephen, 180*n*
Haiti
democratic trends, 2
intervention to restore Aristide, 43, 157
policy, 81*n*
US occupation, 24
Hakim, Peter, 133*n*
Hale, Charles A., 21
Hall, Peter A., 9*n*, 28*n*
Halperin, Morton, 60*n*

Hamilton, Alexander, 14*n*
Harrar, George, 87*n*
Haya de la Torre, Víctor Raúl, 21*n*
Hays, Margaret Daly, 95*n*, 186*n*
Health care initiative
plan of action (text), 233-34
references to women, 120
text, 211
USAID, 93
Hemispheric First Ladies conferences, 169
Hemispheric free trade, end date, 78
Hemispheric free trade initiative. *See* Trade integration initiative
Hemispherism
concept, 4, 8, 185*n*
favored, 9
intellectual climate, 13-38
in US, 36
rise after 1930, 23-24
Henning, C. Randall, 195*n*
Hesburgh, Theodore, 87*n*
Hess, Stephen, 158*n*
High-level meetings, 242-43
Hills, Carla, 48*n*, 49
Hirschman, Alfred, 87*n*
Hispanic population in US, 188
Honduras, 112, 119, 164
Hub-and-spoke approach, 131
Hufbauer, Gary C., 47*n*, 51*n*, 68*n*, 181*n*
Hull, Cordell, 56*n*
Human rights
Brazil, 166
Carter administration, 35, 40
Clinton administration, 42-43
groups in US, 118
ombudsmen, 166
Human rights initiative, 165-67, 220-21
Hurrell, Andrew, 8*n*

Ibero-American summits, 111, 111*n*
Iglesias, Enrique, 143-44, 159, 174*n*
Illía, Arturo, 32
Illiberal politics, 26
Immigration issue, 37, 155
Imperialism, 19-22
Implementation
Chile accession, 160
criticized, 183
mechanisms, 101-02
responsible coordinators, 164
Summit Implementation Review Group (SIRG), 163-64
US government, 183-84
Import-substitution industrialization, 25, 32, 49
Inderfurth, Karl F., 84*n*
Infrastructure initiative, 125-26, 210, 228
Instrumental realism, 42
Intellectual property rights, 28
Intellectual tradition, 9-13
Intelligence reporting, 140
Interagency working groups (IWG), 84-90
analyzed, 88-89
corruption issue, 117-18
decision making, 87
democracy, 90-91
earlier work, 79
economics, 91-92
fourteen initiatives, 93-94, 208-12
Inter-American Convention Against Corruption, 168
Inter-American Development Bank (IDB)
civil society initiative, 167
displaced workers, 115
education initiative, 170
Enterprise for the Americas Initiative, 48
infrastructure initiative, 126
microenterprise initiative, 127
plan of action (text), 242
presidential directive, 53
summit initiatives, 84
summit mandate, 161-62
Unit of State Reform and Civil Society, 167
women's leadership and representation fund, 171
Inter-American Dialogue, 89, 120-21, 164*n*
education initiative, 169-70
women's rights initiative, 171
Inter-American system, postsummit, 161, 162*t*, 186
Interim Trade Program
Caribbean, 113
Central America, 112
described, 70
USTR withdraws legislation, 132
Internal Revenue Service, 92
International Center for Research on Women (ICRW), 120-21, 164*n*, 171
International Monetary Fund (IMF), 36
International organizations, 161, 193, 241-42
Intervention, US, 21

Drago Doctrine, 22
Good Neighbor policy, 23-24
Isolationism, 10*t*, 16-18, 22
Israel, 45

Jagan, Cheddi, 42
Japan, 45
Jefferson, Thomas, 14*n*
Johnson, John J., 27*n*
Johnson, Loch K., 84*n*
Johnson, Lyndon, 32-33
Jordan, Amos, 60*n*

Kahler, Miles, 47*n*, 193*n*, 194*n*
Kantor, Mickey (USTR)
Caribbean accession to NAFTA, 70
Chilean accession to NAFTA, 69
free trade benefits US, 75-76
labor and environmental clauses, 177
Miami summit, 154-55
postsummit, 177-78
Karnes, Thomas L., 16*n*
Katz, Jules, 48*n*
Kennan, George F., 30-31, 31*n*
Kennedy, John F., 32
Kettl, Donald F., 85*n*
Kinzer, Stephen, 40*n*
Kirkpatrick, Jean J., 30*n*, 40-41, 40*n*
Kissinger, Henry, 40, 60*n*, 105, 105*n*
Kolbe, Jim, 177
Korb, Lawrence, 60*n*
Kryzanek, Michael, 12*n*
Kucsynski, Pedro Pablo, 35*n*
Kurth, James R., 33, 33*n*
Kyle, Robert, 75

Labor issues, 153, 177, 178
Lagon, Mark P., 9*n*
Lake, Anthony
idea for summit, 1
promotion of democracy, 42*n*
scheduling summit, 57-59
Lampreia, Luiz Felipe, 178
Lancaster, Carol, 80
Latin America
anticorruption theme, 118
civil society initiative, 145-46
early esteem for US, 15
free trade emphases, 72-73
reactions to summit, 105-07
US motives questioned, 138
Latin American amendment, 35-37
Latin American Common Market, 33
Latin-Americanism, 10*t*, 17, 18*n*

Leadership, 38
Leaders present at Miami summit, 245-46
Lee, Ernest, 87*n*
Left wing, Latin American, 28, 42
Lehrman, Robert, 57
Leiken, Robert S., 96*n*
Levinson, Jerome, 100*n*
Liberalism, 19
Lima Congress (1847-48), 17*n*
Lipsey, Richard G., 51*n*
Lobbying organizations, 68
Lowenthal, Abraham F., 35*n*
Lustig, Nora, 176*n*

McClellan, Andrew, 87*n*
McLarty, Thomas "Mack," III
Airlie House meeting, 149
Brazil, 142
Brazil visit, 140-41
Caricom, 141
date certain, 78
logistics, 94-95
NAFTA parity, 177
special envoy appointment, 190-91
summit follow-up, 184
summit suggested, 58-59
McNamara, Robert S., 85*n*
Manley, Michael, 35
Mann Doctrine, 31
Manning, Patrick, 113-14, 156
Market reforms
Bush administration, 46
Latin American effects, 49-50
Treasury Department, 92
Martí, José, 22, 22*n*
Mayorga, Robert, 121
Mecham, J. Lloyd, 18*n*
Meller, Patricio, 51*n*
Memorandum to President Clinton, 58, 206-07
Menem, Carlos Saúl, 35, 65
poverty theme, 108
White Helmets initiative, 109, 156
Mercosur (Southern Cone Common Market), 40
Brazil strategy, 195
NAFTA, 132
Paraguay coup attempt, 166-67
trade (1988-94), 50*t*
trade integration initiative, 131, 135, 137
Mexico
Brazil competition, 178
Clinton and elections, 43

collapse of peso, 176-77, 186
Congress of Panama, 16
counternarcotics, 173
education initiative, 169-70
energy initiative, 146
free trade agreement, 45
infrastructure initiative, 126
postsummit hesitation over free trade, 178
proposes free trade, 7
reaction to summit, 106
Santiago summit, 196
summit consultations, 110-12
target date, 155
trade integration initiative, 131
"Miami process," 103, 129
Miami summit
background, 39-53
choice of city, 151-52
chronology of events, 202-05
consultations with partners, 73
coordination, 80
Declaration of Principles, 213-14
leaders listed, 245-46
logistics, 94-95
media coverage, 158
Mexican reservations, 111-12
mid-course corrections, 182-83
new issues, 182
rhythm of main events, 154
scheduling, 102
security issues, 88
Microenterprise initiative, 126-27
Caribbean, 114
focus on poor women, 93
plan of action (text), 235-36
references to women, 120
text, 211
Military coups, 167-68
Ministerial meetings, 161-62
capital market regulations, 175
Cartagena, 179-80
plan of action (text), 242-43
trade, 133-34, 167-68, 179-81
Mitchell, James F., 114
Modernization theory, 10*t*
Molina, Fr., 14*n*
Money laundering, 172, 223-24
Monroe Doctrine, 10*t*, 14-15, 20
Most-favored nation (MFN) principle, 44
Mottley, Wendell, 114
Mulford, David, 46-47, 65
Mutual confidence initiative, plan of action (text), 225
NAFTA (North American Free Trade Agreement)
as model, 65
Clinton election campaign, 63-64
collapse of peso, 176-77
EAI trade component, 48
enlargement working groups, 133
Gore on, 59
new ties, 7
trade (1988-94), 50*t*
US firms, 47
US House passes, 55
NAFTA accession, 67-68
Argentina, 108
Bolivia, 108
Brazil, 115
Caribbean nations, 70
Cartagena meeting, 180
Chilean frustration, 177
Deputies Committee, 74
Mexican position, 110-11, 135
trade integration initiative, 132, 135
NAFTA expansion, 68
Canada on, 115
Clinton on, 66-67, 66*n*, 67*n*
retreat from, 177-78
trade integration initiative, 132
working groups, 133
NAFTA parity issue, 39, 69-71, 177
Narino Accords (1994), 124
Nathan, Robert, 87*n*
National Endowment for Democracy (NED), 41, 118
National Resources Defense Council (NRDC), 174
National Security Council (NSC), 84-85, 117
Nationalism, 27-28
Natural resource management initiative, 93
Negotiation, intensity, 193
Neill, Sean, 164*n*, 166, 166*n*
Neorealism, 12*n*
Neutrality, 20
Nicaragua
US occupation, 23-24
women's rights initiative, 164, 170-71
Nicaraguan Institute for Women (INM), 121*n*, 170-71
Nixon, Richard M., 30*n*, 40, 100
No-benefits doctrine, 10*t*, 11*t*, 16, 22
Cold War, 26*n*, 31
NAFTA opponents, 56

persistence, 38
World War II era, 229
Nongovernmental actors (NGAs), 86-87
contribution, 128
corruption issue, 118
environmental, 123
Gore on, 112-13
ideas for summit, 89
initiatives leaked, 116
irregular involvement, 129
OAS, 101
post-Cold War, 188
public-private partnerships, 162-63
summit success, 185
Nongovernmental organizations (NGOs)
civil society, 91, 145
Clinton reception for, 153
environmental, 89*n*
OAS, 101
participation in summit initiatives, 167
presidential directive, 53
summit success, 185
as US interventionism, 145
women's rights, 171
Nonintervention, 10*t*, 12, 34-35
North American Free Trade Agreement. *See* NAFTA
North-Atlanticism, 10*t*, 25
North-South issues, 11*t*
Cold War era, 26
foreign aid, 29
Punta del Este summit, 100
Notecard, Summit of the Americas, 95, 244
No-transfer resolution, 10*t*, 14

OAS (Organization of American States)
in 1980s, 33
anticorruption issue, 119, 145, 164, 168-69
Canada, 115
counternarcotics strategy, 173
democracy initiative text, 209
founding, 23
Inter-American Commission on Women, 171
Inter-American Convention Against Corruption, 168
Miami summit, 101
OAS-IDB Americas Commission, 133
Panama summit (1956), 99-100
Permanent Council, 101
plan of action (text), 241
political crisis management, 91
prodemocracy programs, 89
Punta del Este summit (1967), 100
Santiago Resolution (1991), 35
Serrano crisis in Guatemala, 43
stronger trade role, 136
trade initiative, 132
Unit for the Promotion of Democracy, 166
US summit consultations, 114-15
working group on democracy and human rights, 166
working group on probity and public ethics, 168
OAS-IDB Americas Commission, 133
Oñate, Santiago, 110
Onís, José de, 15*n*, 22*n*, 100*n*
Open regionalism, 8*n*
Organization for Economic Cooperation and Development (OECD), 92, 119-20
Organization of American States. *See* OAS
Ortiz, Guillermo, 111
Oviedo, Lino, 166-67
Oye, Kenneth, 103

Packenham, Robert, 26*n*, 28*n*
Panama, US invasion, 41
See also Congress of Panama (1826)
Panama summit (1956), 31, 33, 99-100
Pan-American Congress
of 1889, 19
of 1926, 22-23
Pan American Health Organization (PAHO), 171
Pan-Americanism, 10*t*, 18-20
Pan-Hispanicism, 22
Panetta, Leon, 7, 177-78
Paraguay, collective actions and, 128, 166-67, 197-98
Pastor, Robert A., 12*n*, 21*n*, 24*n*
Payne, Anthony, 8*n*
Peña, Federico, 178
Pérez, Carlos A., 35
Perot, Ross, 55-56
Peru, pre-Airlie consultations, 140
Peru-Ecuador conflict, 186
Petrella, Fernando, 114-15, 135-36
Pinto, Jorge, 106, 145-46, 148-49
Plan of Action, 144-45
Brazil, 146-47
implementation summary chart, 165*t*
international organizations, 162
monitoring implementation, 164-75

postsummit organization, 180
scorecard of results, 165, 181-82
table of contents, 218
text, 218-43
US composite draft, 146
weaknesses, 148
Plurilateralism, 103-04, 117, 122
Policy planning flow chart, 86*t*
Pollution prevention initiative, 123, 174, 239-40
Porter, Roger B., 83*n*
Poverty issue, 125, 198, 231-32, 215-16
Powell, Robert, 12*n*
Prebisch, RaXC67,1l, 25*n*
Presidential Decision Directive (PDD) number 28, 52-53
corruption initiative, 117
Deputies Committee, 80
multilateralism aids, 128
summit decision versus, 50
Presidential Review Directive (PRD) process, 52
Program to Promote Education Reform in Latin America and the Caribbean (PREAL), 170
Protectionism, fears of US, 51, 135
Public-private sector partnerships, 161-63, 167-68, 180
Puerto Rico, 29
Punta del Este summit, 32-33
authoritarian regimes, 40
impact, 99-100
Latin American reaction, 106*n*
Puryear, Jeffrey M., 164*n*, 170*n*
Putnam, Robert D., 38*n*, 189*n*

Quarrel-thy-neighbor, 10*t*, 17

Rama, Carlos M., 15*n*
Reagan, Ronald, 41
Regional trade agreements
bureaucratic reservations, 72
Latin American motives, 51
systemic goals, 65
US prefers, 35, 44
Regionalism, open, 8*n*
Reich, Robert, 72, 76
Reina, Carlos Roberto, 112, 112*n*, 118*n*
Republicanism, 13
Responsible coordinators, 164
Richardson, Bill, 191-92
Rio Group
corruption initiative, 120
final texts, 148
pre-Airlie consultations, 141-44
Santiago summit, 195
US flexibility, 149
Rio Treaty (1947), 23
Rockefeller, David, 52*n*, 87*n*
Rodó, José,1 Enrique, 20
Rodriguez, Rita, 92, 125-26
Roosevelt, Franklin, 23
Rosen, Howard, 45*n*, 51*n*
Rosenberg, Robin L., 87*n*, 89*n*, 164*n*, 168, 168*n*
Rosenthal, AndrXC41,1s, 110-11
Rothkopf, David, 71
Rubin, Robert, 78
Rusk, Dean, 87*n*

Sabot, Richard, 124*n*
SAFTA (South American Free Trade Area), 178
Saint Vincent and the Grenadines, 114
Salazar-Xirinachs, JosXC41,1 M., 164*n*, 179*n*, 180*n*
Salinas de Gortari, Carlos, summit announcement, 59-60
Sánchez de Lozada, Gonzalo, 107-08, 156
Sandiford, Erskine, 113
Sanger, David, 178*n*
Santiago Congress (1856), 17*n*
Santiago Declaration (1991), 198
Santiago summit (1998), 187, 190-94, 196-97
Sarmiento, Domingo, 19
Scheman, L. Ronald, 33*n*
Scherr, S. Jacob, 164*n*
Schifter, Michael, 166, 166*n*
Schlesinger, Arthur M., Jr., 29*n*, 32*n*, 42*n*
Schlesinger, Stephen C., 40*n*
Schneider, Mark, 124
Schott, Jeffrey J., 47*n*, 51*n*, 68*n*
Schultz, Theodore, 87*n*
Science and technology initiative, plan of action (text), 230-31
Second Lima Congress (1864-65), 17*n*
Security issues, 13, 88
Serra Puche, Jaime, 55-56
Shifter, Michael, 164*n*
Shoemaker, Christopher C., 85*n*
SIRG. *See* Summit Implementation Review Group (SIRG)
Skol, Michael, 118-19
Small business. *See* Microenterprise initiative
Smith, Lee, 52*n*
Smith, Murray G., 51*n*

Smith, Peter H., 13*n*, 24
Socialist ideas, 21, 25
Somoza Debayle, Anastasio, 40-41
Southern Cone Common Market. *See* Mercosur
Sovereignty
  Latin American view, 28, 136
  Santiago Resolution (1991), 35
Soviet Union, 29
Spero, Joan
  Airlie House meeting, 142
  Caribbean consultations, 113-14
  Deputies Committee, 80
  document title debate, 147
  Mexico City consultations, 73, 110-11
  trade expertise, 75
Speth, James Gustave, 174*n*
Stein, Stephen, 87*n*, 89*n*
Stephanopoulus, George, 76, 95
Structural dependency, 26
Summers, Lawrence, 73, 80
Summit of the Americas notecard, 95, 244
Summit Implementation Review Group (SIRG), 163-64, 182, 192
Summits, historical background, 7-38
Sustainable development, 93
  Central America, 156
  Declaration of Principles (text), 216
  Gore on, 95
  Quito conference, 122-23
  Santa Cruz meeting, 168, 189
Sustainable development initiative, 173-75
  Bolivia, 108
  Central America, 112, 156
  plan of action (text), 237-38

Talbott, Strobe, 114
Tariff rates, 50
Tarullo, Daniel, 75
Tattemanti, Pablo, 105
Taylor, William, Jr., 60*n*
Tegucigalpa meeting, 112-13
Telecommunications initiative, 96, 108, 210, 229-30
Tello, Manuel, 110*n*
Terms of trade, declining, 25
Terrorism, plan of action (text), 224-25
Textiles and apparel sector, 70, 112
Texts, summit
  final document, 148
  Plan of Action, 141-45
  Rio Group suggestions, 142-44
  signing ceremony, 158-60
  three rounds, 107
  title of document, 147
Think tanks, 36
Thorup, Catherine, 89*n*
Thuermer, Karen E., 37
Tourism initiative, 147, 156, 231
Trade
  interregional (1988-94), 50*t*
  intraregional, 50
  US-Latin America, 46-47
Trade and commercial forum, 134
Trade fatigue, 72, 176
Trade integration initiative, 131-38
  architecture of postsummit negotiations, 179-81
  Bolivia, 108
  Denver meeting, 180
  intensive consultations, 134-38
  main functional issues, 179
  plan of action (text), 225-27
  text, 209
  three US objectives, 132
Trade and investment councils, 133, 179
Trade policy, decision-making flow chart, 76*t*
Transparency International, 89, 118
Treasury Department (US)
  Bush administration policies, 46
  coordinator for capital markets, 175
  economics working group, 91-92
Trinidad and Tobago, 113-14, 145
Tulchin, Joseph S., 33*n*, 47*n*
Tyson, Laura, 76

United Nations Conference on Women, 171
Universalism, 21-23
Uruguay, trade initiative, 135-36
Uruguay Round, 44, 78
US (United States of America)
  APEC, 45
  border states, 36-37, 37*n*
  energy initiative, 173-74
  GATT shortcomings, 44
  Hispanic population in US, 188
  human rights groups, 118
  interests and strategy, 187-91, 244
  postsummit hesitation over free trade, 176-78
US Agency for International Development (USAID)
  civil society initiative, 167
  education initiative, 169

gender equality, 93
health and education, 124
NGO networks, 91
summit agenda, 83
women's initiative, 120
working group, 93
US government
human rights policy, 2
lack of constituency around Latin America, 189-90
policy planning chart, 86*t*
US Information Agency (USIA), 118
US-Latin America relations
of 1960s, 29-30
early 20th century, 21
foreign policy innovations, 188
hemispherism, 4
low priority problem, 9, 12
power asymmetries, 13*n*
summit diplomacy, 99-129
US as early model, 15
US Trade Representative (USTR)
draft trade initiative, 136
legislation withdrawn, 132
NAFTA accession, 48
postsummit, 177
trade initiative, 132
trade strategy requested, 73-74
See also Barshefsky, Charlene; Kantor, Mickey

VanDeMark, Brian, 85*n*
Venezuela
anticommunist parties, 29
anticorruption initiative, 118-20, 128, 164, 168
British-Venezuelan conflict (1902), 21
coup attempt, 43
energy initiative, 123, 128, 173-74
Vernon, Raymond, 87*n*
Vice president, 95-97
See also Gore, Al
Von Furstenberg, George M., 181*n*

Ward, Justin, 164*n*, 174*n*
Warrenton, Virginia meeting. *See* Airlie House meeting
Washington Consensus, 35-37
Washington Liaison Committee on Latin America, 120
Washington Protocol, 166
Wasmosy, Juan Carlos, 167
Watson, Alexander, 58, 73, 140
Wesson, Robert, 27*n*, 33*n*, 164*n*
Western Hemisphere idea, 13-14, 17-18
Whitaker, Arthur P., 13*n*, 15*n*
White Helmets initiative, 109, 156, 164, 236-37
Wiarda, Howard J., 36*n*, 41*n*
Williams, Eric, 113
Williamson, John, 46*n*, 49*n*
Wionczek, Miguel S., 100*n*
Wisner, Frank, 80
Women
Hemispheric First Ladies conferences, 169
sustainable development, 93
violence against, 171
women's rights initiative, 120-22
Women's rights initiative, 120-22, 164, 170-71, 234-35
World Bank, 36
World Resources Institute, 168
World Trade Organization (WTO)
open regionalism, 8*n*
regional free trade versus, 47, 68-69

Yankeephobia
of 1920s, 23
of 1960s, 27
conservative, 10*t*, 11*t*, 19-20
diminishes, 29
by early 1990s, 2
growth, 20-21
modern, 10*t*
persistence, 38

Zedillo, Ernesto, 158-59, 196
Zegart, Amy, 85*n*

Other Publications from the **Institute for International Economics**

POLICY ANALYSES IN INTERNATIONAL ECONOMICS Series

1 **The Lending Policies of the International Monetary Fund**
John Williamson/*August 1982*
ISBN paper 0-88132-000-5 — 72 pp.

2 **"Reciprocity": A New Approach to World Trade Policy?**
William R. Cline/*September 1982*
ISBN paper 0-88132-001-3 — 41 pp.

3 **Trade Policy in the 1980s**
C. Fred Bergsten and William R. Cline/*November 1982*
(out of print) ISBN paper 0-88132-002-1 — 84 pp.
Partially reproduced in the book *Trade Policy in the 1980s.*

4 **International Debt and the Stability of the World Economy**
William R. Cline/*September 1983*
ISBN paper 0-88132-010-2 — 134 pp.

5 **The Exchange Rate System,** Second Edition
John Williamson/*September 1983, rev. June 1985*
(out of print) ISBN paper 0-88132-034-X — 61 pp.

6 **Economic Sanctions in Support of Foreign Policy Goals**
Gary Clyde Hufbauer and Jeffrey J. Schott/*October 1983*
ISBN paper 0-88132-014-5 — 109 pp.

7 **A New SDR Allocation?**
John Williamson/*March 1984*
ISBN paper 0-88132-028-5 — 61 pp.

8 **An International Standard for Monetary Stabilization**
Ronald I. McKinnon/*March 1984*
(out of print) ISBN paper 0-88132-018-8 — 108 pp.

9 **The Yen/Dollar Agreement: Liberalizing Japanese Capital Markets**
Jeffrey A. Frankel/*December 1984*
ISBN paper 0-88132-035-8 — 86 pp.

10 **Bank Lending to Developing Countries: The Policy Alternatives**
C. Fred Bergsten, William R. Cline, and John Williamson/*April 1985*
ISBN paper 0-88132-032-3 — 221 pp.

11 **Trading for Growth: The Next Round of Trade Negotiations**
Gary Clyde Hufbauer and Jeffrey J. Schott/*September 1985*
(out of print) ISBN paper 0-88132-033-1 — 109 pp.

12 **Financial Intermediation Beyond the Debt Crisis**
Donald R. Lessard and John Williamson/*September 1985*
(out of print) ISBN paper 0-88132-021-8 — 130 pp.

13 **The United States-Japan Economic Problem**
C. Fred Bergsten and William R. Cline/*October 1985, 2d ed. January 1987*
(out of print) ISBN paper 0-88132-060-9 — 180 pp.

14 **Deficits and the Dollar: The World Economy at Risk**
Stephen Marris/*December 1985, 2d ed. November 1987*
(out of print) ISBN paper 0-88132-067-6 — 415 pp.

15 **Trade Policy for Troubled Industries**
Gary Clyde Hufbauer and Howard F. Rosen/*March 1986*
ISBN paper 0-88132-020-X — 111 pp.

16 **The United States and Canada: The Quest for Free Trade**
Paul Wonnacott, with an Appendix by John Williamson/*March 1987*
ISBN paper 0-88132-056-0 188 pp.

17 **Adjusting to Success: Balance of Payments Policy in the East Asian NICs**
Bela Balassa and John Williamson/*June 1987, rev. April 1990*
ISBN paper 0-88132-101-X 160 pp.

18 **Mobilizing Bank Lending to Debtor Countries**
William R. Cline/*June 1987*
ISBN paper 0-88132-062-5 100 pp.

19 **Auction Quotas and United States Trade Policy**
C. Fred Bergsten, Kimberly Ann Elliott, Jeffrey J. Schott, and Wendy E. Takacs/*September 1987*
ISBN paper 0-88132-050-1 254 pp.

20 **Agriculture and the GATT: Rewriting the Rules**
Dale E. Hathaway/*September 1987*
ISBN paper 0-88132-052-8 169 pp.

21 **Anti-Protection: Changing Forces in United States Trade Politics**
I. M. Destler and John S. Odell/*September 1987*
ISBN paper 0-88132-043-9 220 pp.

22 **Targets and Indicators: A Blueprint for the International Coordination of Economic Policy**
John Williamson and Marcus H. Miller/*September 1987*
ISBN paper 0-88132-051-X 118 pp.

23 **Capital Flight: The Problem and Policy Responses**
Donald R. Lessard and John Williamson/*December 1987*
(out of print) ISBN paper 0-88132-059-5 80 pp.

24 **United States-Canada Free Trade: An Evaluation of the Agreement**
Jeffrey J. Schott/*April 1988*
ISBN paper 0-88132-072-2 48 pp.

25 **Voluntary Approaches to Debt Relief**
John Williamson/*September 1988, rev. May 1989*
ISBN paper 0-88132-098-6 80 pp.

26 **American Trade Adjustment: The Global Impact**
William R. Cline/*March 1989*
ISBN paper 0-88132-095-1 98 pp.

27 **More Free Trade Areas?**
Jeffrey J. Schott/*May 1989*
ISBN paper 0-88132-085-4 88 pp.

28 **The Progress of Policy Reform in Latin America**
John Williamson/*January 1990*
ISBN paper 0-88132-100-1 106 pp.

29 **The Global Trade Negotiations: What Can Be Achieved?**
Jeffrey J. Schott/*September 1990*
ISBN paper 0-88132-137-0 72 pp.

30 **Economic Policy Coordination: Requiem or Prologue?**
Wendy Dobson/*April 1991*
ISBN paper 0-88132-102-8 162 pp.

31 **The Economic Opening of Eastern Europe**
John Williamson/*May 1991* ISBN paper 0-88132-186-9 92 pp.

32 **Eastern Europe and the Soviet Union in the World Economy**
Susan M. Collins and Dani Rodrik/*May 1991*
ISBN paper 0-88132-157-5 152 pp.

33 African Economic Reform: The External Dimension
Carol Lancaster/*June 1991*
ISBN paper 0-88132-096-X 82 pp.

34 Has the Adjustment Process Worked?
Paul R. Krugman/*October 1991*
ISBN paper 0-88132-116-8 80 pp.

35 From Soviet disUnion to Eastern Economic Community?
Oleh Havrylyshyn and John Williamson/*October 1991*
ISBN paper 0-88132-192-3 84 pp.

36 Global Warming: The Economic Stakes
William R. Cline/*May 1992*
ISBN paper 0-88132-172-9 128 pp.

37 Trade and Payments After Soviet Disintegration
John Williamson/*June 1992*
ISBN paper 0-88132-173-7 96 pp.

38 Trade and Migration: NAFTA and Agriculture
Philip L. Martin/*October 1993*
ISBN paper 0-88132-201-6 160 pp.

39 The Exchange Rate System and the IMF: A Modest Agenda
Morris Goldstein/*June 1995*
ISBN paper 0-88132-219-9 104 pp.

40 What Role for Currency Boards?
John Williamson/*September 1995*
ISBN paper 0-88132-222-9 64 pp.

41 Predicting External Imbalances for the United States and Japan
William R. Cline/*September 1995*
ISBN paper 0-88132-220-2 104 pp.

42 Standards and APEC: An Action Agenda
John S. Wilson/*October 1995*
ISBN paper 0-88132-223-7 176 pp.

43 Fundamental Tax Reform and Border Tax Adjustments
Gary Clyde Hufbauer assisted by Carol Gabyzon/*January 1996*
ISBN paper 0-88132-225-3 108 pp.

44 Global Telecom Talks: A Trillion Dollar Deal
Ben A. Petrazzini/*June 1996*
ISBN paper 0-88132-230-X 128 pp.

45 WTO 2000: Setting the Course for World Trade
Jeffrey J. Schott/*September 1996*
ISBN paper 0-88132-234-2 72 pp.

46 The National Economic Council: A Work in Progress
I. M. Destler/*November 1996*
ISBN paper 0-88132-239-3 90 pp.

47 The Case for an International Banking Standard
Morris Goldstein/*April 1997*
ISBN paper 0-88132-244-X 128 pp.

BOOKS

IMF Conditionality
John Williamson, editor/*1983*
ISBN cloth 0-88132-006-4 695 pp.

Trade Policy in the 1980s
William R. Cline, editor/*1983*
(out of print) ISBN paper 0-88132-031-5 810 pp.

Subsidies in International Trade
Gary Clyde Hufbauer and Joanna Shelton Erb/*1984*
ISBN cloth 0-88132-004-8 299 pp.

International Debt: Systemic Risk and Policy Response
William R. Cline/*1984* ISBN cloth 0-88132-015-3 336 pp.

Trade Protection in the United States: 31 Case Studies
Gary Clyde Hufbauer, Diane E. Berliner, and Kimberly Ann Elliott/*1986*
(out of print) ISBN paper 0-88132-040-4 371 pp.

Toward Renewed Economic Growth in Latin America
Bela Balassa, Gerardo M. Bueno, Pedro-Pablo Kuczynski, and Mario Henrique Simonsen/*1986*
(out of stock) ISBN paper 0-88132-045-5 205 pp.

Capital Flight and Third World Debt
Donald R. Lessard and John Williamson, editors/*1987*
(out of print) ISBN paper 0-88132-053-6 270 pp.

The Canada-United States Free Trade Agreement: The Global Impact
Jeffrey J. Schott and Murray G. Smith, editors/*1988*
ISBN paper 0-88132-073-0 211 pp.

World Agricultural Trade: Building a Consensus
William M. Miner and Dale E. Hathaway, editors/*1988*
ISBN paper 0-88132-071-3 226 pp.

Japan in the World Economy
Bela Balassa and Marcus Noland/*1988*
ISBN paper 0-88132-041-2 306 pp.

America in the World Economy: A Strategy for the 1990s
C. Fred Bergsten/*1988* ISBN cloth 0-88132-089-7 235 pp.
ISBN paper 0-88132-082-X 235 pp.

Managing the Dollar: From the Plaza to the Louvre
Yoichi Funabashi/*1988, 2d ed. 1989*
ISBN paper 0-88132-097-8 307 pp.

United States External Adjustment and the World Economy
William R. Cline/*May 1989* ISBN paper 0-88132-048-X 392 pp.

Free Trade Areas and U.S. Trade Policy
Jeffrey J. Schott, editor/*May 1989*
ISBN paper 0-88132-094-3 400 pp.

Dollar Politics: Exchange Rate Policymaking in the United States
I. M. Destler and C. Randall Henning/*September 1989*
(out of print) ISBN paper 0-88132-079-X 192 pp.

Latin American Adjustment: How Much Has Happened?
John Williamson, editor/*April 1990*
ISBN paper 0-88132-125-7 480 pp.

The Future of World Trade in Textiles and Apparel
William R. Cline/*1987, 2d ed. June 1990*
ISBN paper 0-88132-110-9 344 pp.

Completing the Uruguay Round: A Results-Oriented Approach to the GATT Trade Negotiations
Jeffrey J. Schott, editor/*September 1990*
ISBN paper 0-88132-130-3 256 pp.

Economic Sanctions Reconsidered (in two volumes)
Economic Sanctions Reconsidered: Supplemental Case Histories
Gary Clyde Hufbauer, Jeffrey J. Schott, and Kimberly Ann Elliott/*1985, 2d ed. December 1990*
ISBN cloth 0-88132-115-X 928 pp.
ISBN paper 0-88132-105-2 928 pp.

Economic Sanctions Reconsidered: History and Current Policy
Gary Clyde Hufbauer, Jeffrey J. Schott, and Kimberly Ann Elliott/*December 1990*
ISBN cloth 0-88132-136-2 288 pp.
ISBN paper 0-88132-140-0 288 pp.

Pacific Basin Developing Countries: Prospects for the Future
Marcus Noland/*January 1991* ISBN cloth 0-88132-141-9 250 pp.
(out of print) ISBN paper 0-88132-081-1 250 pp.

Currency Convertibility in Eastern Europe
John Williamson, editor/*October 1991*
ISBN paper 0-88132-128-1 396 pp.

International Adjustment and Financing: The Lessons of 1985-1991
C. Fred Bergsten, editor/*January 1992*
ISBN paper 0-88132-112-5 336 pp.

North American Free Trade: Issues and Recommendations
Gary Clyde Hufbauer and Jeffrey J. Schott/*April 1992*
ISBN paper 0-88132-120-6 392 pp.

Narrowing the U.S. Current Account Deficit
Allen J. Lenz/*June 1992*
(out of print) ISBN paper 0-88132-103-6 640 pp.

The Economics of Global Warming
William R. Cline/*June 1992* ISBN paper 0-88132-132-X 416 pp.

U.S. Taxation of International Income: Blueprint for Reform
Gary Clyde Hufbauer, assisted by Joanna M. van Rooij/*October 1992*
ISBN cloth 0-88132-178-8 304 pp.
ISBN paper 0-88132-134-6 304 pp.

Who's Bashing Whom? Trade Conflict in High-Technology Industries
Laura D'Andrea Tyson/*November 1992*
ISBN paper 0-88132-106-0 352 pp.

Korea in the World Economy
Il SaKong/*January 1993* ISBN paper 0-88132-106-0 328 pp.

Pacific Dynamism and the International Economic System
C. Fred Bergsten and Marcus Noland, editors/*May 1993*
ISBN paper 0-88132-196-6 424 pp.

Economic Consequences of Soviet Disintegration
John Williamson, editor/*May 1993*
ISBN paper 0-88132-190-7 664 pp.

Reconcilable Differences? United States-Japan Economic Conflict
C. Fred Bergsten and Marcus Noland/*June 1993*
ISBN paper 0-88132-129-X 296 pp.

Does Foreign Exchange Intervention Work?
Kathryn M. Dominguez and Jeffrey A. Frankel/*September 1993*
ISBN paper 0-88132-104-4 192 pp.

Sizing Up U.S. Export Disincentives
J. David Richardson/*September 1993*
ISBN paper 0-88132-107-9 192 pp.

NAFTA: An Assessment
Gary Clyde Hufbauer and Jeffrey J. Schott/*rev. ed. October 1993*
ISBN paper 0-88132-199-0 216 pp.

Adjusting to Volatile Energy Prices
Philip K. Verleger, Jr./*November 1993*
ISBN paper 0-88132-069-2 288 pp.

The Political Economy of Policy Reform
John Williamson, editor/*January 1994*
ISBN paper 0-88132-195-8 624 pp.

Measuring the Costs of Protection in the United States
Gary Clyde Hufbauer and Kimberly Ann Elliott/*January 1994*
ISBN paper 0-88132-108-7 144 pp.

The Dynamics of Korean Economic Development
Cho Soon/*March 1994* ISBN paper 0-88132-162-1 272 pp.

Reviving the European Union
C. Randall Henning, Eduard Hochreiter and Gary Clyde Hufbauer, editors/*April 1994*
ISBN paper 0-88132-208-3 192 pp.

China in the World Economy
Nicholas R. Lardy/*April 1994*
ISBN paper 0-88132-200-8 176 pp.

Greening the GATT: Trade, Environment, and the Future
Daniel C. Esty/ *July 1994* ISBN paper 0-88132-205-9 344 pp.

Western Hemisphere Economic Integration
Gary Clyde Hufbauer and Jeffrey J. Schott/*July 1994*
ISBN paper 0-88132-159-1 304 pp.

Currencies and Politics in the United States, Germany, and Japan
C. Randall Henning/*September 1994*
ISBN paper 0-88132-127-3 432 pp.

Estimating Equilibrium Exchange Rates
John Williamson, editor/*September 1994*
ISBN paper 0-88132-076-5 320 pp.

Managing the World Economy: Fifty Years After Bretton Woods
Peter B. Kenen, editor/*September 1994*
ISBN paper 0-88132-212-1 448 pp.

Reciprocity and Retaliation in U.S. Trade Policy
Thomas O. Bayard and Kimberly Ann Elliott/*September 1994*
ISBN paper 0-88132-084-6 528 pp.

The Uruguay Round: An Assessment
Jeffrey J. Schott, assisted by Johanna W. Buurman/*November 1994*
ISBN paper 0-88132-206-7 240 pp.

Measuring the Costs of Protection in Japan
Yoko Sazanami, Shujiro Urata, and Hiroki Kawai/*January 1995*
ISBN paper 0-88132-211-3 96 pp.

Foreign Direct Investment in the United States, Third Edition
Edward M. Graham and Paul R. Krugman/*January 1995*
ISBN paper 0-88132-204-0 232 pp.

The Political Economy of Korea-United States Cooperation
C. Fred Bergsten and Il SaKong, editors/*February 1995*
ISBN paper 0-88132-213-X 128 pp.

International Debt Reexamined
William R. Cline/*February 1995*
ISBN paper 0-88132-083-8 560 pp.

American Trade Politics, Third Edition
I. M. Destler/*April 1995* ISBN paper 0-88132-215-6 360 pp.

Managing Official Export Credits: The Quest for a Global Regime
John E. Ray/*July 1995* ISBN paper 0-88132-207-5 344 pp.

Asia Pacific Fusion: Japan's Role in APEC
Yoichi Funabashi/*October 1995*
ISBN paper 0-88132-224-5 312 pp.

Korea-United States Cooperation in the New World Order
C. Fred Bergsten and Il SaKong, editors/*February 1996*
ISBN paper 0-88132-226-1 144 pp.

Why Exports Really Matter! ISBN paper 0-88132-221-0 34 pp.
Why Exports Matter More! ISBN paper 0-88132-229-6 36 pp.
J. David Richardson and Karin Rindal/*July 1995; February 1996*

Global Corporations and National Governments
Edward M. Graham/*May 1996*
ISBN paper 0-88132-111-7 168 pp.

Global Economic Leadership and the Group of Seven
C. Fred Bergsten and C. Randall Henning/*May 1996*
ISBN paper 0-88132-218-0 192 pp.

The Trading System After the Uruguay Round
John Whalley and Colleen Hamilton/*July 1996*
ISBN paper 0-88132-131-1 224 pp.

Private Capital Flows to Emerging Markets After the Mexican Crisis
Guillermo A. Calvo, Morris Goldstein, and Eduard Hochreiter/*September 1996*
ISBN paper 0-88132-232-6 352 pp.

The Crawling Band as an Exchange Rate Regime: Lessons from Chile, Colombia, and Israel
John Williamson/*September 1996*
ISBN paper 0-88132-231-8 192 pp.

Flying High: Civil Aviation in the Asia Pacific
Gary Clyde Hufbauer and Christopher Findlay/*November 1996*
ISBN paper 0-88132-231-8 232 pp.

Measuring the Costs of Visible Protection in Korea
Namdoo Kim/*November 1996*
ISBN paper 0-88132-236-9 112 pp.

The World Trading System: Challenges Ahead
Jeffrey J. Schott/*December 1996*
ISBN paper 0-88132-235-0 350 pp.

Has Globalization Gone Too Far?
Dani Rodrik/*March 1997* ISBN cloth 0-88132-243-1 128 pp.

Korea-United States Economic Relationship
C. Fred Bergsten and Il SaKong, editors/*March 1997*
ISBN paper 0-88132-240-7 152 pp.

Summitry in the Americas: A Progress Report
Richard E. Feinberg/*April 1997*
ISBN paper 0-88132-242-3 272 pp.

SPECIAL REPORTS

1 **Promoting World Recovery: A Statement on Global Economic Strategy by Twenty-six Economists from Fourteen Countries**/*December 1982*
(out of print) ISBN paper 0-88132-013-7 45 pp.

2 **Prospects for Adjustment in Argentina, Brazil, and Mexico: Responding to the Debt Crisis** (out of print)
John Williamson, editor/*June 1983* ISBN paper 0-88132-016-1 71 pp.

3 **Inflation and Indexation: Argentina, Brazil, and Israel**
John Williamson, editor/*March 1985* ISBN paper 0-88132-037-4 191 pp.

4 **Global Economic Imbalances**
C. Fred Bergsten, editor/*March 1986* ISBN cloth 0-88132-038-2 126 pp.
ISBN paper 0-88132-042-0 126 pp.

5 **African Debt and Financing**
Carol Lancaster and John Williamson, editors/*May 1986*
(out of print) ISBN paper 0-88132-044-7 229 pp.

6 **Resolving the Global Economic Crisis: After Wall Street**
Thirty-three Economists from Thirteen Countries/*December 1987*
ISBN paper 0-88132-070-6 30 pp.

7 **World Economic Problems**
Kimberly Ann Elliott and John Williamson, editors/*April 1988*
ISBN paper 0-88132-055-2 298 pp.

Reforming World Agricultural Trade
Twenty-nine Professionals from Seventeen Countries/*1988*
ISBN paper 0-88132-088-9 42 pp.

8 **Economic Relations Between the United States and Korea: Conflict or Cooperation?**
Thomas O. Bayard and Soo-Gil Young, editors/*January 1989*
ISBN paper 0-88132-068-4 192 pp.

WORKS IN PROGRESS

Liberalizing Financial Services
Michael Aho and Pierre Jacquet

Trade, Jobs, and Income Distribution
William R. Cline

China's Entry to the World Economy
Richard N. Cooper

Corruption and the Global Economy
Kimberly Ann Elliott

Economic Sanctions After the Cold War
Kimberly Ann Elliott, Gary C. Hufbauer and Jeffrey J. Schott

Trade and Labor Standards
Kimberly Ann Elliott and Richard Freeman

Regional Trading Blocs in the World Economic System
Jeffrey A. Frankel

Transatlantic Economic Cooperation: A Strategic Agenda
Ellen Frost

Forecasting Financial Crises: Early Warning Signs for Emerging Markets
Morris Goldstein and Carmen Reinhart

Overseeing Global Capital Markets
Morris Goldstein and Peter Garber

Global Competition Policy
Edward M. Graham and J. David Richardson

The Global Impact of Economic and Monetary Union
C. Randall Henning

Prospects for Western Hemisphere Free Trade
Gary Clyde Hufbauer and Jeffrey J. Schott

The Future of U.S. Foreign Aid
Carol Lancaster

The Economics of Korean Unification
Marcus Noland

The Case for Trade: A Modern Reconsideration
J. David Richardson

Measuring the Cost of Protection in China
Zhang Shuguang, Zhang Yansheng, and Wan Zhongxin

Who's Bashing Whom? Trade Conflict in High-Technology Industries, Second Edition
Laura D'Andrea Tyson

Canadian customers can order from the Institute or from either:

RENOUF BOOKSTORE
1294 Algoma Road
Ottawa, Ontario K1B 3W8
Telephone: 613 741-4333
Fax: 613 741-5439

LA LIBERTÉ
3020 chemin Sainte-Foy
Quebec G1X 3V6
Telephone: 418 658-3763
Fax: 800 567-5449

Visit our website at: http:/ / www.iie.com
E-mail address: orders@iie.com